The Meaning
of Heidegger

A CRITICAL STUDY
OF AN EXISTENTIALIST
PHENOMENOLOGY

by

THOMAS LANGAN

NEW YORK AND LONDON

Columbia University Press

*This Edition first published
in the United States 1959
by Columbia University Press
New York*

COLUMBIA PAPERBACK EDITION 1961
Third printing and second paperback printing 1965
PRINTED IN THE UNITED STATES OF AMERICA

To My Parents and Janine

Contents

PART I

THE EXISTENTIAL ANALYTIC

PART II

RECALLING THE HISTORICAL DESTINY OF THE WESTERN TRADITION

Acknowledgements

I WISH to thank the Max Niemeyer Verlag, Tübingen, for permission to quote from the German edition of *Sein und Zeit*, and Professor Edward Schouten Robinson for permission to use my own translation of *Sein und Zeit*, since the translation which he is preparing of this work was not yet ready for use at the time my work was being completed. Professor Walter Kaufmann has kindly allowed me to base my own modified translation on his translated excerpt from *Was ist Metaphysic?* published in his book of readings, *Existentialism from Dostoievsky to Sartre*. The Verlag Vittorio Klostermann, Frankfurt am Main, graciously consented to my citing the German of this essay, as well as *Kant und das Problem der Metaphysik*, *Vom Wesen der Wahrheit* and *Holzwege*. The Verlag Günther Neske, Pfüllingen, has consented to my citing *Vorträge und Aufsätze*. Monseigneur van Steenberghen consented on behalf of the Louvain press to my citing De Waelhens' *La Philosophie de Martin Heidegger*.

Acknowledgements

I want to thank the Max Niemeyer Verlag, Tübingen, for
permission to quote from the German edition of...

INTRODUCTORY

To emphasize the root sense of the word *Eksistenz* (existence) as "standing-out," Heidegger frequently uses a hyphenated form: *Ek-sistenz*; he uses similarly the word which expresses the "standing-out" dimensions of time: *Ek-stasis*. Occasionally in this study the hyphenated form is retained in order that the reader will meditate on the root sense of the "standing-out." Where this special attention is not the purpose of the context, however, the words are rendered by the normal English form "existence" (existent), and by the English-sounding neologism "exstasis" (*exstatic*). The word *Dasein* also is hyphenated (*Da-sein*) at times to underscore the root meaning, the Being-there of the existent. Because of the rich and very particular meaning Heidegger builds about this word it is taken over, without translation, as a technical term to stress Heideggerian overtones that go beyond the normal connotations of the English word "existent."

2

Heidegger's Life and Works

ALTHOUGH the philosophy of Martin Heidegger has had a great influence on Protestant theology, on philology and on literary and philosophical history and criticism in Europe, knowledge of his work remains limited in America. Wherever interest in the existential revolution arises, and whenever awareness of the new methods of phenomenology begins to come alive, the American encounters the difficult conceptions of this most systematic of existentialists, and most enigmatic of phenomenologists. But a formidable language barrier blocks the path of the serious student who would see for himself this great philosophy at work—a language barrier that stems from more than a mere accidental lack of translations from the German. Heidegger recreates the German language as he writes. His deeply poetical, utterly original language challenges the literate German—to say nothing of what it does to one who knows the language only from the outside looking in. Translating a philosophy that lives deep in the darkest genius of its language is no easier than translating Hölderlin, Goethe, or Rilke. When Walter Biemel and Alphonse DeWaelhens very competently rethought in French Heidegger's little essay on the essence of truth they found it necessary to wrestle with the key terms literally for months, and in some cases they still found themselves coining neologisms for which they could only feel apologetic. None of the other existentialists' works have posed problems quite this grave. The American reader can find long works of Sartre, Marcel, and Jaspers translated, while Heidegger is still represented only by a handful of essays gathered by Werner Brock under the title *Existence and Being* and a few fragments elsewhere—material that is almost in-

3

comprehensible without a knowledge of Heidegger's major work, *Sein und Zeit*.

There has been a political reason, too, accounting to some extent for the reticent reception of Heidegger's Thought in America. Heidegger's position in the early days of National Socialism's reign in Germany, whose beginning coincided with Heidegger's rectorship at the University of Freiburg-im-Breisgau, has remained upsetting to those who suffered so severely from Nazi barbarism. Heidegger resigned his position some months after the Nazis took office, but, say the critics, he at no time took a strong public stand against this infamous régime. Heidegger's most violent critics would argue that the very nature of his "nihilistic" philosophy prevents the author from taking a strong political stand against any "ism" which might in fact express at a given moment a nation's *"Da-sein."* The official address which Heidegger gave upon acceding to the rectorate in 1933 offers, they believe, strong evidence of the soundness of this criticism,

Sincere opposition to anything remotely suggesting "Heideggerism" has developed in this country among many refugee professors who were forced to flee Germany in the 1930s. We are fortunate to count among these men some of the most influential professors of philosophy. My sympathies are with these gentlemen in their condemnation of any movement that would compromise the freedom and dignity of the individual. I cannot, however, presume to pass judgment in any way on the very unclear circumstances surrounding Heidegger's relations to the National Socialist movement.

Political considerations should not deter us from a thorough and positive study of Heidegger's thought. Not only is Heidegger perhaps the most influential thinker on the Continent today, but, as I shall endeavour to point out particularly in the critical chapter at the end of the present study, his is one of the richest and most challenging statements of a philosophy of finite being that can be forged. Beyond question, Heidegger's phenomenology reveals fundamental aspects of human existence and of the history of the Western tradition that previous philosophies have never adequately underscored. In its claim "to surpass metaphysics" and to stand "beyond the evening of the Eveningland" (i.e. the Occidental tradition), this

Denken, as Heidegger likes to characterize his thought, presents a challenge which the serious thinker cannot afford to ignore. Everyday philosophers in America are groping with problems and struggling with methods of analysis upon which the "fundamental ontology" of Heidegger has thrown a radically new light, and toward which he has directed devastatingly critical questions which the intellectually sincere thinker may not ignore.

Martin Heidegger was born in Messkirch (Baden), in southern Germany, close to the great hills of the Black Forest, whose high woods to this day remain his favorite haunt for writing and meditating. Born and reared a Catholic, Heidegger, after showing signs early in his youth of interest in a religious vocation, left the Church while still very young. As a student in Freiburg, Heidegger was influenced first by Rickert and then very greatly by the father of phenomenology, Edmund Husserl. Indications of this influence can be found in Heidegger's dissertation, presented in 1914, *Die Lehre vom Urteil im Psychologismus*.

Husserl did not come to fix himself permanently at Freiburg until two years later. By then Heidegger had been named *Privatdozent*, and was ready to present the special dissertation required to establish a professorial standing (the *Habilitation*). The title of Heidegger's work, *Die Kategorien-und Bedeutungslehre des Duns Scotus*, indicates both an interest in the kind of theme that would interest Husserl and a serious penetration into the history of philosophy which is not typical of the Husserl of 1916.

In 1923 Heidegger was named professor in Marburg, where he wrote his fundamental work, *Sein und Zeit*, the first and only completed part of which was published in 1927. The work was at once acclaimed a milestone in the history of phenomenological thought (although Husserl viewed Heidegger's contribution, abandoning as it did all pretense of "philosophy without presupposition," as a mile in reverse). In the wake of this great success, Heidegger was named to a chair in Freiburg in 1928, the same year that Husserl was named professor emeritus. Heidegger offered as his contribution to the commemorative book edited by Husserl's former students the brilliant essay *Vom Wesen des Grundes*. The same year saw the completion of a remarkable study on Kant, *Kant und das Problem der Meta-*

physik. Heidegger began this work at Marburg, long a centre of Kantian studies, to prove his competence in the university's traditional strong point. He proved his ability well indeed, for this study now ranks as one of the great contemporary Kantian commentaries.

Another work of this fertile period (whose products I shall treat as adjuncts to the published first part of *Sein und Zeit*) was the inaugural lecture Heidegger delivered upon acceding to the chair at Freiburg—and it was another sensation—the exceptionally difficult *Was ist Metaphysik?* Heidegger was speaking to an audience full of scientists. To this group he could apparently not resist offering the greatest philosophic enigma at his disposal, the problem of the Nothing. The Foreword and the Postscript which he wrote many years later have only complicated the task of interpreting this key pronouncement of the finite philosophy of Being.

Because the 1930s were such troubled years, Heidegger became almost silent, though we now know, in view of postwar publications, that within his retreat in the Schwarzwald he never stopped writing, developing, deepening. At least one good indication of the developments that were taking place reached the world before darkness descended: *Hölderlin und das Wesen der Dichtung* (1937). With its great emphasis on the act of poetizing as formation of language, this work was at once taken to indicate a great change of direction in Heidegger's thought. Critics tended to infer from this work, and from the failure of the later projected parts of *Sein und Zeit* to appear, that Heidegger had worked himself into a trap in the fundamental work, and would not be able to erect the "ontology" that the introduction to this work had proposed. Instead, they said, Heidegger had been forced to abandon any systematic effort and had gone off into the more Dionysiac realms of a *Wortmystik*.

The works published since the war indicate that this judgment was exaggerated. Heidegger's little essay on truth, written in part as early as 1930 but developed until the time of the war years themselves, can and must be read entirely in the light of the works *circa* 1930. *Was heisst Denken?* and *Platons Lehre von der Wahrheit* contain nothing that cannot be read in a way consistent with the intentions of the original program.

As for the varied essays that appeared in two waves, one grouped and entitled *Holzwege* appearing in 1950, the other appearing in 1954 as *Vorträge und Aufsätze*, all make perfect sense when viewed in the light of one another, though they range in date from 1935 to 1952, and all work to fill out precisely the schema outlined in *Sein und Zeit.*

Strangely enough, though, almost all of the commentaries on Heidegger which have appeared to date continue to treat mainly of *Sein und Zeit* and the works that immediately followed it. The present study deliberately reverses the balance. It has been necessary to presuppose a basic knowledge of *Sein und Zeit* (a good study of this work is available in Alphonse DeWaelhens's *La Philosophie de Martin Heidegger*), though enough of a sketch of the main movement of the fundamental work is provided to permit the reader to follow the later developments. I have shown (1) the consistency of the whole range of Heidegger's thought; (2) the necessity to understand the enigmas of *Sein und Zeit* in view of the vast wealth of explanation offered in the later works; and (3), most importantly of all, that the basic program proposed in *Sein und Zeit* appears, to the extent that it probably ever shall, in the pieces and patches of later essays. Consequently, I have sketched here, I believe for the first time, a fairly complete picture of Heidegger's "philosophy of the history of philosophy"—the Western tradition as Heidegger has rethought it.

This study reveals Heidegger to be something of each of the things critics have accused him of being. Existentialist? Yes, but he develops a conception of existence that bursts through the bonds of what is often thought of in these terms. The important thing is to realize that Heidegger discourses on the Being of the things-that-are, and therefore he has to do essentially with ontology, in the sense that his philosophy poses a new solution to the traditional problem of the *Sein des Seienden.* Phenomenologist? Yes, but he gives a new cast to what phenomenology means, one that is strongly opposed to some basic Husserlian principles, and one which leaves not the remotest grounds for wondering about Husserlian idealism, with which Heidegger will have nothing to do. Heidegger's phenomenology is indeed so personal that it forms the very epicenter of this thought and is the point which we have found most fruitful to consider as the touchstone for a criticism. Kantian? Hegelian? Nietzschean nihilist? It is impossible to understand the sense in which Heidegger is all of these and more—pre-Socratic, realist, Kierkegaardian, Husserlian—without thoroughly comprehending what he means by the *Nachdenken* and *Andenken* of Being in the "destruction of the history of ontology." Being is revealed and dissimulated in each of its great manifestations in time throughout the Western tradition, from the pre-Sociatics to the present day. For Heidegger the pursuit of Being requires the liberation of what is positive in each of the great metaphysics, in a way that succeeds in de-metaphysicizing the truth contained in each position. Consequently, strong and recognizable elements of each great philosophical position appear in Heidegger's thought, in perfect unity with one another, and essentially changed to fit the requirements of Heidegger's existential notion of Being. It is a tragic error then, and one not infrequently made, to try to interpret Heidegger in terms of one of these recognizable "influences." Heidegger's thought will fit no such category; no more than Hegel can be presented as a Platonist or Kant as a follower of Leibniz and Hume. It is equally foolish to say that Heidegger is just Kierkegaard de-Christianized, or Nietzsche systematized, or Hegel de-absolutized.

Latent in these last remarks is a conviction which I might as well confess, rather than leave it to be discovered by the perceptive reader. I consider Heidegger's philosophy one of those extraordinary manifestations of man's forging of a knowledge of Being which the ages cannot but reckon with. Heidegger comes to grips with the basic and traditional—indeed the *perennial*—problems of Being, Existence, and Truth. His solutions, in their consistency, originality, and profundity, approaching the "pure position" of a finite explanation of all that is positive in Being, provide a challenge which I cannot imagine the sincere thinker not taking up, not only today, but whenever man shall try to grapple with these problems in the light of an entire philosophical tradition. Today's intellectual, challenged by the problems which Husserl presents, might still argue that he can dialogue on these questions almost as well with Kant; the study of Jaspers could send us to Kierkegaard. But the study of Heidegger must send us always to the only adequate original source, *Sein und Zeit* itself, and from there, once we have understood what is really at stake, to the entire range of Western philosophy.

To concern oneself with the limitations of Heidegger's thought involves nothing less than coming to grips with the problem of conceiving Being. More than any other thinker of our time, Heidegger challenges those who have recourse to a transcendent Absolute as base for their conception of the world. Heidegger represents the ultimate consolidation of the effectiveness in the attacks of Kant on metaphysics and of Nietzsche on God. For the man of faith, his is a challenge that causes one to put every aspect of the presence of God in history and in ontology to a supreme test. Those whose rational structure for a faith in God can meet this challenge will draw from the experience a deeper insight into the way that structure must be built if it is to withstand the batterings of the last two hundred years as they are concentrated in this finite philosophy.

I shall never forget the day in 1955 at the manor in Normandy, Cerisy-la-Salle, when Heidegger met for eight days of discussion with leading French thinkers who were still somewhat hostile toward him politically and very much so philosophically. He delivered himself of an *explication de texte* on one of the thorniest passages from the introduction to the *Phenomenology of the Spirit*. The reason why Gabriel Marcel, Paul Ricoeur, and all those present rose to their feet to cheer, sums up the attitude of respect that I hope this critical study will, despite its criticisms, convey to the reader. These men were of course not "converted" to Heidegger's *Denken*. But they all knew that they had overheard a dialogue with Hegel that marched boldly along on the great philosopher's own level. That doesn't happen every day.

The Twofold Task

I N the introduction to *Sein und Zeit*, Martin Heidegger laid down a plan for the existential philosophy which was to be his life's work. The parts of *Sein und Zeit* published in 1927 represented only the first steps of the ambitious and truly revolutionary philosophical project outlined there. Why have the remaining projected parts of the fundamental work never appeared?

Some suggest that the original project was, as planned, fundamentally impossible to accomplish. They claim that Heidegger himself came to see that the refounding of ontology he had proposed could never come to fruition; that he consequently was forced to change direction, and to abandon hope of answering in a radically new and properly ontological fashion the *Leitfrage*: What is the Being of the things-that-are?

In the present work I maintain the contrary thesis. I atttempt to show through an analysis of the whole course of Heidegger's work, from *Sein und Zeit* to the most recent essays, that the original project was never abandoned. Though the sense may have deepened with the development exposed in the later works, the original thesis of *Sein und Zeit* is never denied and in fact only comes to fruition in the works after 1936. An attempt to understand Heidegger's commentaries on Hölderlin, for example, or the difficult Postscript added in 1949 to the even more difficult *Was ist Metaphysik?*, precisely in terms of the perspective of *Sein und Zeit*, clearly brings to light Heidegger's perfect consistency. In fact, the later works take on in the process a fuller sense than they enjoy when read without reference to the analysis of the original *Existentiale*.

But, while disagreeing with commentators like Löwith and

the DeWaelhens of 1940[1] on the problem of whether or not the later works constitute steps along the road laid down originally, I cannot but agree with them on the even more important question of this philosophy's fundamental incapacity to realize its project.

Heidegger's original plan proposed nothing less than a renewal of philosophy on a basis missed by the entire metaphysical tradition of the Occident. The history of Western philosophy begins with the Greeks posing the question of the Being of the things-that-are; it ends with Nietzsche answering that question in a way that renders impossible any further inquiry, at least on traditional grounds. Heidegger proposes to create a climate in which the questioning of Being might reopen; this can only be achieved by founding ontology on completely new grounds; it requires above all a rejection of the old effort to search for the *Sein des Seienden* (the Being of the concrete things-that-are) beyond the totality of things, a search that found itself severely judged when Nietzsche, announcing "the death of God," planted the gravestone of all inquiry *meta-ta-phusika*.

The true fundament of Being does not lie in a world beyond our world. In looking *meta-ta-phusika* the tradition failed to discover what really founds the horizon in which the light of Being comes to illumine the things that are: the human existent. The new, the fundamental ontology, must rectify this error. Armed with a new method of analysis and a new perspective, the existential phenomenology must show (1) that human existence, as source of intelligible light, horizon, time, is the key to interpreting the history of philosophy, the fate of all of the historical questionings about Being; (2) that the tradition's having missed the very fundament of Being in the *Dasein* (*Ek-sistent*) is no simple suite of accidents but is due to the very nature of existence itself. The exposition of the essence of the existent as fundament of Being and the exposition of the course of the history of the revelation of Being in Dasein constitute a twofold task (*Doppelaufgabe*), in which each leg of the exposition requires the other for its realization. The

[1] The latter shows a tendency in his more recent works to interpret Heidegger as though the program of 1927 never changed.

Introduction to *Sein und Zeit* proposed that the work should be divided into two parts corresponding to the two facets of this task.

The first would seek, through phenomenological analysis, to achieve for the first time a methodical exposition of the fundamental reality of existence: a temporal horizon within which the things "in the world" come to have meaning and hence come "to be" in time. To this end, phenomenology had to be developed as a new method, involving a new conception of the phenomenon based on Heidegger's radically ontological view of what it is to know: the *Seiende* came to be, by coming to mean something to historical Dasein. Armed with such a conception of the nature of phenomenal existence, the new method becomes the key both to the grasp of the essential Being of the things-that-are, and to their history, i.e., to their insertion into a particular place and a particular time in the stream of human events. The title of the proposed first part of *Sein und Zeit* should not be misleading. Though it reads "The Interpretation of Dasein in Terms of (*auf*) Temporality and the Explanation of Time as the Tradscendental Horizon of the Question concerning Being," it is no mere philosophy of man. It is intended to be the most fundamental ontology, laying the analytic basis for an ontology of history, i.e., for an examination of the details of Being's own revelation in time.

Having succeeded in exposing the roots of Being in the existence of that Dasein which makes possible time, meaning, history, Heidegger can hope to turn to the details of Being's historical unveiling in time. But because Being's revelation of itself in the historical existence of Occidental Dasein has in fact also been Being's dissimulation of itself, the phenomenology of Dasein's history must become a critique of Western philosophies to show how and why the foundation of Being in Dasein has remained unperceived by Dasein himself. The second part of *Sein und Zeit* was proposed then as a "Destruction of the Historical Destiny (*Geschichte*) of Ontology." The goal of such an analysis of Being's progressive, epochal dissimulating-revelation of itself is the quest for a way beyond the impasse of metaphysics: explanations of Being which ignore the central-ity of Dasein by explaining the ground of the things-that-are as itself some "thing"—a God, the Idea, the Absolute Ego—have been so discredited that the *Seinsfrage* has been left historically in a lurch from which it must be rescued.

The published pages of *Sein und Zeit* contain but two of the three projected sections of that interpretation of Dasein as temporality which itself is only the first part of the twofold task. The first published section, entitled "A Preparatory Fundamental Analysis of Dasein," contains the phenomenological exposition of Dasein as founder of the temporal world horizon; the second section, "Dasein and Temporality," carries the theme forward, showing how the Dasein, in projecting the world's horizon, founds history. The unpublished third section was to be entitled "Time and Being." In it Being was to achieve its optimum positive expression in terms of time. All of the second part, which was to be devoted to the phenomenological destruction of history, remains unpublished.

There is nothing to add to the published parts of *Sein und Zeit*, say Heidegger's critics, because the essence of Being, it turns out, cannot be expressed. Having been forced to abandon hope of achieving an essential expression of Being, having been driven into a negative expression of Being bordering on the chasm of nihilism, Heidegger, say such commentators as DeWaelhens, Jean Wahl, and Karl Löwith, turned the works after 1935 into the dusky ways of a kind of mysticism, a poetical expression of the dark, unfathomable, irrational presence of the mass of *Seienden*, the kind of presentation which only Dionysiac terms can express.

It is true that Heidegger now holds that Being is not prepared for an essential revelation of itself, that the expression of Being still remains negative, progressive, preparatory (*vorbereitende*)—and probably always will; this is because Being is finite, revealing itself through finite Dasein, and consequently is of its nature epochal, and thus can never truly manifest itself as an evident, simply penetrable essence. Heidegger deliberately substitutes phenomenology for metaphysics, and in so doing realizes that he destines philosophy to being always preparatory to Being's own finite, progressive revelation of itself. It is not, then, a legitimate criticism simply to accuse Heidegger of having failed to express Being's essence. The cryptic nature of the remarks in *Sein und Zeit* may have left the erroneous impression that Heidegger looked forward to the discovery of the essence of Being. We shall see later that Heidegger has felt compelled to correct this misimpression, along with some others to which the term "fundamental ontology" gave rise. As long as we stay within his own terms, we cannot legitimately reproach Heidegger for not expressing the essence of Being; he never presumed to attempt it. We can only try to judge the adequacy of Heidegger's phenomenology as an expression of Being. The central question facing any properly internal criticism of his work is the following: Has Heidegger's phenomenology worked to discover all that a phenomenology can discover?

In his early work on Heidegger, Alphonse DeWaelhens criticized his fundamental conception of the primordial contact of the existent with the things that are. Convinced that Heidegger's notion of "interpretation" was bound to frustrate any effort to achieve an essential expression of Being, DeWaelhens construed Heidegger's first commentaries on Hölderlin as a flight from reason. Because we at last possess all the works which accumulated during the Nazi years and could be published only after the war, we can now take up DeWaelhens's criticisms in a fuller light. We shall find, as I have already suggested, no flight from reason toward Dionysos, but instead a great rational consistency. But we shall also find— a point that the last chapters of the present analysis will develop—that DeWaelhens's basic criticisms of Heidegger's phenomenology are justified. We shall see that every line of phenomenological investigation he pursues encounters the same impasse—the Nothingness of the finite freedom of Dasein which Heidegger sees as the source of the light of the things-that-are. We shall see that the Nothing does not provide a natural resting place for any line of investigation, but raises more questions than it answers. We shall see that the conceptions underlying Heidegger's notion of interpretation, i.e., what it is to know and what it is to exist, artificially limit inquiry and stop the development of phenomenological analysis.

Once the reader has seen enough of the general scheme of Heidegger's philosophy to realize that, for the phenomenologist, will is comprehensible only in terms of knowledge, and the engagement of knowledge only in terms of freedom; that both will and knowledge, constituting as they do together the single reality of the Dasein's presence among the things-that-are, are comprehensible only in terms of the kind of emotional complexus which alone makes up the totality of the human's life in its original unity; once he has understood that phenomenology is at once scientific and passionate, that there is no science without passion, no passion without intentionality, no freedom without knowledge, no life without poetry, no poetry without truth—only then will he begin to understand where, how, and at what a valid criticism of Heidegger's "phenomenology" must aim.

We have to do here, it is becoming apparent, with a philosophy that is an exceptionally tight-knit whole. Because of the extremely integrated nature of this existential phenomenology, the reader must be warned not to be discouraged by the strangeness and seeming incomprehensibility of what he will meet in these pages. When he has seen an outline of the whole structure, he will begin to perceive the sense of the parts; what is presented in this book will be strange and difficult, then, until the whole picture starts to form.

Taking Heidegger at the letter I have followed in this study the order proposed in the introduction to *Sein und Zeit*. Consequently, Part I summarizes as much of the "interpretation of Dasein in terms of temporality, and explanation of time as the transcendental horizon of the question concerning Being" as can be garnered in what has been published up to now. This analysis of the *Existentiale* contains, first, in chapter one, a summary presentation of the two published sections of *Sein und Zeit*, containing the body of the Dasein analysis. (Not wishing to duplicate the more detailed analysis already accomplished by DeWaelhens, I have not gone into the details of this remarkably rich book. Only enough of the essential argument is presented to found the more detailed analyses of those later works in which the phenomenology of Heidegger begins to manifest more clearly its basic problems.) The works published after *Sein und Zeit* are then shown to contain all of the projected "Zeit und Sein" that we can ever reasonably expect to see. In *Kant und das Problem der Metaphysik*, in *Vom Wesen des Grundes*, in *Vom Wesen der Wahrheit*, and in the works on the nature of authentic existence as originative thinking (inspired by the analysis of Hölderlin), there is ample foundation for the analysis of history, and enough evidence to show why Heidegger's philosophy, without essential transformation, will never satisfactorily overcome the profound and destructive enigmas that lie at its roots.

Part II assembles (for the first time, I believe) the main moments of the phenomenological destruction of the historical destiny of ontology proposed originally as the second part of *Sein und Zeit*. From essays published in *Holzwege*, and even more recent essays in *Vorträge und Aufsätze*, we can discern enough of Heidegger's conception of the destiny pursued by Being in its revelation through Occidental Dasein to discern the outlines of the second half of the twofold task.

The two parts of the *Doppelaufgabe* are, then, interrelated in every way. We shall see that every trait of human existence exposed by the *Existentiale* aids in bringing out the ontological, destined sense of the history that Dasein has unfolded from itself. Conversely, every moment of the Occidental historical destiny becomes the source of a new revelation of the essential possibilities of Dasein—therefore of Dasein itself; for what is Dasein, after all, for Heidegger's kind of phenomenologist, but the sum total of possibility which he has forged from the resources of his liberty? If the *Existentiale* precedes in Heidegger's —and our—exposition the destruction, this is more a result of the limitations imposed on analysis by human finitude than an expressly desirable state of affairs. But the order laid down by Heidegger is not purely arbitrary. If the perfect circle of interpretation must be broken, this is the way to break it, because the dialectical essence should be presented before the details of the dialectic itself are unfolded. It is in examining the existent he finds himself to be *now*, that Heidegger discovers Being, but a Being whose essence it is to be historical. Consequently, though it might precede a historical exposition, the essential analysis of Dasein necessarily calls forth that historical exposition. Dasein is what Dasein does.

Heidegger begins the quest for essence in *Sein und Zeit* by analyzing the "average" Dasein encountered in everyday life. The phenomenological analysis that would uncover the essential structure of the Dasein must pass by way of the

Dasein's free, concrete acts.[2] Every concrete act is a manifestation of the ontological structure of the Being positing the act.
In the language of *Sein und Zeit*, the road of the *Existentiale*
(which seeks the *Wesen* of *Ek-sistenz*) passes by way of the
concrete realities of the *Existentiellen*, the concrete determinations of daily existence.

But the freedom of Dasein further complicates the analysis
of the human existent. In projecting any given concrete act
Dasein is free to do so either in view of an adequate notion of
what he really is, i.e., in view of his authentic end—in which
event the act itself will be "authentic"; or he can plunge
blindly ahead, substituting means for ends, the lesser for the
greater, the act for the agent (the act being then, of course,
"inauthentic" [*ineigentlich*]). Since Dasein's finite grasp of his
own nature is always bound to be limited, the acts of any
given Dasein are always tainted with some inauthenticity—
for much the same reason that any philosopher's revelation of
Being is always of its very nature also a dissimulation. (Thus,
as we shall see later, inauthenticity is to the *Existentiale* what
the forgetting of being is to the destruction of history.)

The complicated *Existentiale* which we shall now expose
reduces, then, to the scheme just sketched. The concrete
determinations of daily existence reveal a double-faced
ontological structure of Dasein, the authentic and the inauthentic. Both bespeak the nature of Dasein as discursive,
temporal. Authentic existence grasps the meaning and directs
the destiny of its true temporality. Inauthentic existence hides
the real meaning of time as the expression of Being. From the
interplay of the two is born the continuing drama of history—
history in possession of itself, or history losing itself in the
tragedy of inconscient, unguided destiny.

[2] "Ohne ein existenzielles Verstehen bleibt doch alle Analyse der
Existenzialität bodenlos." Heidegger, *Sein und Zeit*, p. 312.

PART I
THE EXISTENTIAL ANALYTIC

I Being and Time

DASEIN'S MODES OF STANDING-IN

THE first of the two published sections of *Sein und Zeit*, the part entitled "The Preparatory Analysis of the Dasein," begins with an analysis of the concrete situation of the Dasein as "Being-in-the-World." It unfolds through 175 pages of description of the many aspects of the Dasein's average inauthentic and authentic *Ek-sistenz* among the natural things and instruments it encounters in its "world." From this wealth of rich phenomenological material we shall limit ourselves to seeking the main line of argument which leads to Heidegger's unification of all the basic aspects of Dasein in their common essential structure, the Being of the Dasein as Care (*Sorge*).

At the root of every philosophy of Being lies a conception of how the knower relates himself to the things known. Realism is distinguishable historically from idealism because the former conceives the truth relationship in terms of a conformity of the intellect to the "reality" presented by the immediately intuited presence of the things that are; while the latter conceives the relationship in terms of the internal discovery of the ideal to which the concrete changing things must form themselves in order to be vested with the light of intelligibility. The Heideggerian phenomenology is deliberately neither realistic nor idealistic. On the contrary, the new phenomenology would occupy a place in history lying beyond the traditional metaphysical opposition of realism-idealism. It would achieve a fundamentality capable of undercutting the root "metaphysical" dichotomy that has plagued Western thought since Plato's time—the very opposition of subject and object.[1] Indeed the

---

[1] Heidegger, *Sein und Zeit*, pp. 214 ff.

phenomenology of the Dasein's "standing-in" in a world would establish fundamentally the nature of the relationship of Dasein to the things-that-are in a way susceptible of resolving the age-old epistemological conflicts, by revealing in a new light the conditions of Being's opening into the world, which is the basic situation making the rise of such conflicts possible.[2]

Heidegger claims that the key to a proper understanding of Dasein's *Inständigkeit* lies in the phenomenon of human concern (*Besorgen*) for things.[3] Man is in the world, of course, as a body, occupying a space among other objects like any material thing. But this spatial standing-in is not what characterizes most essentially the human relationship to things and to other people. Man's relationship to the tools he uses and to the people he knows involves something more consequential than mere spatial relationship, namely relationship of intention, of concern, of meaning.[4] When I am hungry, I stand among trees, rocks, weeds— spatially related but unconcerned. Were I to spy a wild blackberry bush I would at once situate it at the centre of my universe of concern. The phenomenon of concern shows that Dasein's world is a world of meaning radiating from the only kind of being capable of grouping, relating, using, willing things. The first step of the phenomenology of *Sein und Zeit* is to analyze the structure of comportment that makes such meaning possible.

Heidegger discovers three aspects or moments basic to the structure of world-projecting concern, each an indispensable building stone in Dasein's rapport with the things-that-are. Each is a mode of Dasein's standing-in, i.e., of his freely relating himself to things. Consequently each is open to the possible variations which freedom introduces. Dasein, in projecting the fundamental acts of standing-in, can, in the case of each of the three modes that we are going to examine, do so either authentically or inauthentically. An authentic (*eigentlich*) mode of standing-in is based on Dasein's relating himself to things in view of the whole structure of what he really is. An inauthentic (*uneigentlich*) mode of standing-in finds Dasein so concerned with the necessities of daily life that he relates himself to things by

---

[2] *Ibid.*, pp. 130 ff.

[3] *Ibid.*, p. 131. *Inständig* means "instantly'"; hence Heidegger's "standing-in" is a play on the word in both its routine and its root meanings.

[4] *Ibid.*, pp. 134 ff.

projections which ignore the implications of the full structure of his possibilities. For each mode of comportment toward the things-that-are—discovery of self as already in the world (*Befindlichkeit*), understanding (*Verstehen*), and discourse (*Rede*) —there exists a corresponding inauthentic form: ambiguity (*Zweideutigkeit*), curiosity (*Neugier*), and prattle (*Gerede*).

Each mode is only one aspect of the main basic act of standing-in and hence is always to be found with the others, just as the future, the present, and the past are only modes of time, each essentially inseparable from the others. Understanding, for example, Dasein's central way of existing, would be impossible without that basic presence to the things-that-are, natural to Dasein from birth. Likewise, there could be no such *Befindlichkeit* if it were not of the very essence of Dasein to stand-in by interpreting, i.e., by understanding (just as there could be no past if there were no present). Nor would there be an understanding were there no expression of what is understood. Expression being the function of discourse, it follows that *Rede* is the essential fulfillment of *Verstehen* and hence as basic a form of Dasein's finding itself in the world.[5]

From this analysis of the authentic modes of Dasein's standing-in we can conclude that the basic concern (*Besorgen*) of Dasein, if true to his own essence, is an involvement in things of an intentional kind, understanding; this self-assertion among the things-that-are is supposed to be at once docile, drawing its substance from things as they are, and creative, bringing the illumination of meaning to things in the act of discourse.[6] The authentic act of standing-in is an act of existence involving a self-extension toward what is unknown and *is* not yet, so that meaning may be brought to be and new explanation offered for the things-that-are.

The Dasein as understanding projects from out its possibilities . . . . The projection of understanding has as its proper possibility [the capability] of building itself out (*sich ausbilden*). This building-out of understanding is what we call "explanation" (*Auslegung*).[7]

Authentic existence, Heidegger explains in later works, is "poetic" in nature. Poetry, as he conceives it, is respectful of things, respectful of the meanings created by past generations

[5] *Ibid.*, p. 160.　　　　[6] *Ibid.*, p. 148.　　　　[7] *Ibid.*, p. 148.

as expression of correct possibilities of those epochs, while remaining conscious of its own responsibility as creator of new meaning in casting original light on the things-that-are. The fruit of authentic existence is the creative, revealing, renewing language forged for the poetic expression of discourse.[8]

Before attempting to disengage the ontological structure which roots and makes possible the authentic modes of standing-in, Heidegger must still complete the second half of the basic description of Dasein. The possibilities of inauthenticity must be described. These are no mere negations of the authentic modes, nor are they simply lesser forms of the same thing. The inauthentic acts of standing-in are as much positive, concrete realities of Dasein as the authentic. Ontologically both are on the same footing, and both go always together to form the two faces of finitude, somewhat as act and potency always go together in the Aristotelian conception of the finite thing. As a result of Dasein's finitude, he is thrown into a world dominated by concern (*Besorgen*) for the necessities of survival. Everyday life takes its stamp from the concern of the crowd. Its forms are the formula's "they" develop—that mysterious, anonymous "they" which appears in everyday man's answer for doing what he does: "Well, they say that. . . ." So, if Heidegger delays for a long moment[9] to describe the inauthentic forms, it is because he recognizes not only that this is half the picture of Dasein's standing-in, but also that it is the half that establishes the dominant tonality of existence for the average man.[10]

Heidegger speaks of this condition of the "everyday Dasein" as his *Verfallensein*.[11] The author expressly informs us that he is not attempting in the paragraphs devoted to man's fallen state a phenomenology of the traces of original sin. Nor does Heidegger intend to pass judgment on the forms of daily existence. He does seek to express the *Verfallensein* as a positive phenomenon, "This not-being-itself functions as a positive

[8] *Ibid.*, pp. 160 ff.   [9] *Ibid.*, pp. 167-75.

[10] "Das Dasein zunächst und zumeist im Man aufgeht und von ihm gemeistert wird." *Ibid.*, p. 167.

[11] "Die Verfallenheit an die 'Welt' meint das Aufgehen im Miteinandersein, sofern dieses durch Gerede, Neugier und Zweideutigkeit geführt wird." *Ibid.*, p. 175.

possibility of Dasein, resulting from the Dasein's con[...] involvement in the world."[12] We should understand that we a[...] encountering here the reality of Dasein's essential finitude. Because he is finite, the Dasein never achieves a pure revelation of Being in a perfect relationship to the things-that-are, untrammeled by narrow considerations. Each revelation, each "interpretation" is partial; consequently its very affirmations must exclude.[13] Authentic existence, in fact, can only be something of an ideal, a direction to aim at amidst the dark reality of the dissimulation of everyday life.

The average man lives, then, less in a state of pure *Befindlichkeit*, of marvel before the discovery of self as the founding act that opens a horizon onto the world of things, than in a state of ignorance concerning his own fundamentalness, his true ontological status. The Dasein becomes so involved in the necessary search for bread and in concern for what "they" say that he ignores above all the reality of his own existence. The egoist, vaunting his talents and position, is really, in his "fallen being," the man who has lost sight of himself.[14] The authentic existent, who has discovered the miracle of his presence to the things-that-are, is ready to sacrifice all to the service of the creative renewing powers of his own poetic nature. The effort to surpass metaphysics, to which Heidegger's philosophy is devoted, should be viewed in the existential perspective of *Sein und Zeit*. The forgetting of being that has characterized the Western tradition is the counterpart on the level of philosophical criticism of the *Verfallensein* on the level of the concrete existential act. The surpassing of this tradition is the act required of the authentic Dasein who would renew an awareness of the holiness of *Ek-sistenz*.

Heidegger terms the kind of involvement which characterizes the Dasein of the daily world a *Zweideutigkeit*. The curious phenomenon signalled by this term is that the man who is caught up in the whirlpool of daily activity is the least straightforward in his dealings with things.[15] Dasein gets so involved in "going along with the crowd" that soon he can no longer distinguish their catchwords and pat formula answers from

---

[12] *Ibid.*, p. 176.
[13] This is a notion fundamental to the Hegelian dialectic.
[14] *Sein und Zeit*, p. 178.   [15] *Ibid.*, p. 173.

in pure understanding." This goes to prove
the very nature of the act of understanding,
.oes not function in a vacuum of pure reason
.tally based on the projections which underlie
.ting myself to the world. I do not just observe
the .... .g before me, but rather I go to them forearmed
and forewa... ed by the interpretations of others and what they
have told me about them. This determines how I shall look at
things and what I shall see when I do observe them.[16] The
ambiguity arises from the interplay of conflicting elements
in my interpretation: the influences of the *echte Verstehen* and
the point of view and presuppositions I bring to the thing. In
examining the other two modes of daily standing-in we shall
see that the average Dasein's involvement in things once
infected with ambiguity lacks the foundation to achieve
anything but a superficial handling of reality.

The second mode of standing-in becomes, in the fallen state,
curiosity (*Neugier*) instead of genuine understanding.[17]
Heidegger's later essays on the poetic nature of thought will
clarify what *Sein und Zeit* explains here in a language still very
difficult because of its newness. In later works Heidegger
contrasts an "originative thinking," i.e., the understanding
that brings new light and new meaning to the things upon
which it is exercised, with mere "calculative thinking," which
discovers nothing new but instead feeds on what others have
already provided in the way of meaning, dividing and re-
combining old ideas until their staleness becomes the very
odour of death. Curiosity, which often passes in the world as
a virtue and sounds so original, just as the practical man seems
so wonderfully in control of things, is, in its superficiality,
only interested in uncovering what is trite and can never
invent new horizons of its own. "He is interested in seeing, but
only in seeing," says Heidegger of the curious man, "and
not in understanding, that is to say, *in ein Sein zu ihm zu
kommen.*[18]

This way of putting things may sound too narrowly epistemological. Yet Heidegger is trying to describe here not the logical
conditions of scientific understanding, but the universal, ontic,
i.e. concrete conditions of all human comportment. We can see,

[16] *Ibid.*, p. 173.   [17] *Ibid.*, pp. 170-73.   [18] *Ibid.*, p. 172.

for example, that the opposition—understanding vs. curiosity or originative thinking vs. calculative thinking—would apply with perfect ease to the love relationship. A love that feeds on another's contributions, on another's constant renewal, is not really love at all, but a parasitical relationship drawing its sustenance from a source it will soon wither by its constant drain.

The expression of the curious Dasein is prattle (*Gerede*), the inauthentic counterpart of genuine discourse (*Rede*).[19] If Heidegger again draws his figure from the world of speech, it is because spoken and written language are the most common forms of the poetic act, i.e., of the authentic act of human existence, not because he would restrict the conception literally to the spoken or written word. Prattle serves very well indeed to dramatize the doubtful fruit of inauthentic existence. The prattle of the market place is not just nothing. Rather it serves as a positive block to genuine discourse, the clanging noise that drives away that great silence indispensable for the kind of discourse that touches the essence of things.[20]

Once the ontic, concrete description of the three authentic modes and their everyday inauthentic counterparts is completed, the next task is to disengage from these descriptions the ontological structure to which they belong, and which is the source of their underlying unity: the necessary structure of Dasein's essential possibility. Heidegger carefully disassociates this phenomenological endeavor from the efforts of the realists to abstract a universal essence from the particular individual and of the idealists to intuit an idea in the spirit applicable imperfectly to many individuals.[21] The complex structure of the in-standing existent is neither a general idea nor super-characteristic, from which the three modes can be deduced, nor an *ego cogito* separable from the three modes though present in them.[22] Here again, the relationship of the temporal horizon to its exstases is our model for understanding

[19] *Ibid.*, p. 167.

[20] The reader may have been struck already by what could seem to be gratuitous assumptions underlying these positions. It is better to wait, however, until we have presented a fuller picture of the Dasein as Heidegger conceives him before attempting to justify or criticize any of the details.

[21] *Sein und Zeit*, pp. 180 ff.   [22] *Ibid.*, p. 181.

the existential structure: the time span is neither the past, nor the present, nor the future, nor is it just the three added together. It is something unto its own, giving reality to the extases, incapable of independent existence but not simply equal to the sum of the three modes. This comparison is not fortuitous; we shall see below that the three modes of the Dasein's standing-in among the things-that-are correspond to the three aspects of a discursivity essentially temporal because of its finite nature.

In seeking the ontological structure underlying the three modes of the Dasein's discursive standing-in, the phenomenologist is seeking the fundamental phenomenon itself, i.e., the operational essence of the free *ek-sistent* seized in the very act of exercising its *Da-sein*. What is sought here is, if you will, an attitude, an ultimate form of concern touching all the things that can enter the horizon of the world of meaning, a form of concern that puts the horizon itself in question and consequently involves everything involving the very root of there being a world in the first place. Heidegger discovers this attitude to lie in the very existentialist notion of *Sorge*, a word which we can only approximately translate as "care."

The problem is to show how a human existent can be brought to a state of extraordinary self-penetration (*eine ausgezeichnete Erschlossenheit*) so fundamental that what he grasps in all lucidity is the very structure of his own existence.[23] What lies open to him in that extraordinary moment is the intentional lucidity of his own fundamental possibility. In the state of *Sorge* Dasein grasps his own reality as projection of the world horizon and, at the same time, as radical finitude. The Dasein who manages, in this sense, to *care* realizes his responsibility as the unique source of meaning in the world and realizes in the same instant, his own nothingness as finite being. How, concretely, can Dasein arrive at such a fundamental questioning of his own Being?

The revelation of the structural whole of the Dasein involves, very evidently, a quite special act of self-discovery, a *Grundbefindlichkeit* that can throw my whole being-in-the-world into question. When the whole structure is thrown into question, there arises a hope of discerning its essential elements

[23] *Ibid.*, p. 184.

in their authentic relationship to one another. This threshold to authentic self-discovery Heidegger terms *Angst*.[24] Anguish is not a mere emotion, nor is it just one among many harrowing experiences. Rather it is one of those extraordinary manifestations of man which is proper to Dasein alone. Only Dasein can experience anguish. Even an animal, by contrast, shares with man the possibility of encountering fear. Fear differs from anguish in that it is always experienced in reference to a concrete something: I fear the storm, for it is a threat to my continued existence. In the case of anguish, on the other hand, it is not violence, or destruction, or any danger from a particular source that conquers me. Rather, I begin to feel that I am losing my grip on my world. I begin to call into question the reality of my being and my place in the world; they both seem to slip through my fingers. The solidity and "givenness" of the things that are present before me suddenly dissolve as I doubt the possibility of there being anything at all.[25] It is in such a moment that I can suddenly come to realize that I am thrown into a world where I find myself among the things-that-are, that their presence before me depends on my opening a horizon of interpretation (*Verstehen*) through the projection of a comportment in relationship to them, and that my dwelling by the things-that-are requires that I actively let the objective thing (*Vorhandensein*) be through the discourse (*Rede*) which is the outcome of my acts of interpretation. The source of each of these modes of standing-in is traced immediately to my own finite reality, and the unity of the three is discovered to be rooted in my finite existence. Because of this revelation of the dynamic unity of the three modes, the essential temporality of care becomes attainable. My recognition of my total responsibility for there being a "world" can lead, in my efforts to care about Being, to at least a dumb, inchoate grasp of the authentic temporal existence this infers. I can come to see that every moment of authentic existence must unite care for each of the extases, the past, the present and the future—the past which I must actively assimilate as part of an authentic

[24] *Ibid.*, pp. 184 ff.
[25] *Ibid.*, p. 187. An excellent description of the clinical aspects of this experience is given by Stephan Strasser in "The Concept of Dread in Heidegger's Philosophy," *Modern Schoolman*, XXXV (1957-58), pp. 1-20.

Befindlichkeit, the future which I build out through the projections of *Verstehen,* and the present of that dwelling with the
things-that-are that takes place in the *Rede* which expresses my
grasp of things.

How does a feeling of *Angst* come over one, so that the
discovery of self which is called care becomes a real possibility?
Of course, any great shock that forces me to question what
I had taken so much for granted, my place in the world among
the things-that-are, can cause me to realize suddenly my
Unheimlichkeit in the world.[26] But just the extreme of inauthentic existence can bring on the kind of *nausée* that might
force some fundamental questioning of myself. The inauthentic
existence is a flight before the stark realities facing the finite
existent thrown in the world. We are driven into a frenzy
of activity as we plunge into the whirlpool of concern,[27] seeking
security and assurance in the friendly presence with "them"
among the things-that-are. A soul that retains deep down a
modicum of sensitivity, driven so far in this pursuit of happiness
that the unrealness of the chase after an always just-escaping
security begins to manifest itself, can suddenly, when least
expected, be forced to throw the whole quest of the average
man into serious doubt. It is then, as all dissolves into the
nothingness that waits at its base to engulf the flimsy structures
of a fabricated life, that Dasein is forced to question radically
where he is from, and where he is going.

Through *Angst* the caring Dasein comes to discover the
nature of that dynamic, finite structural whole which is his
existence. He discovers that the "where-from" and the "where-
to" of Dasein present constantly recurring dimensions rooted
in the "where-now" of the self-unfolding Dasein. In the very
act of this *Grundbefindlichkeit* Dasein can see how the three
modes of standing-in imply one another mutually. The kind
of self-discovery in the world which is *Befindlichkeit* would be
unthinkable were there no fundamental act of understanding.
But, there could be no future-producing projection of understanding were it not rooted in a past, i.e., if the Dasein did not
already find himself in the world. Likewise, the Dasein's

[26] *Sein und Zeit,* p. 188. Something akin to this happens to Mersault when
he is condemned to death in Camus's, *L'Etranger.*

[27] *Sein und Zeit,* p. 178.

being-in-the-world would mean nothing *now* nor would the acts of understanding come to anything if they did not issue in the present in that grasp on things which expresses itself as *Rede*.

Heidegger has sought to unify the three modes in an expression which underscores the characteristic temporality of each. In *Sorge*, he says, Dasein discovers himself as *Sich-vorweg-im -schon-sein-in-einer-Welt-als-Sein-bei (Seienden)*, i.e., as self-projecting Being (expressing the futurity of the projection in *Verstehen*) that is already in a world (expressing the past nature of *Befindlichkeit*) as Being in company with the things-that-are (which expresses the essential present act of coming to dwell with the *Seienden* in the discursive, temporal fruition that is *Rede*).[28]

This master phrase defining *Sorge* we can take as something of a climax and a symbol of the complexity and dense organic unity of this first section of *Sein und Zeit*—"the preparatory fundamental analysis of Dasein"—remembering that all we have reproduced here are the barest outlines. The exposition of the first section remains preparatory because it is aimed at the discovery of the existential (ontic) structure of Time, the full ontological significance of which will only be revealed in the following section.

DASEIN AS BEING-TOWARD-DEATH

The phenomenological movement of the first section of *Sein und Zeit* climaxes, we have seen, in the discovery of the dynamic structure underlying the three modes of standing-in. This discovery of care as key to the structural whole of Dasein is not, however, the final answer to the question posed at the start of the first part of the twofold task, for the inner ontological nature of the discovered structure—its nature as temporality—remains to be explored.

The second section of the existential analysis of Dasein begins by coming to grips with the basic problem raised by the discoveries that have just been made. At the root of the Dasein's standing-in-a-world we have discovered the exstatic structure of the free existent. The essence of Dasein has been discovered to lie in its ability for self-extension in time by free

[28] *Ibid.*, p. 192.

projection beyond the here and now toward a future that is not yet. This freedom is possible because Dasein alone of all finite things is capable of grasping the whole structure of his self-extending being. Because the Dasein is at once self-penetrating and limited, the key to his understanding his own self-extension lies in his grasping the outer limit or end of the process which his own liberty unfolds. In other words, now that the basic unity of the ekstatic structural unity has been discovered, there arises the problem of discovering its limits by discovering its end.

Dasein exists by projecting himself toward a future that is not yet (*noch nicht*). Consequently Dasein is a being that lives very much in prospect of this and that—in prospect of tomorrow's feast, in prospect of finishing this house or of seeing it destroyed by the war that is about to come. But what is the sole prospect that everyone shares, a prospect absolutely unavoidable, and which touches in some way every other prospect? Death. And when I grasp fully the prospect of death, do I not put into prospect my very possibility to be? This is what Heidegger means when he declares that Dasein's death is *die Möglichkeit des Nicht-mehr-dasein-könnens*,[29]—the possibility to be able not to be Dasein anymore. This is indeed an "extraordinary prospect,"[30] constituting as it does the "most proper, unavoidable and unsurpassable possibility" of the finite existent.

Because he knows that he will die, Dasein takes possession, like no other thing does, of the course of his personal destiny, even before it is in fact realized. Consequently, when Heidegger speaks of Dasein as Being-toward-death (*Sein-zum-Tode*) he signals the finite self-possession which characterizes the free being who in projecting himself unfolds the reality of his own destiny.

Consider how I must grasp my death for it to become the reality that can introduce me to the whole structure of my existence and, consequently, open the possibility of authentic projection. It does not suffice to see somebody else die,[31] nor even to take cognizance, more or less vividly, that I am going to die someday. This kind of realization is incapable of rendering any special meaning to the present moment. It is only when

[29] *Ibid.*, p. 250.   [30] *Ibid.*, p. 251.   [31] *Ibid.*, p. 240.

I come to realize that my every moment and my every act share the same fate, all destined to the same all-dissolving end, all capable of being swept up and fixed in the complete picture of a terminated existence, that the reality of my finite destiny reveals the meaning of the moment.

According to Heidegger the anguished grasp of the meaning of death as outermost possibility reveals my true essence to me. Because Dasein, knowing his destiny, can change his concrete decisions accordingly, this special self-possession in the end renders me free to develop my essence as I will, within the limits imposed by my essential finitude. And because I am the kind of being that knows I am going to die, I can realize my ultimate separation from a world that cannot really contain me. The anticipation of death dissolves the grip of overriding importance that the event of the moment might enjoy. The realization that I am Being-destined-to-death tends to put all external influences on the same level, freeing my own self-extension from any bondage, permitting me to reengage myself in the details of the present freely and nobly, with the realization that it is up to me to afford things a place in the course I choose to carve out between now and that inevitable future event. In a word, grasping the significance of his own finitude, Dasein, before the spectacle of the Nothingness of his own Being, cannot authentically root himself in anything but his own freedom, his own finite self-possession.[32]

---

[32] Does this affirmation of Dasein's end as *Sein-zum-Tode* exclude a Christian perspective which would affirm the immortality of the soul? Heidegger explicitly states that this analysis neither affirms nor excludes such a possibility; it only affirms the realities that are consequent to the realization that every life, Christian or not, is ended in this world at death (*Sein und Zeit*, p. 248). Even if one believes firmly in life after death, this belief itself should be rooted in the full grasp of Dasein as he exists now as Being-in-the-world; for he is factually "thrown" into the world, owing his existence to whatever has thrown him, and losing it at death, when, undeniably, he goes out of the world. A notion of immortality of the soul can only take on its fullest meaning in view of the realities of Dasein as Being-destined-for death (*ibid.*). It is evident that Heidegger does not adequately bring out the problems that the doctrine of *Sein-zum-Tode* poses to a Christian when formulated as he presents it. We shall wait to present any criticism, however, until we have developed the whole picture of Heidegger's thought. In the last chapters we can approach the question of the *Sein-zum-Tode* in a fuller and more meaningful perspective.

The act of freedom involves Dasein in the responsibility of accepting, or of refusing to accept, the full reality of the destiny of his worldly acts. He must choose to project either authentically (which we now see means in view of his full essence as Being-destined-for-death), or inauthentically (which concretely means proceeding toward the future without pausing to see what it really has in store). Because the grasp of self required for authentic existence is indeed, as Heidegger says, "extraordinary," we see why the forms of daily existence tend to be dominated by inauthentic projection. The whirlpool of daily activity excludes that retirement into an inner silence, what Gabriel Marcel would term *le recueillement* necessary that "the quiet voice of Being" can speak its message of human destiny. Heidegger dramatizes the difficulty of achieving authenticity by terming the need for the extraordinary self-penetration which we have been describing *eine phantastische Zumutung*—a fantastic requirement.[33]

The Dasein who can succeed in carrying through the exigencies of the fantastic requirement of authentic existence will come into possession of his true Self. Heidegger's notion of the *Selbstständigkeit* of the authentic Dasein forms a kind of summit in *Sein und Zeit*'s analysis of the human existent. Consequently, it is important that we understand this conception and distinguish it carefully from traditional notions of "Selfhood." Heidegger himself goes to some pains at this point to distinguish existential selfhood from Kant's notion of the *Ich*.

The Kantian *Ich* resembles the Heideggerian Dasein in following in its discovery from the effort of the existent to grasp his subjectivity. Again like Heidegger, Kant refuses to reduce the *Ich* to a simple substantiality of the human essence. But Kant, reducing Dasein to a transcendental subject, lacks an adequate conception of the existent's Being-in-the-world. Too severely distinguished from the things-that-are, the *Ich* becomes too much of a pure "I think." It becomes an unchanging *Vorhandenes* "outside the world."

This sketch of a criticism[34] is sufficient to tell us something of

---

[33] *Sein und Zeit*, p. 266.

[34] Heidegger attempts no fundamental "destruction" of Kant before *Kant und das Problem der Metaphysik*.

what the self-ness of Dasein is not. After thus denying the subjective isolation of the Dasein, Heidegger quickly makes it clear that the true notion of self should not be perverted in the opposite direction either—through an overinvolvement in things, the kind of depersonalization which overcomes the "*I*" in the unself-possessed manifestations of everyday existence. The self that loses itself inauthentically, by freely committing itself to an essentially blind projection into the whirlpool of often meaningless daily activity, substitutes for the personal affirmations of an "I," who knows the profound secrets of its own Being, the" they say that . . . " of the crowd's rumor.

The true Self, the caring Self, the Dasein who understands himself in the structural whole of his Being as temporality, realizes itself as conscience (*Gewissheit*). Conscience suggests a note of awareness, the kind of awareness that is born of a steady gaze directed at things as they are. The German *Gewissheit* translates this note better, for the stem *Gewiss* basically signifies certitude. What is the nature of this certitude that opens the Dasein into the authentic existence of a life of conscience? It is the certitude of death as it is known by the *Sein-zum-Tode*. Conscience understood thus fundamentally is not a voice calling from outside, but a still and resolute address of the authentic Dasein to himself. This call (*Ruf*) is the voice of care (*Sorge*). It is a call to salvation from the daily self-loss in "what *they* say" issued by the roots of my Being from out the act of self-transparency. It is a call to the discovery, by a Self that is thrown into the world, of its own real possibilities in their death-directed reality. Conscience is the silence of my Being before the call of its own situation.

What is the call of the still voice of Dasein's own Being? In Heidegger's answer, we feel the abyss that divides his thought from, for example, the Christian existentialism of Gabriel Marcel. The latter would respond to a like question, *L'appel à devenir soi-même*, which would mean the call to fulfill the destiny of a vocation which I must freely work out in union with God's love and God's plan. Heidegger is attempting an explanation of man within the limits of a strict finitude without making appeal to a transcendence of the kind Marcel exposes in his analyses of love. This difference is more far-reaching than it might at first glance appear. It is far reaching enough to affect, in the philosophical option upon which the two thinkers divide, the phenomenology itself in those areas where its range is affected by differing conceptions of what it is to *know*.

An *Ek-sistent* whose possibilities begin in the darkness of the *Geworfenheit* ("throwness") and end in the certitude of death, can never in its *Da* be far from a realization of its own Nothingness (*Nichtigkeit*). Earlier in *Sein und Zeit*, when speaking of the revelation of anguish, Heidegger declared, "In anguish the Dasein discovers himself confronted by the Nothingness of the possible impossibility of his existence."[35] The Dasein's ultimate possibility is death, i.e., the radical impossibility that a finite being should continue to exist forever. "Throwness" at one end and death at the other—these are the signs that Dasein draws its reality from Nothing and is destined to return it to the same indefinite night. Conscience is "the call of the Nothing," the call of the ultimate in a finite world, addressed to an existent, who is asked to shoulder the burden of his own ultimate impossibility.

The Nothingness of Dasein is the Nothingness of Being, and is therefore the ultimate. The Dasein is not the things-that-are and is not even like the things-that-are. The Dasein is *die Transzendenz schlechthin* because it is capable of responding to the call of conscience. Alone of all beings it is capable of grasping and willing the reality of its own Nothingness. Therein lies its freedom—in the acceptance or rejection of that destiny. Therein lies the source of its prerogative as the being that lets Being be. It is Dasein who opens the space within which the light of Being can reveal itself. It is Dasein who opens the horizon of time, inserting from out of nothing the disengaging nothing, the distance that makes the interpretation of things possible. The full significance of the perspective dominating the phenomenology of Heidegger lies in the conception of Nothingness as the ultimate in a philosophy of finitude. The Heideggerian phenomenology is founded in the conviction that the originative element in any truly fundamental act of revealing in knowledge—as for any truly existential act extending the Being of Dasein—is drawn from out this absolute, the only possible finite absolute, Nothingness itself.

[35] *Sein und Zeit*, p. 266.

The justification of the option manifesting itself here should be the main concern of an evaluation of Heidegger's philosophy that would wish itself fundamental. Heidegger's choice of the Nothing as ground of a philosophy of existence will become, therefore, a subject of importance for the concluding chapters of the present study.

Conscience, then—the call of the Nothing—can only be truly meaningful when viewed in the light of the option which we shall call "the Heideggerian perspective." This perspective becomes even more dramatically underscored when the analysis brings us to the result of the authentically attended call: The Dasein called from out the depths of his own Nothingness shoulders in positive resolution the burden of his guilt.[36] Two notions, guilt and resolution, grow so intimately out of the one integral analysis of the Self that it is difficult to explain the one without invoking the other. The reader will see why resolution follows the assumption of guilt if he bears in mind the meaning of the latter. *Schuld* in German, it should be remarked, has a double sense lacking in English; it means both guilt, in the sense of a responsibility for past acts that have been found wanting, and also a debt, in the sense that there remains something in the situation that needs filling up. In the Heideggerian perspective, the first sense is meaningful in terms of the rectification that is imposed upon us by the whole limiting structure of the past acts of inauthentic existence. This past endows the present Dasein with a heritage to be surpassed (in the same sense that the ontological past must be overcome through a destruction of the history of philosophy so that the question of Being might be rejuvenated). The limitations of past existence make themselves felt on every level of the individual's life, from the limitations of a tradition down to the

[36] Heidegger explicitly denies that the terms "conscience," "guilt," and "resolution" replace the Christian conceptions or secularize them. Rather these fundamental discoveries about Dasein would, according to him, have to precede and found an explanation of man that would avail itself of the givens of a faith. Consequently, the Dasein's assumption of guilt should not be interpreted as a kind of mute recognition of the universal presence of original sin. Rather, it involves an acceptance of human finitude that would have faced even man-before-the-Fall—for he too was finite. It is the acceptance of those same limitations of the human condition which makes sin possible (*Sein und Zeit*, p. 286).

ns deep within the structure of the life that I have
r myself amidst the cries and hews of daily existence.
In the future I must pay the "debt" of limitations inherited
from the past, in the sense that I must be determined to struggle
beyond the more crippling limitations. This is in part what
Heidegger means by resolution (*Entschlossenheit*).[37] "Resolution is an extraordinary mode of the openness of Dasein."[38] It
is the only appropriate basis for action. Resoluteness is a
constant fight to maintain the extraordinary openness in the
face of a world formed by the inauthentic existence of others
and against the burdens of our own condition which tend
always to pull us back toward inauthenticity. Facing the reality
of the Nothingness that he really us, Dasein must free himself
resolutely for action based on recognition of the full reality of
his concrete situation.[39]

There has perhaps been a tendency among students and
critics to emphasize a bit disproportionately the negative role
of anguish as self-revelation of Dasein, to the detriment of the
counterbalancing positive side of Heidegger's doctrine as it
unfolds in *Sein und Zeit*. *Angst* is not, after all, an end in itself,
but only a step to the full birth of conscience. Anguish is
destined to fruition in resolution, and resolution is positive,
even though not unlimited. Resolution opens up a field for the
authentic exercise of freedom, for in projecting on the basis
of my essential situation I am freed from the tyranny of the
meaningless domination of the anonymous "they." It is only
when authentic resolution has thus cleared the field that an
authentic *Mitsein* of Dasein to Dasein becomes possible.[40]
And, too, deep in this self-revelation and in the full freedom to
be oneself that it permits, lie the roots, as Heidegger sees it,
of truth itself. This is a subject to which we must later devote
a full and careful analysis. The point of insertion for our later

[37] One thinks again of Meursault in *L'Etranger* of Camus. His creator
has said of him that his whole life was based on one dominating principle,
his honesty. Nowhere in the course of that life was that honesty more
"authentic," in the Heideggerian sense, than when it was rendered its
full reality in those hours of lucidity which followed Meursault's conviction
that he was going to die.

[38] "Die Entschlossenheit ist ein ausgezeichneter Modus der Erschlossenheit des Daseins." *Sein und Zeit.*, pp. 297, 331, 335, 336.

[39] *Ibid.*, p. 310.   [40] *Ibid.*, p. 264.

discussion of the essence of truth as freedom lies, within the structure revealed by the phenomenology of Dasein in *Sein und Zeit*, in the notion of resolution as the positive coming to grips with things as they are, made possible by Dasein's resolute, authentic grasp of himself.[41]

Heidegger terminates the climactic exposition of resolution with a positive note too often overlooked by critics anxious to make Heidegger look as much like Sartre as possible:

> Along with sober anguish, which brings [the Dasein] up before the reality of his central existential possibility, goes a supporting joy over this very possibility. In [grasping this possibility] the Dasein becomes free from the "accidents" of subsistence problems which arise out of the goings-on in the world of a life of busy inquisitiveness.[42]

Far from being dominated by an anguished sentiment of abandonment in a hostile world, the authentic tonality of the resolute Dasein is a joy before the prospects of an exercise of freedom worthy of a mortal man. The Dasein, as Heidegger conceives him, is noble in his poverty, and free in his finitude. Devoid of delusions or degrading involvements he can involve himself freely, thus engaging his "Being-there" in "a true and realizable (*ein faktisches*) Ideal."[43]

These considerations of "fantastic requirement," "guilt," "conscience," and the like raise a question which we cannot let pass without at least a preliminary remark.

In describing this "fantastic requirement" is Heidegger telling us what we *should* do? If this is so, are we not obliged to consider *Sein und Zeit* in some respect a work of ethics?

Though we shall leave the final consideration of the epistemological and moral status of Heidegger's philosophy to the end, the problem of the ethical status of the pronouncements on authentic and inauthentic existence and upon the fantastic requirement of achieving a perfect self-transparency has posed itself sufficiently, I believe, to justify an aside to help us from the very beginning to locate ourselves tentatively in this respect.

Nowhere in *Sein und Zeit*, nor for that matter in any of his

[41] *Ibid.*, pp. 264, 298, 384.   [42] *Ibid.*, p. 310.   [43] *Ibid.*

subsequent works, does Heidegger discourse upon what *should* or *should not* be done. The tone of the phenomenology is always matter of fact, deliberately descriptive. But, of its very nature, the material treated can not be rendered ethically neutral, nor does the author believe that any intentional consideration can be isolated from the question of freedom. And nowhere more than in *Sein und Zeit* is the reader more directly and personally touched. For here Heidegger analyzes the essence of that thing we ourselves are; and he does it existentially, i.e., precisely in terms of the liberty of that essence which we must choose to be and work at to realize.

In fact, the phenomenological consideration of the human essence as self-constitutive freedom, we are beginning to see, cuts across the traditional division between ontology and ethics. This is a sign, as Heidegger sees it, that the phenomenological analysis is more fundamental than the objective categorical analysis of the traditional metaphysics. The discoveries of the *Existentiale* are, if you will, both ontological and ethical, since the result is the grasp of the ontological structure of an essence —a free essence, grasped not as an object to be contemplated, but as a challenge to be lived.[44]

A judgment on the status of this philosophy in terms of the traditional, and, to the phenomenologist, less fundamental analysis of man which divides him between psychology and ethics, would be questionable. I personally would affirm confidence in the value of the *Existentiale* as a legitimately "different" kind of analysis at least to the point of not attempting any such classification of it. But in considerations such as conscience, guilt, and understanding of the call, as well as *Sorge*, *Angst* and authentic and inauthentic existence, it is impossible not to raise questions which border on the "should." These words of Werner Brock state the fact succinctly: "Care, as the Being if Dasein, does not allow for a separation between

[44] This is, of course, not the first time in history that philosophizing has been "personal." But it is new—a phenomenon of the second phase of the existentialist movement (if we may think of Kierkegaard and Nietzsche as forming a first phase, and of Jaspers, Heidegger, and to the extent that we can consider him "methodic and organized," Gabriel Marcel, as a second phase), that a rigorous and methodic effort should be made to reveal Dasein where an Augustine or a Pascal only touch on him in brilliant flashes.

a 'theoretical' and a 'practical' kind of behaviour."[45] The analysis of the authentic self-ness (*Selbstständigkeit*, i.e., self-ness with the note of substantiality underscored) of Dasein plunges to the dynamic unity of existence where *theoria* and *praxis* are one in the concrete act of self-extension.[46]

DASEIN AND TEMPORALITY

The analysis of conscience, guilt, and resolution has enriched our knowledge of the anguished self-resolution of Dasein without, for all its complexity, revealing the full ontological significance (*Sinn*)[47] of *Sorge*. It has not uncovered the explicit nature of the ontological structure of the Dasein. The *Dasein* has been described as "horizon-opening resolute projection" without our even having raised the question of the *woraufhin*— the "in-virtue-of-what"—of the projection. Consequently the existential-ontological unity of the three modes of standing-in remains to be explored.

This unity, according to Heidegger, is a temporal one.[48] Without our realizing it, the entire analysis has been aimed at revealing the essential temporality of the Dasein's ontological structure, and the stamp of time has been on the description of

[45] Footnote in Introduction to *Existence and Being*.

[46] In this respect, I do not believe that Gabriel Marcel's analysis of the exigencies of a concrete philosophy versus the dangers of systematization penetrates to the heart of the problem. Both Jaspers and Heidegger, in fact, appear to achieve an analysis of Dasein in the concrete determinations of existence, which is personal in the sense that it is not presented disinterestedly, but as a challenge to be lived. This, without sacrificing the coherence and methodicalness associated with traditional systematic philosophical analyses. They have demonstrated in fact that what is advantageous in the systems, namely rational consistency and full development of themes in an organized way, is not of itself destructive to genuine ontological mystery and "openness." One is tempted to think that Marcel's requirements for "concreteness," go so far in attacking systematization that they become more an *apologia pro opera sua* than an adequate statement of the systematic possibilities of an existential analysis.

[47] For the Heideggerian phenomenology, the *Sinn* of a phenomenon is the *Wesen* (essence, understood not as *essentia*, the form and matter of Aristotelian ontology, but as existential structure), grasped in a way that makes possible an existential projection in regard to the phenomenon. *Sein und Zeit*, p. 324; see also pp. 148 ff., esp. pp. 151 ff.

[48] *Sein und Zeit*, pp. 331-33.

every aspect of every mode of the Dasein's way of standing-in, in a world. Each of the three modes unified in that complex structure of which *Sorge* has been the touchstone, viz. *Befindlichkeit*, *Verstehen* and *Rede*, corresponds to an exstasis or dimension of time,[49] whether in an authentic or inauthentic form. Let us examine each of the natural exstases of time, the future, the past and the present, to see in what way a mode of the Dasein's standing-in in the world corresponds to what each exstasis represents:

The future

The experience of care (*Sorge*) reveals the Dasein's structure as *vorlaufende Entschlossenheit*, as the resolution that projects itself forward in the horizon-opening act of exsistence.[50] It is precisely because the Dasein cares that he is different from the tree or the rock; for caring signals a freedom that permits the existent to disentangle himself from a passive, total involvement in the here and now—as though the tree, suddenly caring not to catch cold tomorrow, were to free itself from its roots and take cover from the rain. Because it can know its potentialities, it can anticipate them and be present to them now, which makes the Dasein's future in some sense already *now*, just as his now is always already to some extent being lived in the future. Because it is my grasp and direction of these possibilities that determines my becoming, this futurity becomes the basis of the Dasein's whole self-development. Hence Heidegger's conclusion: The fundamental extasis of the Dasein is the future.[51]

The futurity here is evidently a very different one from the "future" as it is understood by the man in the street as part of the everyday conception of time—the one adopted by the Greeks as the basis of their philosophical conception of the future. The "future" in a conception of time that is concerned with a commerce with things is dominated by the "now" which characterizes possession of concrete *Seienden*; to the man in the marketplace the future is a state of possession of things now

[49] The word *Ek-stasis* recalls the standing-forth of the Dasein's self-extension which makes possible the standing-in of the existent.

[50] *Sein und Zeit*, p. 335.

[51] *Ibid.*, pp. 337, 325. This is because Dasein viewed existentially is authentically *creative*.

that is anticipated because it is not yet. In such a conception, the now itself becomes a discrete moment, manipulable, even priceable, for "time is money." Such a temporality, conceived as a flow of self-important moments, based on the possession of things, is blind to the inner transparency and intentional interpenetration of the exstases of authentic temporal existence. Because the authentic Dasein projects in view of his genuine possibilities, his "now" is never isolated for consideration from the future. Nor is his future ever separated from present responsibility, which might be shoved aside while we wait for some future discrete moment to make its appearance. A future that grows out of a respected past and whose importance is felt even now is authentic because of the continuity of existence it fosters. And thus it is in turn for each of the other exstases.

The contrast between the average Dasein's concern over the possession of things and the authentic Dasein's dwelling with the *Seienden* in the light of resolute future projection can be summed up in the distinction *Sein-Seienden*. Care for the Being of the things-that-are recognizes that Being transcends the limited horizons of present concern, to embrace and keep alive the richness that the past has brought in other peoples' interpretations of these same things-that-are, and that to do so we must actively comport ourselves to things in view of an essential, authentic projection giving direction to our relations. The commerce with things carried on in the *besorgenden Welt* is reprehensible only when its projections ignore the full, authentic exstatic dimensions of Being. The authentic form of each ekstasis, consequently, will derive its full reality from its openness to and union with the complementary dimensions grasped actively.

The past

Similarly, we can see that the "past" of an authentic existent is not a "now" that was and is no longer.[52] The Dasein must possess his past *now*, in virtue of the future that he forges for himself. A final consideration of the Dasein's ultimate finitude brings out the root-involvement of past and future in one another quite clearly: Because I am revealed to myself as Being-toward-death, I come to possess my beginning as thrown-

[52] *Ibid.*, p. 337.

into-the-world.[53] Dasein must assume responsibility for what he is and accept it, which means to will it in those acts that are capable of creating a future. Grasping his limits in the experience of guilt thus makes possible absolute projection of an authentic future, in an act of conscience which sees the unity of the past and the future accomplished in the moment of the now. Dasein unifies through care his past, his present, and his future. The Dasein who knows what he was, knows what he is and can project a future based on the authentic structure of his own existence, making present the past in extending its authentic structure toward the *not yet*.

This existential notion of the significance of the past is evidently the ruling conception founding the later Heideggerian phenomenology of the history of Western philosophy. When, in Part II, we examine in detail the "Destruction of the historical-destiny of ontologies" proposed in the introduction to *Sein und Zeit*, we shall see in action, so to speak, the Heideggerian conception of the existential past. Just the little that we have said about it should serve, too, to show *why* Heidegger's refounding of ontology must necessarily be grounded in such a "destruction." The Heideggerian refounding of ontology is a projection toward the future of thought achieved now in view of a past—a past which must be made actively present by the very projection of a new ontology whose destiny it is called upon to guide. The circularity apparent in such a statement does not escape Heidegger, who explicitly wills it as a characteristic of any finite act of existence.[54]

The present

The Dasein absorbed in the concerns (*Besorgen*) of daily life takes the presence of things for granted. The apples, the people, the town are present, now, before me. The profit, the relaxation, the weekend are absent from my present enjoyment, but, in a "now" that is "just around the corner," they will be there. This, we have seen, is the kind of gross presence, the kind of making-present which pays no attention to *how* what is present

[53] *Ibid.*, p. 260.
[54] The question of Heidegger's notion of the circularity of finite thought will be expanded upon later and will be critically discussed in the final chapter.

is made present, upon which the vulgar time conception and the traditional being conception are founded.[55] The contrast of such a materialized time with the authentic present is now becoming clear. The man of affairs, concerned with manipulating the things present before him ignores the creative possibilities of authentic Dasein because his approach to things "takes so much for granted." On the other hand, in the place of a time fragmented into instants regulated to the presence and absence of particular things, the authentic existent, recognizing his originality as the creative making-present of what is present (the *Anwesen des Anwesendes*), bases his conception of the "now" on a temporality that includes the whole exstatic structure of existence, with its past, present, and future dynamically interpenetrating in a structure of time which draws its newness from my projections. The authentic present takes its place, not in a stream of incremented instants, but in the full *Augenblick* which Kierkegaard described, where it is linked to a past made-present by a future which I possess already in my resolute act of future projection. The transparency and unity of the intentional horizon is allowed fullest play in those temporal acts which affirm the maximum self-possession—the mastery that is only possible for a being who freely forges his own future.

Each of the modes of standing-in in the world takes on an entirely different complexion depending on whether the standing-in follows the forms of authentic or of inauthentic temporality. The fundamentally temporal nature of human existence becomes even more manifest when we see how the basic nature of understanding, self-discovery, and discourse change following the Dasein's decision to project, either in keeping with his transcendental reality as horizon-opener or in keeping with his daily necessities as a negotiant in the world of thingly concerns. Let us consider each mode in this way, beginning with "interpretation" (*Verstehen* as translated by DeWaelhens), since, as a matter of fact, what we are doing is "interpreting" time.

Verstehen[56]

All understanding is grounded in the futurity of projecting resolution. Every act of understanding is grounded in a point

---

[55] *Sein und Zeit*, pp. 421-23.   [56] *Ibid.*, pp. 336-38.

of view, a projection, in virtue of which the thing is understood. This, like any projection, can be either founded in the whole structure of real Being as its ultimate point of view, or substituted for it in the particular preoccupations of daily activity which, per force, dissimulate the full Being of the projection. In an authentic understanding I view things in their ultimate light, i.e., I engage myself in the act of interpretation of the present situation from the point of view of the full past, which constitutes me in my encounter with things, and the true "end" to which I am destined in my act of engaging myself in this interpretation. If I lose my grip on my essential futurity I narrow the horizon of things to a coarse now, a *Gegenwärtigen*, that awaits a now that is not yet, so that I may get hold of something for the sake of consuming it.[57] In this way I forget what things are really for and how I should relate myself to them. From this arises the incredible vanities of a humanity that all too quickly forgets its real destiny—Being-for-death.

A forgetting of the past, the ignoring of origins—mine and the thing's—is an essential step in the process of achieving the thing-absorbed preoccupation of daily life. On the other hand, the authentic understanding in approaching the *Seiende* is originative because it takes possession of a past, the significance of which it can, out of the realization of its own liberty, continue toward the not-yet in an act that brings new meaning and new light to the thing understood. The existent who projects in his interpretation inauthentically can not (ironically, because his projection is thing-centred and now-absorbed) find in the thing any more light than that with which it is commonly endowed. Care for Being, Heidegger affirmed in 1949 (in the Postscript to *Was ist Metaphysik?* which we shall examine in chapter five), is the real devotion to *Seienden*, which means, in effect, that the man devoted to the liberation of human creativity is alone truly concerned for the Being of the things-that-are. In Part II of the present book we shall find an exact and rich exemplification of authentic interpretation, when we come to analyze the details of Heidegger's own interpretation of the history of Western thought.

---

[57] *Ibid.*, p. 337.

Befindlichkeit[58]

Just as understanding is grounded in the futurity of projection, so in like manner the primary extasis of *Befindlichkeit*—the Dasein's awareness of his fundamental situation—is rooted in the past. The basic perspective of the discovery of my Being-there is oriented toward the event that is my beginning. Because my past is given, my existence is "tuned" by what has come before. Heidegger uses the word *Stimmung*, rather than a word suggesting determination, to underscore the freedom in human development. The assimilation of the past by the authentic Dasein in no way resembles the missile's following a predetermined course, but is rather like the recapitulation in a sonata, where the earlier material becomes a field of possibilities for new development rather than a track demanding rigid obedience. Inauthentic existence fails to take advantage of the possibilities the past presents, because of its absorption in concern for what is happening just now. Thus, when I am afraid (to develop a contrast employed earlier to bring out the nature of anguish) I cannot for the moment be bothered by the fact that I represent a tradition and have a responsibility to make something out of a past which I alone can keep vital. Anguish, on the other hand, brings the reality of my past before me in clear relief as I come to question the outer limits of my whole existence. Note well the active note that characterizes this conception of the past; I must take possession of my past by keeping the possibilities it represents alive in view of my own projections for the future. Heidegger accents the active nature very well when he speaks of the *Stimmung* as "a turning-back-to-bring-forward-out of what has been."[59]

When it comes to the mode representing the present, we must join two aspects of the previous discussion whose connection has perhaps been unclear to the reader up to now. When the present concerned is that of average, everyday, undifferentiated Dasein, then we must consider the temporality of that *Verfallensein* in which the being of everyday Dasein is dispersed. The Dasein who, by contrast, achieves an existence in which the three temporal extases are perfectly integrated enjoys a very

---

[58] *Ibid.*, pp. 339-45.

[59] "Ein Zurückbringen aus einem ursprünglichen Gewesensein," *Sein und Zeit*, p. 344.

47

special kind of life in the present, which Heidegger, following the tradition established by Kierkegaard, names "the Moment" (*Augenblick*), existentially represented by authentic *Rede*. Let us consider each in turn.

Verfallen[60]

Each aspect of the Dasein's factual fallen state—the curiosity, prattle, and ambiguity which characterize his life among the anonymous "they"—results from an overinvolvement in what is going on at the moment. The kind of surfeited plunging of superficial intelligence into the flow of daily events— "curiosity" as Heidegger terms it—seeks neither origins nor destinies and assiduously avoids disquieting questions about ultimate meanings, beginnings, and ends; it seeks only advantage for now, sensation for the instant. The daily prattle of the market place is the commentary on the events rasped by curiosity. These become frozen into those sayings of the anonymous "they say that . . . " which everyday Dasein comes to accept as a basis for his inauthentic projections. Nothing is more "natural" than this average state of affairs. The finitude of Dasein explains why his Being-in-the-world must be first of all an affair of concern for the *Zuhandene* (the instruments) with which he must treat in order to make his way among the things-that-are. Nothing could be more automatic. What is not automatic is his someday rising above the preoccupations of the here and now to look toward the receding future and to wonder about the realities of his past. Until a fundamental shock of the order of anguish jars him out of his daily course, an inauthentic present will keep him *Verfallen* among the *Zuhandene* with "no time to spare" for anything else.

Rede[61]

The Dasein who finds himself in the world, in all that that implies for authentic existence, has the basis for the true act of interpretation which Heidegger terms *Verstehen*, the act which, in bringing new light to the things-that-are, is truly creative i.e., creative of a future. The realization of this new "Being" as it takes place in the dense moment of authentic existence takes the form of a discursive unveiling of new reality which

[60] *Ibid.*, pp. 346 ff.   [61] *Ibid.*, pp. 349 ff.

Heidegger terms *Rede*. The choice of this term to express what we might, rather grossly, term the *result* of authentic existence emphasizes two things: that its nature is progressive, unfolding (discursiveness being the form that an existence at once dynamic and finite would have to take), and that the basic manifestation of this conquering activity is speech. We shall gain a much richer idea of Heidegger's conception that Being comes to lodge itself in time in the words of speech as we progress. For now, it suffices for the reader to recall that the conviction that the activity of Being-producing-itself issues in "the Word" is no unprecedented position; for is this not a fundamental Christian notion, though we are encountering here the Christian doctrine of the Word as radically transformed by a finite philosophy.[62]

The revelation of new Being through the authentic resolution that terminates in the expression of *Rede* (*Aussagen* for Heidegger being derived from, and made possible by *Rede*) represents, as we have said, the integration of all three temporal exstases in a dynamic whole where no one exstasis dominates. As a matter of fact, it is unavoidable that the expression of discourse should take on a slight cast from the present—because of the language that even the authentic Dasein is forced to employ. The words we inherit are too impregnated with the concerns of daily life, not to lose some of their power to evoke the whole fabric of authentic existential temporality.[63] Later, when we examine Heidegger's meditations on poetizing, we shall see that he contrasts an authentic poetical *Sprache* with the dissimulating *Gerede* of daily concern.[64] This consideration becomes one of utmost concern in Heidegger's works as the analysis of authentic-inauthentic existence comes, in his more recent writings, to be couched in terms of the notion of "originative" and "calculative" thinking which we have promised to examine in Chapter V.

Though each of the three elements analyzed above temporal-

---

[62] This subject is treated in the last chapter.

[63] *Sein und Zeit*, p. 349.

[64] When Heidegger, inspired by Hölderlin, asserts later that *Sprache ist das Haus des Seins*, we should understand that he means all speech as it stands stamped with daily usage. For Being itself, in its revelation through Dasein, dissimulates itself necessarily because of its finitude.

izes (*zeitigt*) itself primarily in one rather than another of the exstases, nevertheless in each, as in *Rede*, Dasein must be understood to temporalize itself completely, manifesting in every act all three exstases, whether in an authentic or in an inauthentic form. The entire *Sorge*-revealed complexus of Dasein reveals itself in some way in every moment. As Heidegger puts it:

> Temporality temporalizes itself totally in each exstasis, that is to say, that in the exstatic unity of the ever-present full temporalizing of the temporality the totality of the structural whole of Eksistenz, factuality and Fallenness (*Verfallensein*) is grounded, this being the very unity of the structure of Care.[65]

The Dasein's *Ek-sistenz*, i.e., his ability to extend himself toward the future, despite the evident domination of the forward projection, is an act based in the past, and unfolding in the present. Whether the futurity underlying existence is the *Vorlaufen* (projection) of authentic existence, or the *Gewärtigen* (the waiting-for) of the inauthentic, both involve a past and a present. Likewise the factuality of *Befindlichkeit*, whether it gives rise to an authentic *Wiederholung* (a repetition of past possibility), or whether it leads only to inauthentic *Vergessenheit* (a forgetting or ignoring of past possibility), the nature of the Dasein's future projections is what decides, and this in turn fashions the form of the present. And so too, though the *Verfallen* is first of all in the present, whether the present take the form of *Gegenwärtigen* (the kind of making-present that puts the *Zuhandene* before me), or of the authentic existential *Augenblick* (moment), again all is determined by the Dasein's projections and by the way he makes present his past. The discursiveness of Dasein permits the dynamic unification into one temporal whole representing different exstatic directions. This discursiveness is the fundamental characteristic of the finite horizon opened by Dasein within which Being is revealed in time. Speech, in which the Being that is thus revealed is passed on to posterity, manifests the movement and intentional interpenetration of this same discursiveness. The discursiveness which permits Being's revelation in time is the fundamental characteristic of the ontological structure of time itself. Consequently, the analyses of time and history with which *Sein*

---

[65] *Sein und Zeit*, p. 350.

und Zeit terminates will reproduce the same movement that we have just seen analyzed on the plane of the individual existent, now on the level of a discussion of the possible kinds of temporality.

MUNDANE AND INTERMUNDANE TIME AND THE ORIGIN OF THE POPULAR CONCEPTION OF TIME

The description of the existential-ontological structure of time just summarized seems to have nothing in common with the customary conception of time that we depend on to regulate our everyday affairs. Nor does it seem related to those traditional philosophical conceptions which seemed based on the "common sense" experience of time. Heidegger finds it necessary, then, to contrast the existential interpretation of time with "time" as the world thinks of it, and as philosophers such as Aristotle have explained it, in a way that will help us to see the relation between these differing conceptions.

The "world's" time is the time of the *besorgende Umwelt*, the world of everyday concerns,[66] in which authentic and inauthentic Dasein alike are forced by the insufficiency of their finite natures to take a hand. When I am concerned with securing my place in a world where my continued presence is by no means guaranteed, my problem is to deal with the instruments and objects that can actually affect my present well-being. Consequently I am interested in having the situation well in hand and in being certain that when tomorrow comes I shall once again be able to handle things satisfactorily. It is evident that the scope of consideration is very limited when it is only a question of handling the instruments necessary for the protection and comfort of my life, and of materially securing my place in the world. It is much less evident, though the reader of *Sein und Zeit* is beginning to see that it is important, that the kind of temporality involved in this sort of concern is also of a very definite type. Dealing with objects and going to work (*zu Werke gehen*) do not require that I wonder how these things can be intentionally present before me, or that I pose fundamental questions about ultimate goals or first origins. Rather my concern is fastened on the kind of "now"

[66] *Ibid.*, pp. 352-56.

that finds the thing before me, bristling with significance for other things that can affect me. The duration of its instant of importance is conditioned by the intersection of its influence with other influences, its competition for attention with other *Vorhandene* and instruments that can aid me in my mission of concern. Hence, these various interacting elements begin to take their place in a time fabric in the form of discrete periods of concern. My meeting with *A* is succeeded by an interview with *Z*, which in turn gives way to lunch, etc. In every instance, however, my moment of action is now when *A* or *Z* or the lunch is before me and therefore susceptible of acting on me or of being acted upon by me. From the exigencies of this kind of concern flow two consequences for the mundane notion of time: its concern is absorbed by the now, and its movement is essentially a flow of identifiable nows which follow one after the other. From this, two more results: the future and the past are looked upon strictly in terms of their becoming or having been a now for action; and, since there can be an infinity of objects and of concerns, there can be an infinity of moments stretching out along a line of time indefinitely. Hence Heidegger's characterization of daily time as "a following of now-points" (*Jetzt-Punkte*).[67]

The everyday Dasein finds a natural system of measurement which permits an effective regulation of the flow of events that swarm by each day. The sun's light casts a benevolent illumination over the totality of things with which I am concerned, and at night, in its absence, I have only the stars to orient me in my comings and goings. Here are events of universal importance, concern to all the Mitdasein active in their *besorgende Umwelt*.[68] "Concern makes use of the 'instrument' of the light-giving and warmth-giving sun."[69] The division of the day into daytime and nighttime, and of both into hours, follows, again naturally, from the need to regulate the events of the day on the basis of some absolutely common concern.[70] The public time, made possible by the Dasein's *geworfene-verfallende* presence in the world of concern and made necessary by the need to regulate commonly the flow of the *Jetztfolge* of interlacing concerns, is born simply and naturally into the existence of everyday Dasein.

[67] *Ibid.*, p. 423.　　[68] *Ibid.*, pp. 412-13.　　[69] *Ibid.*, p. 412.　　[70] *Ibid.*, p. 413.

Aristotle's definition of time as "the measure of motion according to the before and after"[71] is a perfect formulization of this self-evident, common-sense kind of time. The "before" and "after" (*kata to proteron kai husteron*) are viewed either as instants that are not yet, but are awaited, or as instants that are no longer, but were present. Is such time objective? This natural *Weltzeit* is neither objective nor subjective. Or as Heidegger says, it is "more objective than any object"—because it springs ultimately from the very transcendental horizon of Dasein which makes possible any "objects"—and "more subjective" than any particular subject "because this time first becomes possible with the Being, understood in the sense of care, of the factually existing self."[72] For the public time finds its possibility in the ontological root of Dasein as the care-structure opening the horizon for *Being-in-the-world*, which is of course the prior, ultimate condition for there to be any subjectivity or objectivity.

From the tone of the preceding remarks it is evident that Heidegger does not "find anything wrong" with there being a public time, or in our normal activities with it—anymore than he "finds anything wrong" with our functioning as *alltäglich* Dasein. Being part and parcel of the finitude of our being as "thrown-fallen" into the world, there can be no question of passing moral judgment on such a state of affairs. It is not even a question of applying the troubling qualification "inauthentic"—so long as this is not where we let the matter lie.

The point is that the mundane time, like the daily existence of which it is part, is not fundamental, but depends on the ontological structure of Dasein as *Sorge* for its very possibility. As long as the authentic Dasein recognizes this, and thereby goes beyond the life of concern to the life of care, he can remain authentic while necessarily continuing to have something to do with the time and the instruments of daily affairs.

But the trouble is that, to really plunge into "the time of concerned affairs," a specific *forgetting* is required; we are required to forget ourselves.[73] And the philosophy that erects

---

[71] *Physics*, D 11, 219b 1 sq., cited in *Sein und Zeir*, p. 421.

[72] *Sein und Zeit*, p. 419.

[73] "Um an die Zeugwelt 'verloren', 'wirklich' zu Werke gehen und hantieren zu können, muss sich das Selbst vergessen." *Ibid.*, p. 354.

a definition like Aristotle's into the fundamental expression of time "forgets" the ontological structure of the possibility of time in the exstatic *Sorge*-structure of the Dasein. This has been the fate of the entire Western philosophical tradition: the fundamental ontological basis of time has been ignored; and the Being of Dasein, that makes possible the coming to be of historical Being, has been "forgotten."

Is Heidegger suggesting that Dasein, of his very nature, is doomed to a certain degree of inauthenticity? After all, his *geworfen-verfallene* finite nature forces him first and foremost (*zunächst und zumeist*) into the everyday world of concern. The problem here, of course, is to understand precisely Heidegger's complex conception of the plight of finite existence in its struggle through its essential limitations toward an adequate, authentic existence.

The first thing we must realize is that no Dasein is ever purely authentic in every respect all of the time. Because we are "thrown, fallen into the world" we cannot avoid some involvement in the concerns of daily life, and these are inevitably going to involve us in that mundane time where a forgetting of self takes hold of us. But because this is a constant, and even an overwhelming tendency, it does not mean that domination by concern to the point that the essential direction of my life is set by such concerns, need be inevitable. Heidegger points this out very clearly by explaining what he means when he repeatedly employs the phrase "first and foremost" in referring to the daily forms of existence. *Zunächst* indicates the way the Dasein opens up into the world, involved automatically in relations of *Mitsein* and *Zusein*, but in a way that provides in the very *Grund* of the daily situation a way of overcoming its bounds.[74] *Zumeist* means the way that Dasein, "as a rule, but not always," manifests himself in the forms of *Jedermann*.[75]

Authenticity remains the essential possibility in the most inauthentic life, just as the genuine *Sorge*-structure is always the hidden source of the most involved daily time. Conversely, the most authentic life will never be free of the necessity of *besorgende* involvements; but the essential authenticity of the ruling projections in such a life, forces the narrow *Jetztpunkt* of daily time into continuous oscillation toward the deeper

[74] *Ibid.*, p. 370.   [75] *Ibid.*

54

horizons of an authentic futurity, by always revivifying the realization that I am *Sein-zum-Tode*, and toward the authentic past, by always viewing the now in terms of the rich possibilities presented by my tradition.

Looked at functionally from the standpoint of the person's concrete life, authenticity and inauthenticity are, then, in a certain sense, relative terms. Though Heidegger nowhere uses such terminology, I think it might help the reader to visualize the tension that is always going to exist in any life between these two poles, neither one of which is ever going to exclude the other. Were I to orient the temporal structure of my existence on the *Sorge*-achieved balance of extases dominated by projections, never losing sight of my essential structure in its true possibilities and limitations, I should probably still find myself forced at times to forget the *Selbst* and to absorb myself provisionally, only for a few moments, in problems arising from the *Umwelt*.

The same problem—understanding Heidegger's conception of how the authentic and the inauthentic interplay concretely— arises when we endeavour to grasp the relationship of the revelation and the dissimulation that takes place in the course of Being's unfolding in history. We can see now that the domination of one or the other conception of time in any one epoch could serve as a kind of indicator of "how goes it" for the essential revelation of Being during that period. This is why the last published chapters of *Sein und Zeit* are concerned not only to draw a more explicit picture of how the *Geschicht-lichkeit* of Dasein follows from his temporality, but also to give some indications of the development of the conception of time throughout the history of philosophy. Heidegger's remarks provide a kind of thumbnail sketch of this development from Plato and Aristotle[76] to Hegel[77] and Dilthey and Graf Yorck.[78] We shall leave any further consideration of this historical development to Part II, where we can sketch in one unified plan the whole sweep of Heidegger's "destruction." But to clarify the fact that history only projects through centuries the pattern of existence of the average individual as Heidegger conceives it, we can say this here: The time conception has moved from an expression of the natural *Weltzeit* viewed in its

[76] *Ibid.*, pp. 421-23.   [77] *Ibid.*, pp. 428-35.   [78] *Ibid.*, pp. 397 ff.

55

self-evidence and common-sense naturalness by Aristotle to an increasing awareness of the deeper ontological structure of time in Hegel. This structure is conceived, however, in terms involving the ultimate "forgetting"; for the absolutization of time renders as inauthentic as possible the projections of the Hegelian Dasein, who, instead of basing his existence on *Sein-zum-Tode*, comes to participate in an absolute and immortal process. The revolt against this deification of Time brings Western man to the brink of the Nothingness in nihilism, where his *Angst* can begin. Thus in the throes of the worst inauthenticity begins the deepest night. It is this night of *Angst* which can give birth to the Heideggerian *Sorge*, and an authentic, existential revelation of Time.

THE HISTORICITY OF THE DASEIN

The above remarks give some indication of the importance of the last published chapter of *Sein und Zeit*, the chapter on the historicity of the Dasein. This is truly the summit of the fundamental work, the closest Heidegger comes to explaining formally in what sense *Sein* itself is *zeitlich*. That the conception of Being emerging there remains the basic cadre for all the philosophy to follow, Heidegger himself has re-affirmed formally as recently as 1946. In the letter to Jean Beaufret (*Brief über den Humanismus*) he says that we should consider the analysis in *Sein und Zeit* a "regional ontology" founding the entire effort to recapture Being through its basis in Dasein.

"A regional ontology" is a fundamental study of one kind of being; but we should remember that the kind of being that figures as the subject of the Existentiale is a very special one. Not only is it "that thing which we ourselves are," but it is the *Da-sein*, the being which, by its fundamental, essential act, opens the horizon within which Being itself is revealed. Consequently the essential historicity of this particular subject of a "regional ontology" is not an isolated, curious phenomenon, but the central conditioning fact in the revelation of the Being of the things-that-are.

For this reason the lessons taught about historicity in the last chapter of *Sein und Zeit* should be viewed ontologically, i.e., in their bearing on Being's own way of unfolding itself.

Heidegger begins the task of exposing the *Geschichtlichkeit* of the Dasien's existence by contrasting the historical course of a human being with the "life span" of something that lives out an allotted course in time. The rather physical conception of a life span as a coarse between two temporal sign posts (beginning and end) waiting to be filled up with a quantity of fragmented events might be suitable for a *Vorhandensein*, but not for an existent. We have already seen the great importance of recognizing that the Dasein's death is not just a capital moment waiting to be fulfilled someday. It is rather the fact, the awareness of which will, through anguish, keep the Dasein in a state of *Sorge*, in other words in a grasp of the structural totality of that thing which I am. Nor is the other pole of my existence, my birth, simply a moment over and done with; rather for the caring Dasein it becomes a present, conditioning reality grasped as fundamental throwness—that radical contingency which touches as an essential consideration all of my concrete possibilities as Being-toward-death. "The factual Dasein exists *born*, and is dying already *as* born, in the sense of 'thrown' as Being-toward-death."[79] In the full "now" of authentic existence, all projections are made in view of my radical throwness, with death before me as the ultimate conditioning possibility, so that existence becomes a self-extension (*sich erstrecken*) from birth to death lived in the dense moment of caring projection. Because the Dasein knows the course it is taking and resolutely wills it, the historical motion is not a passive undergoing, such as the material living thing experiences, but an active "letting itself happen," the free shouldering of a destiny. For this reason Heidegger terms the motion of the Dasein's self-extension a *Geschehen*—a "happening," from which of course he would derive the word *Geschichte* (historical destiny).

The sense of the word *Geschichte*, as Heidegger employs it, must be worked out then against the whole context of the existential analysis. Ordinarily when we speak of history, Heidegger warns us, we mix indiscriminately several different notions. When one says "history" he may mean, for example, simply the "gone," the "past," in much the sense of the *Vergangenen* that figures in the public conception of time. Or he

[79] *Ibid.*, p. 374.

could be referring to the origin of a particular monument, or of a town, in some past time. Or perhaps he means a sum total of things that are changing through the course of time, so that the reference may be to the long destiny of a country of men. Perhaps he means simply all that is handed down by tradition. What is common to all four of these examples chosen at random is what is least commonly brought to light—their root in the historicizing possibilities in the *Geschehen* of the Dasein. Until this is brought out into the light, seen and understood as the origin of all "history," of all the past and of time itself, any affirmation about history must remain less than fundamental, and affirmations about the essence of history run a very real risk of becoming inauthentic.

To avoid any such unfortunate occurrence, let us proceed with Heidegger directly to the central question: How does the concrete temporal existence of the particular Dasein insert him into a "history"?

The *Existentiale* has brought to light the fact that authenticity requires that we grasp our Being in its outermost possibilities. "Possibility" is, of course, basically future-directed. But Dasein's possibilities, we have seen, are founded on a past that has revealed what it is possible for Dasein to do, and in the very act of revelation has laid the ground for future possibilities.[80] Consequently, the Dasein's realization in the present of certain possibilities requires that he make present, in view of his projects, the possibilities offered by the past.

Any failure to realize his full possibilities would be due to projections that suppress or underemphasize either the futurity of projection, or the need to apply to the past in order to actualize the possibilities that are present there. When I turn to the past as though it were a passive "object" waiting to reveal its secrets to me, I am overlooking the fact that the past reveals itself to me in terms of human possibility, and that it is my projections, i.e., what I count possible, that determines what I shall objectively "see" or overlook.[81] If I fail to take account of the influence of these projections, that does not mean they do not exist; rather, their role simply becomes more dangerous, since they can operate without my ever suspecting that they are there. The opposite oversight—projection without sufficient

[80] *Ibid.*, p. 391.　　　　　　[81] *Ibid.*, p. 395.

reference to the past as source of concrete possibility—is just as disastrous, for then subjective aspirations become blind, without reference to real possibility and without control from consciously considered experience. Consequently, the Dasein that does not shoulder the burden of his destiny (*Schicksal*), either because he ignores the past or because he ignores his responsibility toward the future, becomes the tool of fate and blind arbitrariness, both of which are only aspects of his own inauthenticity.

Wiederholung and *Ueberlieferung* are the names Heidegger gives to the two aspects of Dasein's authentic historical development. Repetition, the act of making present the possibilities of the past in view of his resolute projections,[82] is the basis of "handing on a tradition," which is what occurs when I actualize historical possibility on the basis of what has been done, and thus make possible new advances for the future.[83]

Heidegger's "destruction" of the historical destiny of ontology is an effort to approach the Western philosophical tradition authentically, by regarding the various developments as so many possibilities for a philosophy wishing to refound the Being-question. This means that Heidegger will have to repeat these possibilities in a way that will transform them to hand them on to the tradition now being formed and transmitted. The truth of the destruction resides in its maintaining the integrity of the *wiederholend-überliefernd* movement in perfect balance. Hence, though Heidegger will approach past philosophies from a definite point of view, he will expect that point of view to be in turn regulated by the revelations that are found in history.

A vicious circle? A circle, Heidegger admits, and in fact even joyfully admits, for, in the existential view of things, this is a sign of authentic explanation. The interpretations of a finite understanding will always be circular. We cannot understand unless we bring a viewpoint to things, and there would be nothing to be seen from this viewpoint if there were nothing understood. This circularity, in Heidegger's opinion,

---

[82] "Die Wiederholung kennzeichnen wir als den Modus der sich überliefernden Entschlossenheit, durch den das Dasein ausdrücklich als Schicksal existiert." *Ibid.*, p. 386.

[83] *Ibid.*, p. 385.

can never be broken. This in no way dooms Dasein to subjectivity or arbitrariness, for there is a kind of justification or critique possible interior to this understanding. It lies in the ability of the projections upon which the interpretation is founded to render present, and thus make meaningful for the future, the greatest range of possibilities from out the tradition.

I shall reserve a closer scrutiny of this conception of the circularity of interpretation to the last chapter of the book. I bring it up here to suggest to the reader something about the kind of balance it is necessary to maintain within the Heideggerian universe, between subjectivity and objectivity, idealism and realism, revelation and dissimulation, past and future, *Wiederholung* and *Ueberlieferung*. Heidegger's position has something in common with Nietzsche's notion of the historical return of the similar in its attempt to achieve a self-sufficiency within the circle *Sein-Seienden*. What is real is what is revealed by Dasein. Further revelation of the real requires that I make present what has already been revealed, which I can only do in view of future possibility. But since future possibility grows only out of the field of past possibility, a circle of interpretation is formed. Is there, then, nothing new in Being? Nietzsche seems to have faced this problem squarely in his last works and to have answered "No!"—the movement of history and the revelation of Being is only the *ewige Wiederkunft des Gleichens*! Heidegger will not accept this solution. He wishes to maintain the perfect circle of interpretation; this prevents subordinating the understanding to an objective order which could move it toward a transcendent Absolute; yet he insists that the Dasein's self-extension toward the future does involve real originality. It must be so, otherwise all meaning would be drained out of freedom. Heidegger cannot see Nietzsche any other way than as one who has capitulated freedom to the Eternal Return, in the interest of reestablishing a metaphysical, stable order under the guise of motion. But from whence comes the *newness* which this originality represents? The works which follow *Sein und Zeit* will reinforce the answer already suggested there somewhat timidly: from out the Nothing, the *Nichts* of Dasein's originative finitude. But how can the originative element come forth from Nothing to be inserted into the circle of interpretation without compromising its basic balance? In effect, does not this solution destroy the balance in favour of a subjectivism? "The authentic repetition of a past existential possibility—the Dasein's choice of a hero—is existentially grounded in projecting resolution."[84] This interesting statement comes as close as any to suggesting the dangers of subjectivity which lurk in Heidegger's solution, despite his horror, so explicitly and abundantly expressed, for any "solution" that might upset the subject-object balance.

It is with this problem lurking in the background that Heidegger seeks to explain how history can be a concrete and personal affair, and still remain, in some sense, scientific.[85] Rethinking the meaning of "science," he is led to reject two of the most sacrosanct notions of its traditional "metaphysical" conception: first, the notion that a science, to be worthy of the name, must be "universal"; second, the notion of "science without presupposition." To these positions Heidegger opposes two discoveries of the *Existentiale*: (1) all knowledge is based on a governing projection, and hence cannot be without presupposition; (2) the interest of scientific conception lies not in ideal generality (that *Allgemeinheit* which Heidegger sees as the most telling symptom of idealism, of "metaphysicalism"), but in the validity of that which is real (and therefore concrete in origin) for two or more parallel situations.

The first discovery, we see at once, is dictated by the Heideggerian conception of what it is to know, by the conviction that *Verstehen* involves the Dasein in an act of interpretation, which requires that the Dasein in his freedom take a stand in order to open the meaning of a thing. Applying this to the sciences, Heidegger has only to point out that the sciences are divided according to formal and material objects. The establishment of *Forschungsbereiche* is based on the decision flowing from a point of view, i.e., from the kind of question the scientist wishes to pose.[86] This *Thematisierung* involves both the projection just mentioned, and a presupposition, namely that the object can sensibly be divided the way the scientist decides to do it.

[84] *Ibid.*, p. 385.
[85] We shall only touch on Heidegger's conception of science here, reserving to chapter XII a more extended discussion. Cf. *Sein und Zeit*, p. 392.
[86] *Sein und Zeit*, p. 393.

Against the notion of "science without presupposition," and particularly in reference to the science of history, Heidegger states:

The selection (*Auswahl*) of what shall become the possible object has already happened in the factual existential *decision* (*Wahl*) of the *Geschichtlichkeit* of the Dasein, in whom history first of all comes to pass, and to whom it is proper.[87]

Concerning the universality of scientific notions, we should first point out that Heidegger has nothing against a science being general, as long as the nature of its chosen object is susceptible of general treatment without risk of essential distortion. As long as a particular kind of knowledge need not be concerned with what touches the individuality of beings, there is no inconvenience in generalization. But in the study of man in his freedom, i.e., man as real existent, it is precisely the concrete possibilities manifested by different men that concern us. History, then, above all other sciences, is properly concerned with the concrete, "In no other science is the 'generally valid' . . . a less possible criterion of truth than in authentic history."[88] Heidegger explains why this must be so:

Because existence is "thrown" [into the world] only factually, the nature of history, as the quiet force of the possible (*die stille Kraft des Möglichen*), becomes most revealingly exposed the more singularly and concretely In-the-World past being is understood in terms of possibility and only thus.[89]

No *Geschichtswissenschaft*, then, can ever legitimately be general and fundamental at the same time.[90]

How then can historical research be said to have scientific value? How can the historical *factum* have an interest transcending the moment? If history has to do neither with the facts, which as purely concrete can have no applicability elsewhere, nor with "general laws" which would abstract from the concreteness of existence to the point that it loses its validity, then history's scientific value evidently depends on a new kind of applicability, concrete but not limited to the here and now circumstances of the original fact. Heidegger speaks of this existential applicability of the concretely possible in a paragraph that may well become a classic in the philosophy of history:

[87] *Ibid.*, p. 395.   [88] *Ibid.*   [89] *Ibid.*, p. 394.   [90] *Ibid.*, p. 395.

The "thema" of history is concerned neither with that which happens only once, nor with some generality that hovers over the facts, but with the factually existent past possibility. Such possibility can never be repeated, i.e., historically understood authentically, as long as it is turned into the paleness of a super-temporal model. Only factually authentic historicity as resolute destiny (*Schicksal*) can so reveal past history that in the repetition the force of the possible will affect existence strikingly, which is to say will be allowed to affect its futurity.[91]

Because the existent today can grasp the human significance of the past act in terms of the possibility it represents for his own future projections, the historical event can become meaningful in other places and in other times than its own. Hence its becoming meaningful for others need in no way compromise its concrete status as factual.

If the reader is still somewhat astounded by the audacity and the newness of such a conception of the science of history, he should at least see that it all follows from what Heidegger has discovered to us phenomenologically about the nature of existence and about the nature of that interpretation which becomes for the phenomenologist the basis of our relationship to the things-that-are. Concerning the nature of that *Ek-sistent* which it is proper to history to study, let us recall what *Sein und Zeit* has already taught us about this *Wesen* when viewed in the roots of its liberty. The Dasein is not an *essentia*, a fixed structure corresponding to an idea expressible in several intelligible notes, like the "animal having logos" of Aristotle. This kind of crude designation, derived from an "objective" consideration of the human being as a kind of *Vorhandensein*, reveals nothing of the nature of its liberty, of its true reality as foundation for Being; in fact it reveals nothing about the true meaning of that *logos*, and indeed dissimulates the true historical nature of Dasein's revelation of Being. Because the nature of Dasein is existential, it can only be grasped as possibility, i.e., in the concrete unfolding of its dynamic nature in the movement of time. "Since Dasein 'authentically' can only be real in its existence, then it constitutes its own proper 'objective factuality' (*Tatsächlichkeit*) directly, in resolute self-projection in view of a chosen possibility of Being (*auf ein gewähltes Seinkönnen*)."[92]

[91] *Ibid.*   [92] *Ibid.*, p. 394.

Heidegger asserts that the objective analysis of a human nature as a kind of thing is not fundamental; but, from this insistence on grasping the Dasein as concrete possibility, the reader should not too quickly conclude that Heidegger sees no sense in the term "human nature." First, note that Heidegger does not consider false the definition of man as "rational animal." It is true up to a point; it is not fundamental. It becomes a dissimulation when it satisfies the mind as *the* expression of the *Wesen* of man, and thereby blocks further discovery of the existential nature of *Dasein*. This suggests that there is still something in common between all Dasein of all eras, though their differences are more than accidental. When Heidegger locates the subject of history on a plane that is neither purely factual nor general, it is evident that he is applying a different kind of analysis—phenomenology—in order to get at man on that deeper, common level, where distinctions of substance and accident, factual and universal, do not apply.

The best way to bring out the kind of unity that runs through the epochs of the dynamic, exstatic self-extention of Dasein would be to consider the contrary of this unity, the dispersion and lack of cohesion that brand, according to our author, inauthentic histories. It is when men are viewed as objects, and their relationships as oppositions and unions of forces, that the true, existential, exstatic unity of humanity is dispersed. The externality and non-intentionality of the unphenomenological, *vorhandenlich* objective analysis, building as it does on its exterior view of everyday, inauthentic Dasein, forces the inauthentic historian to seek in general ideas and imposed conceptions, such as movements, currents, and other such constructed organizing devices, some way of overcoming the dispersion which his kind of approach has caused.[93] In other words, historical unity has to be "constructed" once we have missed the way of access into the true source of human unity, which lies in the *Selbst* building out of a tradition which he must freely repeat, toward a future which will continue in his free projections the tradition he has brought forward.

Heidegger compares the structures of inauthentic history to that "flight before death" which characterizes the existence of daily Dasein.[94] The suggestion is that "constructed" histories

[93] *Ibid.*, p. 390.　　　　　　　　　[94] *Ibid.*

erect out of the *vergangenen* (past) material a series of static, monumental structures which dissimulate more than they reveal the freedom and responsibility of the concrete existent. Determinism in history, and the absolutisation of history, both find their root-possibility in a particular "fundamental existential interpretation of the Dasein's happening-structure (*Geschehensganzheit*),"[95] namely that of the inauthentic Dasein, who views man in the image and likeness of his own flight before the realities of his finitude.

Authentic history, on the other hand, brings Dasein immediately (*unmittelbar*) before the reality of the past, that is *zeitlich ekstatisch zurück*.[96] Brought face to face with the true existential possibilities that history represents, Dasein can accept the reality of his death and of his birth in terms of the responsibilities they imply. He will see that his birth into a historical tradition is not automatic, but something he has to face up to, assimilating this past, and thereby causing it to live again. He will see that the only escape from his finitude lies, not in ignoring the reality of death, but in accepting the responsibility of making possible the only real kind of immortality, i.e., the kind that lies in the "protection of being."

Here, then, in true historicity, lies the real sense of fidelity for Heidegger, and the only meaning worthy of man's freedom *reverance* and *authority* can have for the Dasein-doomed-to-die. "Resolution constitutes the *fidelity* (*Treue*) of existence to its own self (*Selbst*). As resolution prepared by anguish, this fidelity becomes at the same time possible reverence (*Ehrfurcht*) before the sole authority that a free existence can recognize—before the repeatable possibilities of existence."[97]

---

[95] *Ibid.*   [96] *Ibid.*, p. 391.

[97] *Ibid.*, p. 391. With this explanation of the nature of the authentic science of history in view, and with the knowledge of what has been said already about the need for achieving an "existential balance" between subjectivity and objectivity, we can understand Heidegger's criticism of the two major kinds of inauthentic, or non-fundamental, historical sciences. It is as possible for the historian as for the philosopher to sin either on the side of subjective over-systematization (which corresponds roughly in history to the temptation to idealism in philosophy), or on the side of a pretended objectivity (which like philosophical realism really shares with idealism, down deep, the same unhappy cause: the arbitrary projection of an ideal contrary to the exigencies of human nature as it really and

"The authentic repetition of a past existenz-possibility—Dasein's choosing of its heroes—is grounded existentially in projecting resolution."[98] This admirably sums up the importance of history in Heidegger's eyes. It would hardly be going too far to say that history, understood in terms of that *eigentliche Geschichtlichkeit* which I have been describing, becomes for him the new philosophy; for certainly it is now conceived as our source of understanding what man is and how Being is revealed through him. History is *the* important science—this is the profound sense of Heidegger's assertion: "The primary thematisation (*Thematisierung*) of the historical object projects the past Dasein from out its most proper *Eksistenz*-possibility."[99]

Like the *Existentiale* which gives it birth, this fundamental conception of history achieves an exposition of reality that has undeniable and extremely precious value; it may move the thinker of the Western tradition a step beyond the battles over subjective versus objective history, and goes far in revealing to us why so many discussions on the question, "Is history scientific?" have been rather sterile. The notion that we should find in history real existential possibility is an exciting answer for the professional historians who, confronted by intelligent students who find history dull, have sought the key to giving history the life they knew certainly it should possess. The existential-phenomenological conception of history invites an approach to historical reality that promises to help retain in its study the integration, dynamism, liberty and profundity of human life itself. It makes eminently clear on the level of philosophical

authentically exists). The subjective historian substitutes a fabricated general structure abstracted from selected facts of history in place of that interest in the facts of historical events viewed as concrete possibility for existing which alone constitutes the authentic matter for historical science. The objective historian, believing that he uncovers the facts as they really are, ignores the point that the meaning of facts is a question of interpretation, and that interpretation involves inclusion of the thing within a temporal world opened by the projections of Dasein. Any given historian *must* himself subsume the facts of history into a particular temporal horizon and therefore must interpret them from the point of view of a given *Geschichtlichkeit*. The sad thing is that the objective historian, having never examined phenomenologically the exact conditions of interpretation, ignores the influence shaping subterraneanly his own *Geschichtlichkeit*, his own projections.

[98] *Sein und Zeit*, p. 385.   [99] *Ibid.*, p. 394.

explanation, for instance, something that many have long suspected, but have never found reason to justify—namely that the division of history into political, social, economic, cultural, and intellectual segments was basically dangerous, and that, even when most intelligently approached, each branch tended somehow, somewhere to lack vitality. Heidegger forces us to see why vitality has been lacking—because our point of view has not revealed the past in its exciting reality as receptacle of possibility for us.

Yet, despite the magnificent positive gains of this conception of history, the problem of the originative source, and hence of the ultimate guide, of interpretation remains unsolved; it is, in fact, only heightened by Heidegger's profound analyses of the fundamental existential themes. The question we posed above about Dasein's central act of existence: how is the circle of "interpretation" broken by the originative element in new revelation? what is the origin of that new element?—can be posed about existential history, in a suitably altered form. Granting that Heidegger would have us approach history in a way that will reawaken and pass along the maximum of what is real and valuable among the human possibilities accumulated in the course of a tradition, is the problem of a guide for choice, of direction for our resolute projections, any the more solved by the realization that Dasein must choose its heroes? Possibilities conflict and heroes differ, as St. Francis differs from Caesar. If the answer is offered, "Choose the hero that demands of his followers the maximum self-extension to preserve the greatest past heritage," then the question is thrown on an altogether different plane, that of an objective consideration of the relative value of the Being-concepts presented in the programs lived by now this hero, now that. The realization that the truth of historical positions is something we must make our own by living it is a precious gain, and to the extent that the Heideggerian analysis makes us aware of this, we should be grateful. But the real problems of the direction of life are not confronted seriously by this analysis as we have seen it evolve to this point.

It is in this sense that *Sein und Zeit* remains incomplete. Whether the later works continue along the *Holzweg* laboriously prepared by the published parts of the basic work, sufficiently deep into the forest so that decision, and therefore guidance, becomes necessary, is something that can only be determined, of course, when we have come to the end of our survey. Before we attempt to make any such fundamental judgment, we should follow the course of Heidegger's own concrete analysis of the history of Western ontology. This is where Heidegger intends us to watch truth as he sees it unfold; we must examine with him the various stations along that historical-destiny, to see what they reveal of Being, and to criticize their ways of dissimulating it.

But before we can do that, we shall have to first follow, in the works immediately succeeding *Sein und Zeit*, Heidegger's efforts to ground phenomenologically in the freedom of Dasein the notion of truth which bases the historical analysis of ontologies: truth conceived as *a-letheia*, as the continuous dynamic dissimulating-unveiling of Being. The first step in this effort, which culminates in the lecture "On the Essence of Truth," was the firmer establishment of the distinction between his own existential notion of truth, and the notion implicit in the transcendental idealism of Kant.

II   Kant and the Problem of Metaphysics

THE part of *Sein und Zeit* published in 1927 contained 427 pages of careful analysis of Dasein. Following the radical method of "the Heideggerian phenomenology," it is couched in a new philosophical language and expresses its discoveries in new categories. That even major implications of this monumental work are only now coming to light is not surprising. Heidegger himself, in the thirty-two years that have intervened, has come to see in a different light some of what is most original in the fundamental work.

The following text, written in 1949 as part of an Introduction to the difficult lecture of 1929, *Was ist Metaphysik?*, gives us some idea of the form this clarified basic conception of *Sein und Zeit*'s aims has taken in Heidegger's mind.

The attempt to inquire back into what conceals itself [in the ὄν ᾗ ὄν of traditional metaphysics], looked at from the point of view of metaphysics, is a seeking after the fundament of ontology. Therefore, this attempt is called in *Sein und Zeit* "Fundamental Ontology." Yet this title, as any title would be in this case, is misleading. Considered *metaphysically*, it would be correct, and that is the very reason it is misleading; for what is at stake is getting beyond metaphysics to a thinking that recalls the Truth of Being. As long as this thinking continues to call itself "Fundamental Ontology" it at one and the same time puts itself on the right road and leaves that road in the dark. For the title "Fundamental Ontology" suggests that the thinking that seeks to think the Truth of Being, and not, as all ontology, simply the truth of beings (*Seienden*), is nevertheless itself a kind of ontology.... [However] in trying to think the Truth of Being, and thus in going into the ground of all metaphysics, this thinking, by its very first step, has left the region of ontology.[1]

This text suggests that *Sein und Zeit* was indeed moving in the right direction; but having in the Introduction proposed to prepare the way for a thinking of the Truth of Being, its very first step had led it beyond all metaphysics, and therefore beyond the very title that Heidegger then attached to the effort it was undertaking—"Fundamental Ontology." He admitted in 1949 that the full implications of what he had accomplished in 1927 were not then clear to him. Let us, from the more recent, more profound perspective, seek to determine more adequately than was possible in our analysis of *Sein und Zeit* what is really at stake in a "surpassing of metaphysics."

In the concluding paragraphs of the Inaugural Lecture of 1929—now the body of *Was ist Metaphysik?*—Heidegger wrote, "Metaphysics is the fundamental event (*Grundgeschehen*) of the Dasein. It is the Dasein himself."[2] Does this mean that in surpassing metaphysics, the Dasein would surpass himself? Heidegger affirms exactly that. The Dasein building on his old self, would surpass it, in founding the self of a new tradition. The Introduction of 1949 states:

A thinking that recalls the Truth of Being no longer finds mere metaphysics sufficient; but it does not for all this oppose metaphysics. To put it figuratively, it does not rip up the roots of philosophy. It tills the ground and plows the soil for it. Metaphysics remains the first of philosophy; it does not succeed in being the first of thinking (*Die Metaphysik bleibt das Erste der Philosophie. Das Erste des Denkens erreicht sie nicht*). In the recalling of the Truth of Being metaphysics is overcome. . . . Yet this *Überwindung* of metaphysics does not set metaphysics aside. So long as man remains the "animal rationale," he remains the *animal metaphysicum*. But if our thinking should succeed in its efforts to go back into the ground of metaphysics, it would be the occasion for a change of the essence of man, accompanied by a transformation of metaphysics.[3]

Man, to surpass his nature as *animal metaphysicum*, must go back into the historical ground of that nature, into that *Erste* of philosophy, to take full possession of it. To take full possession of historical reality, he must grasp the structural whole of the act involved. The structural whole of a man is grasped when we

---

[1] Heidegger, *Was ist Metaphysik?*, p. 21.　　[2] *Ibid.*, p. 41.　　[3] *Ibid.*, p. 9.

view him in the total span of his existence from the "throwness" of birth to the "end" of death. Similarly the structural whole of a metaphysics is seen, in the case of the particular ontology, when we grasp it in its outer limits, in the *Grenze* of its dissimulation, and in the case of an entire tradition, when we think beyond it, to something hyper-metaphysical. If we indeed achieve such a thinking, that is, if we achieve a surpassing of metaphysics, the new thinking will not be against the old, but built upon and beyond it. Again a comparison with the existence of the individual man is enlightening. Authentic existence is, in a sense, a surpassing of the primordial, natural condition of the individual in the *Verfallensein* in which he finds himself as he is "thrown" into a world. This surpassing does not declare war on the "undifferentiated structure of everyday Dasein"; it builds upon it, and out beyond it in a fuller, freer exercise of the Dasein's possibilities. This—and we shall return to the notion for a more leisurely consideration later—is what is involved in the Dasein's "changing his nature."

The same Introduction to *Was ist Metaphysik?* situates very exactly the perspective of the first major work to follow *Sein und Zeit*, the profound critique of transcendental idealism entitled *Kant und das Problem der Metaphysik*.[4] For Heidegger, surpassing the level of ontological existence means achieving a grasp on existence more fundamental than one which reduces Being to a consideration of transcendence. In the words of the Introduction, "Every philosophy which revolves around a direct or indirect representation of 'transcendence' remains of necessity an ontology, whether it achieves a new foundation of ontology or whether it assures us that it repudiates ontology as a conceptual freezing of experience."[5] There is no question but that Heidegger is thinking here of Kant. For him Kant is *the* philosopher of transcendence. Kant is in a sense the spiritual father of Heidegger, since he was the thinker who rescued temporality from the periphery of philosophical consideration and installed

[4] Heidegger, then recently named to a chair of philosophy at Marburg, must have found it ideal to undertake the kind of historical analysis expected of a new master by preparing this work on Kant, which responds so exactly to the need to situate the revolutionary perspective of *Sein und Zeit* in relation to that earlier revolution to which Heidegger owes so much, the revolution wrought by *The Critique of Pure Reason*.

[5] Heidegger, *Was ist Metaphysik?*, p. 21.

it at the center of a new analysis of man as transcendental horizon. But Heidegger is no Kantian, any more than Aristotle can be termed a Platonist because he continued his master's search for the definitions of things.[6] Because Heidegger continues the master's search for the meaning of the transcendental horizon of the world, he owes a great debt to the Kant against whom he is revolting; but, in seeking the existential significance of the transcendental horizon, Heidegger proposes to surpass metaphysics, and this means explicitly and as a first consideration to surpass Kantian idealism.

Kant was indeed seeking the ground of metaphysics—that was his greatness. But he failed to do so existentially, i.e., by seeking to recall (*Andenken*) the Truth of Being. He sought the fundament of metaphysics only metaphysically—he stopped with a consideration of the transcendence that makes knowledge possible. He did not seek into the Being which is revealed historically within the transcendental existence of Dasein. Kant made no effort to get beyond the metaphysical nature of man, by recalling the historical destiny made possible by the temporality of his transcendence. Thus, though Kant puts the form of Time at the center of knowledge, he has missed the truly temporal nature of Being itself. The most evident result of this failure to understand the fundamental ontological implications of the exstatic nature of Dasein was his erection of the static forms and categories of the mind as principles *meta-ta-phusika* to explain the revelation of the things-that-are. But that is getting ahead of our story.

What, more specifically, were the results of Kant's endeavor? What did Kant achieve in the famous "deduction of transcendental categories"?

Heidegger's interpretation in *Kant und das Problem der Metaphysik* is squarely opposed to the post-Kantian analyses that interpret the deduction of categories as the affirmation of the domination of the transcendental logic over the transcendental

---

[6] Kant is not the only spiritual father of Heidegger. There is a real sense in which each of the philosophers figuring importantly in the destruction is a spiritual father. Kant, Kierkegaard, Hegel, Nietzsche, Husserl, and Dilthey—and the pre-Socratics, Plato and Aristotle—have all contributed something real, some "Being," which, freed by the destruction from its metaphysical limitations, enters into the Heideggerian doctrine in the role of essential principle.

aesthetic. Rather, Heidegger claims, the *Critique of Pure Reason* affirms the unity of apperception, showing that finite intuition is possible only because of the unity of conception and sensible intuition. This intuition, the *Critique* asserts, is achieved through the medium of the pure form of Time, which Kant views as a product of the "transcendental imagination."[7] It is to this notion of a transcendental imagination that we must turn if we are to understand this first effort to explain how Dasein can open a gap between himself and the things-that-are—how he can separate himself from the *Seienden*, regarding them as objects of his knowledge. Heidegger in his analysis put great emphasis on this Kantian notion of a *Gegenstehenlassen von* . . . , the objectivizing encounter with the things-that-are which renders all knowledge possible.

How is such an objectivizing encounter possible? Heidegger answers (and this assertion is so fundamental that we must return to consider its implications at length) that the Dasein's objectivizing encounter is rendered possible through the service of "no thing."

It can be *no* thing. But if it is not some being, it must consequently be *Nothing* (*Nichts*). It is only because the *Gegenstehenlassen von* . . . is a maintaining of oneself out-ahead in the Nothing that representation can encounter in the place of the Nothing and interior to the Nothing a *non-nothing*, something like a being (*Seiende*), provided of course that such a being manifests itself empirically. This Nothing, however, is not the *nihil absolutum*."[8]

At this point in our analysis, we are not yet prepared to enter into a definitive discussion of the Heideggerian notion of the *Nichts*. Yet if we do not seek to see something of what Heidegger is driving at in interpreting the fundamental act of encounter with things as a *Gegenstehenlassen von* . . . achieved from out the Nothing, we shall evidently profit little from his rethinking of the *Critique*. I ask the reader, therefore, to consider the few remarks that we shall make here only as preliminary, awaiting discussion in a later chapter for their full sense.

The question of the Nothing arises within a metaphysical dimension such as that in which Kant is working when he determines that ontic knowledge depends for its Being upon no

---

[7] Heidegger, *Kant und das Problem der Metaphysik*, p. 34.   [8] *Ibid.*, p. 71.

thing (*Seiende*) as thing. Kant saw that ontic knowledge depends rather on a dimension very different from that of *Seiendheit* (*thingness*), the dimension that Heidegger has termed, already in *Sein und Zeit*, the "ontological," the dimension in which the things-that-are take on their meaning by being placed within a horizon of significance. This ontological foundation for the concrete knowing acts is what is rooted in "no thing." Far from being essentially dependent on a self-evident thing, representation takes up the *Seiende* creatively, by actively rendering the knower present to it.

> Pure intuition insofar as it is finite, is certainly a receptive representation. But that which must be received *now*, where it is a question of Being, not of *Seienden*, cannot be a *vorhandenes* thing which offers itself up. On the contrary, the pure receptive representation must give *itself* a representable. Pure intuition must, therefore, in some way be creative.[9]

We see here another example of that ontic-ontological distinction, so strongly emphasized in *Sein und Zeit*, which will play an important role throughout Heidegger's works. To grasp something "ontically" is to grasp it in its full determination as a concrete phenomenon. To grasp it "ontologically," i.e., in its Being, one must think behind the phenomenon to grasp the ground of its possibility—what it is that makes it possible for this phenomenon to be as it is. This is not the same thing as grasping its causes. An Aristotelian causal explanation is part of an objective analysis (*Kategorien Analytik*) proper to metaphysical thinking, which the phenomenologist would surpass. Heidegger seeks rather to discover how it is that the Dasein's founding of the transcendental horizon makes it possible for the ontic phenomenon "to be" in *Time*. This analysis he terms *Existentiale Analytik*. The pure intuition understood then not just "ontically," as this concrete grasp of this concrete thing, but as the very rendering of meaning to things, must be seen as basically *creative* when viewed in its function as the "ontological" basis of ontic knowledge, as the universal, exstatic, horizontal condition of all concrete acts of intuition.[10]

The creativity of the transcendental imagination is centered in its providing the synthesizing, exstatic figure of Time. For

---

[9] *Ibid.*, p. 47.   [10] *Ibid.*, p. 266.

Kant, according to Heidegger's interpretation, Time is the universal condition of the possibility of phenomena as such, and therefore, is something positive and fundamental. The neo-Kantians, with their special absolutistic bias, missed this point, and therefore looked upon Time as the limitative and purely negative condition which thought imposes upon itself when it becomes a knowledge of things. Therefore the neo-Kantian interpretations are forced to fall back upon the idea of an in-temporal totality, i.e., the cosmological idea, to sustain the cognitive whole. Transcendence in such a conception can only be assured by recourse to a thing-in-itself which depasses the limitative temporal condition of finite knowledge. But the Heideggerian analysis perceives precisely in Time the two essential characteristics of transcendence and its object: the exstasis and the horizontality. Thus, the existential analysis does not seek to depass time, but to discover its true ontological foundation. Time is central because it realizes in itself a proper synthesis, a *synopsis*, alienating the consciousness of self to convert it into an ontological consciousness of the object by the self. We seize in Time, then, the subjective transcendental at work. This is why Kant makes of Time the origin of Space—because Time is the very subjective condition of there being any *Gegenstehenlassen von* . . . in the first place.

Kant locates this ultimate synthesizing function of Time in the imagination. He distinguishes two types of imagination, the reproductive (*exhibitio derivata*) or, in terms of Heidegger's analysis, ontic imagination that reproduces images of things previously intuited, called *derivata* because it is dependent like every ontic activity on the ontological structure of the Dasein for its meaning. The productive or ontological imagination (*exhibitio originaria*)[11] creates its figuration freely; this creation is ontological, i.e., exstatic and horizontal, and, therefore, sense-giving. Its form is the pure figure of Time.

This figure is a priori and present to all possible experience. In furnishing this figure the imagination sees a priori, absolutely and

[11] Heidegger distinguishes two kinds of *Denken*, a calculative derived kind of thinking, which dominates every-day existence; and the more exceptional *anfängliche Denken*, the originative thinking of fully authentic existence, which opens new horizons of Being. The distinction of imaginations achieved by Kant provides some basis for such a distinction of *Denken*.

always something other than a *Seiende*. It sees something other than a *Seiende* because its own preconstitution of a pure scheme, for example of substance, or for example of permanence, presents in general, in the foreground of our grasp of some thing, a continuous *view*, in the horizon of which, once it is formed, this or that presence of an object can manifest itself as object.[12]

We are now in a position to understand more fully how the creativity of the imagination can be said to provide this—the "figure of Time." The first important clue is the affirmation that Time is prior to Space. Time is prior to all "heres" and even to all "nows" because it creates itself as an exstasis *within which* the "nows" and the "heres" are encountered. This exstasis is more original than any moment or any point because it is the very act of giving of sense by the self, of generating out of one's own being the intuitive grasp which, transcending *this* object, *this* place, or *this* moment, renders possible, as long as I am I, my grasp of any object in any place at any time that I intuit it, so long as it becomes present to me in some fashion empirically. This *exhibitio originaria* is properly termed "imagination" because it produces the intuitionable in this sense: In our perception of any image this "giving of self" has to provide the original figure within which the objective encounter can take place. This figure is called "synoptic" because it does not just permit synthesis but a "seeing of the unity" through intuition.[13] A synthesis would be the unification achieved by reflection; the unity in intuition is not that. It is rather the unity apperceived in the very creation of the horizontal and exstatic figure of Time.

Such a synopsis must be at one and the same time receptive and creative, which is what renders Time effective as the liaison between pure concepts of the understanding and the intuitions it joins to them in the verifying synthesis. It is to explain the essence of this synthesis that Kant developed the famous paragraph in the *Critique* entitled "The Schematism of the Pure Concepts of the Understanding." Heidegger considers this the *Kernstuck* (the kernel) of the entire Kantian analysis. The judgment is itself a key for us to Heidegger's very personal interpretation of the transcendental idealism. This, according

---

[12] Heidegger, *Kant und das Problem der Metaphysik*, p. 124.
[13] *Ibid.*, p. 134.

to Heidegger, is the lesson of the *Kernstück*: One must not try to conceive the synopsis—that horizontal totality of diversity—as one would an abstract universal. The synopsis, unlike the universal, cannot be isolated from its particular content. For the synopsis, in its role as "rule" (so Kant terms it) is nothing more than the unification of spontaneity and receptivity. This unity cannot be seized thematically and in itself, but rather, being the unity of *our* knowledge, it must, to see itself, catch itself "on the fly," by discovering itself reflectively in its very act of unification within the intuition itself.

This rule of unity Kant terms the *Schema-bild*. In Heidegger's words, "it draws its character as figure not only and not primarily from its content precisely as perceived image, but from that out of which, and from the way in which it surges up from the possible exposé represented in its regulation: It is thus that the *Schema-bild* maintains the rule in the sphere of possible intuitivity."[14] The concept owes its reality to the schema because the schema can always provide visible unity synoptically through intuition. The pure notion has meaning only for the imagination, and, inversely, it is the imagination which purifies the intuition in relating it to an image which is possible rather than necessarily actual. For example, number as schema is the way of rendering possible at any given moment the image of some given, determinate number.

One important conclusion must be drawn from this discussion: The transcendental schematism really founds the internal possibility of ontological knowledge. It forms the objectivization in the pure encounter in such a way that that which is given in pure thought necessarily gives itself intuitively in the pure image of Time.

Time, then, is that which, inasmuch as it is given a priori, attributes primordially to the transcendental horizon a comprehensible offer. But that is not enough. Inasmuch as it is a unique pure universal image, it gives to the transcendental horizon its fundamental limits. This ontological horizon, unique and pure, is the condition of possibility for there to be *Seienden* given in such and such a particular horizon, that is, it is the condition of ontic possibility for *Seienden*. It is not enough, then, for Time to furnish to the transcendental horizon its unique, primordial cohesion, but

[14] *Ibid.*, p. 93.

inasmuch as it gives itself freely, it must furnish the horizon something like a *stop*. It renders comprehensible to a finite being the opposition (the *Dawider*) of objectivity, which belongs essentially to the finitude of a transcendence which-must-turn-towards. . . .[15]

It is because Time is for us a singular, closed totality that it renders possible the various regional ontologies and their concepts—because it renders possible the apparition of objects as objects in rendering possible the open horizon of finite, empirical knowledge. Finitude itself, for us, *is* this very necessity of objectifying, of putting ourselves over-against an *ob-jectum* which we then re-present to ourselves by forming concepts; this finitude, in a word, manifests itself in the uncreative, receptive core of what is an essentially creative act, knowledge. But liberty and necessity meet in the centre of the unity achieved between the contraries "to know" and "to receive," and it is the liberty, the act, which remains at the basis of it all. The necessity which manifests itself in the objectivizing encounter of the transcendental horizon is only accorded a place as "pressure of encounter" because a "being-free-for . . . " makes an encounter possible in the first place. Even "in the essence of the pure understanding, that is to say in pure theoretical reason, is already to be found liberty insofar as it signifies that one places oneself under a necessity *which gives itself*."[16] However, the theoretical understanding does not owe its freedom to an all-powerful and infinite spontaneity, but rather remains spontaneous only to a limited extent and in union with intuitions, for which it provides pure receptivity through the mediation of the image of Time.

Later we shall consider at length Heidegger's own conception of the foundation of truth in liberty. Let us, however, note this in passing: (1) Heidegger finds in Kant's doctrine a prefiguration of his own, in this respect: The liberty upon which knowledge is founded, being a finite one, is not an act of total spontaneity; it is rather a spontaneity fulfilling a certain necessity. It will be our task in our evaluation to show what is at the root of such a conclusion and what it implies for Heidegger's philosophy. (2) Heidegger finds Kant's doctrine a prefiguration of his own in a second important respect: Kant roots the horizon of values in the horizon within which we objectively

---

[15] *Ibid.*, p. 102.   [16] *Ibid.*, p. 147.

encounter the things-that-are. For Kant pointed to the pure image of "respect" in the *Critique of Practical Reason* as the counterpart of Time in the verifying synthesis. In so doing he discovered the truth, very central to the Existentiale, that ontology and ethics are rooted in a deep unity within the one concrete existent. The two principles just named are indeed only aspects of the same problem, the nature of a free existent that is finite. Heidegger says of the conjuncture of necessity and freedom which such an existent manifests, "The immediate gift . . . is pure receptivity, but the free act of primordially giving oneself a law is pure spontaneity; the two are originally, in themselves, *one*."[17] The "one" considered ontologically is Time; considered ethically it is Respect.

Now that we have reviewed some of the details of Heidegger's interpretation of the theoretical and practical synopses, we come to the real conclusion of the whole analysis: a judgment upon the adequacy of the Kantian analysis as an explanation of the ontological basis for the exstatic horizon. To what extent, in Heidegger's opinion, has Kant succeeded in bringing to light in the exposition of the schematismus, and indeed in the entire *Critique*, the ontological roots of the threefold exstatic nature of Time? If he has not succeeded completely, what has he left undone in the task of providing an ontology of the transcendental horizon?

Here, in a word, is the conclusion of *Kant und das Problem der Metaphysik*: The basic lines of an authentic exstasis are present in the Kantian analysis, but they are not recognized as such; above all, the temporality of finite transcendental knowledge is never explicitly rooted in the authentically dominant exstasis— the future.[18] This last, coming from Heidegger, we can now recognize as a serious accusation. For the fundamental and originative futurity of the free Dasein is the very *sense* of the verifying synthesis, as ontological reality of the apophantic and predicative syntheses of conception. In Heidegger's own words:

Just as a pure reproduction constitutes the possibility of the act of presenting-anew, so a pure recognition must, correspondingly, offer the possibility for a type of identification. But if that pure synthesis is an act of recognizing, that means also that it does not announce a being that it can present to itself by maintaining it as

17 *Ibid.*, p. 152.   18 *Ibid.*, p. 205.

identical, but rather that it announces *the horizon of the possibility of maintaining in general that which it announces*; it is, insofar as it is pure, the originative constitution of that prefixation, that is to say, of the *future*.[19]

If Kant did not realize explicitly the dominant ontological importance of futurity as foundation of the possibility of an exstatic horizon, he did at least provide implicitly a place for Heidegger's insertion of this insistence—in any event, this is how Heidegger would interpret Kant's assertion of the primacy of the transcendental logic. This assertion implied neither a suppression of the schematism in favour of Time, nor even a reduction of Time to a negative condition of knowledge; it was rather, according to Heidegger, Kant's discovery of the phenomenon of the dominance of the future as the fundamental exstasis of Time[20]—a discovery Kant made without really being aware of it.

Such an interpretation illustrates well the method of that destruction announced in *Sein und Zeit*; we are now witnessing its first important act of digestion. In the last chapter of the Kant analysis Heidegger describes explicitly the attitude that should dominate a destruction: it must look beyond what an author has said, to what his achievements mean for a *Denken* that seeks to consider the earlier position in view of its own authentic projections. If we look upon the Kantian effort as an endeavour to achieve a *Grundlegung der Metaphysik*—a new founding of ontology (the last chapter of Heidegger's book is entitled "The Repetition of the Fundament of Metaphysics"), then the real achievement of the *Critique* must not be looked for in the *results* of the transcendental deduction and the schematismus. These conceptions were not definitive, "the insight into the transcendental imagination was not strong enough to permit the subjectivity of the subject as totality to be seen in a new light."[21] We must seek somewhere else the true meaning of this grounding of metaphysics in the subjectivity of the subject. Kant is indeed the first thinker to have grounded metaphysics purely in man as subjective source of transcendental horizon. The real test of the significance of the Kantian achievment lies, then, in determining the adequacy or inadequacy of the Kantian philosophical anthropology.[22]

[19] *Ibid.*, p. 178.   [20] *Ibid.*   [21] *Ibid.*, p. 152.   [22] *Ibid.*, p. 188.

"Philosophical anthropology," the reader must be warned, is not a complimentary term in Heidegger's vocabulary. Indeed, it plays roughly the role in the earlier works that the word "metaphysics" assumes in the later ones; that is, it stands for the inauthentic, truncated philosophical effort which can only be looked upon as a necessary stepping stone toward a more adequate era of fundamental ontology. Speaking of anthropology in general, Heidegger, after affirming that it is not one but a complex series of inquiries about man in his relations with every manner of thing, asserts that this series of inquiries has today made us the best informed people in quantity and variety of information about man—yet the least informed about *what man really is.*[23]

It would seem at first glance to be the task of a "philosophical anthropology" to answer just that question—what is man?—distinguishing him from the other types of *Seienden,* from trees and plants and animals.[24] And if anthropology discovers man to be "the kind of thing that grounds absolutely certain knowledge," it will thus establish itself as the *Ausgang* —the exit—of philosophy itself, since man will be the first given and most certain of *Seienden.* But the problem of determining the value of a philosophical anthropology is not that simple; in fact, given the present stage of philosophical development, it is hardly approachable at all. The function of a philosophical anthropology is not at all "self-understandable" as some would have us believe, because it depends upon a conception of what it is to philosophize. The problem of a philosophical anthropology is unapproachable because the question of the nature of philosophy itself has not been broached. The final chapter of Heidegger's analysis proposes to do precisely that: to consider the Kantian anthropology in the light of what has been discovered in *Sein und Zeit* about "the way back into the ground" of metaphysics.

The previous analysis has already indicated that Kant's questioning about the essence of man is, despite his own use of the term "philosophical anthropology," more, at least potentially, than a *mere* anthropology.

Not that the transcendental imagination is presented as the sought-for "ground," nor that this grounding becomes [explicitly]

<hr />

[23] *Ibid.*, p. 189.　　　　[24] *Ibid.*, p. 191.

a question concerning the essence of human reason, but Kant has, through illuminating in this way the subjectivity of the subject, led back to the real ground itself.[25]

Kant thus took *the* philosophical step that would finally lead back to the very "bottom" (*Boden*) of metaphysics. What is more, he discovered that "bottom" in fact to be an abyss (*Abgrund*, referring to Kant's opening the way to the discovery that metaphysics is grounded in no thing, but only in the *Nichts*).[26]

Because Kant raised the question of possibility, he became the real prophet of man's metaphysical finitude; for the very raising of the question of what man can or cannot do indicates finitude —the infinite has no doubts. Since metaphysics is the inquiry that has traditionally raised the Being-question, it must be determined, once the question of finitude rears its head, to what extent the problem of the finitude of man and the problem of the proper founding of metaphysics (which to the phenomenologist is dependent on the conception of man) affect the *Seinsfrage*.[27] "The Being-question as question concerning the possibility of forming an idea of Being springs originally from that possibility of understanding Being which is prior to the formation of all ideas."[28] The *vorbegriffliches Verstehen des Seins* which Heidigger invokes here recalls the entire horizons of *Sein und Zeit*. Dasein as horizon is the fundamental possibility of Being. The "understanding which is prior to the formation of all ideas" is that unquestionable, unanalyzable, mute grasp of the Being of something which is present as the very atmosphere in which any grasp of any kind of thing takes place—a notion of Being present, necessarily and prior to all other notions— ample in extension (*weite*), constant (*ständig*), and undetermided (*unbestimmt*).[29] Heidegger, in recalling the central lesson of *Sein und Zeit*, affirms that it is this presence amidst the things-that-are, that makes Ek-sistenz possible. An infinite knower may need nothing present before him to intuit, for intuiting he creates from nothing. But that finite thing that I myself am can intuit only as a *Seinsverständniss* that does not create but merely co-creates in union with the multitude and variety of the things that can fill his horizon.

[25] *Ibid.*, p. 194.   [26] *Ibid.*   [27] *Ibid.*, pp. 196-97.   [28] *Ibid.*, p. 204.
[29] *Ibid.*, p. 205.

All questions of a *Grundlegung der Metaphysik*, and any evaluation of the notion of a philosophical anthropology, must first
be rooted firmly in the notion of a *Seinsverständniss* as the
fundamental *Bedürfniss*—the fundamental need of finite Dasein.
The notion of Dasein as a need requiring Being to fill itself up
underlies Heidegger's analysis of Kant because it touches on
the basic projections of the Heideggerian philosophy: a philosophy of freedom and a philosophy of finitude—of a freedom
that is finite. These notions already rule this first step of the
"destruction." The finite knower depends, in order to know,
on his ability to encounter things which he does not create,
but which he has only to let be as they are.[30] Existence itself
means, Heidegger affirms, "instruction by the *Seienden* as such,
through an act of making the *Seiende* as such render itself up."[31]
Being, therefore, is interpreted here, and in the works following,
as it was in *Sein und Zeit*, as essentially connected with the finite
act of engagement of the human existent. The generality
which Being enjoys is itself a result of the transcendence of the
finite ground of Dasein.[32] And it is this same finitude which
accounts for the dissimulation hidden in the essence of truth,
for the *lethe* in the *aletheia*. The root of everything human and
the ground of all Being must be understood in terms of the
all-conditioning finitude of the Dasein: *Ursprünglicher als der
Mensch ist die Endlichkeit des Daseins in ihm*.[33]

The fundamental criticism of Kant requires that the great
Kantian discoveries be rethought in terms of the later and even
more fundamental discoveries of *Sein und Zeit*. *Sein und Zeit's*
discoveries of the domination of futurity in the opening of the
exstatic horizon, of the finitude of Dasein as the ground of the
Seinsbedürfniss, and of the dissimulations which are always
hidden at the heart of any finite revelation of truth, welded
into a unified fundamental conception of Dasein's role as
exstatic horizon for the revelation of Being, must serve as the
framework into which the Kantian discoveries can be absorbed
and rendered a more ultimate significance. This application of
the very positive method of destruction to Kant's *Critique*
reaches its climax in Heidegger's insistence that the transcendental horizon functions as the locale for the *Geschehen* of
a Dasein whose revelations, being those of a *Verfallensein*, must

[30] *Ibid.*, p. 206.   [31] *Ibid.*, p. 206.   [32] *Ibid.*   [33] *Ibid.*, p. 207.

bear the inevitable mark of finitude: dissimulation in the heart of every revelation.[34] Because Kant missed the sense of Dasein as *Geschehen*, he failed to bring to light the true transcendence of the human exstatic horizon. Instead Kant tended to conceive of Dasein as a mind endowed with forms and categories viewed much too much as another kind of *Vorhandenes* reality. This is the sense of Heidegger's ultimate remark, the criticism that returns again and again throughout the course of the de-destruction as the very sign of inauthenticity: "To Kant the distinction of Being and the things-that-are remains hidden."[35]

Kant's failure to reach a clear understanding of the true ground of metaphysics in the Nothingness of the Dasein can be expressed another way, using the categories of *Sein und Zeit*. In effect he discovered the structure of *Sorge* without penetrating to the heart of its exstatic unity. The door to this inner understanding leads through the dark corridor of *Angst*. Any ultimate insight into the Being-question must grasp the real meaning of the Nothing revealed through this *Angst*.

Anguish is that fundamental self-discovery [as Being-there] that places [us] before the Nothing. The Being of the things-that-are is basically only understandable—and therein lies the deepest finitude of transcendence—because in the fundament of its essence Dasein holds itself in the Nothing. This holding of itself in the Nothing is no particular and occasionally thought-out "thinking" of the Nothing, but an event that is rooted in the self-discovery [of the Dasein] amongst the *Seienden* and which must, in a fundamental-ontological analysis of the Dasein, be illumined in its inner possibility.[36]

Kant overlooked in the *Nichts* the only possible ground for an analysis of the finite Dasein and, therefore, the only possible answer to the question he himself raises of the *possibility* of metaphysics. This failure to go all the way in explaining the finitude he had discovered at the root of metaphysics explains why it was still possible for the German idealists who followed Kant to lose sight of it almost entirely.[37]

The task which Kant left unfulfilled becomes the central concern in the works of Heidegger that appear in the years just

[34] *Ibid.*, pp. 210-11.   [35] *Ibid.*, p. 212.   [36] *Ibid.*, pp. 214-15.
[37] *Ibid.*, p. 220.

following the study on Kant. In *Vom Wesen des Grundes*, which we shall consider in the next chapter, he bases his further grappling with the *Grundlegung der Metaphysik* in accordance with the notion of radical finitude presented in the *Critique*; this is why the later Heidegger speaks no longer of "laying the ground" for metaphysics, but of surpassing it altogether.

III   The Essence of Fundament

Vom Wesen des Grundes, published in the same year as the book on Kant, pursues the question on the ground of truth in the finite transcendence of the Dasein. This short but very rich lecture affirms in the language of the *ontologische Differenz—das Sein* is not *die Seienden*—the same fundamental negation discovered in the Kant book when it was stated that the transcendental horizon of Dasein is founded in the Nothing.

In the brief preface to the third edition of *Vom Wesen des Grundes* Heidegger warns us that we must not conceive of this Nothing in purely negative terms. When it is affirmed in the early works that the transcendence of Dasein lies precisely in his capacity to enfold everything that is within his horizon, and that the Dasein owes his horizontality to no thing, this is not tantamount to affirming that Being itself is absolutely nothing at all: Being *ist kein nihil negativum*; while not *Seiende*, nevertheless the root of its horizon *is* positive possibility, a need to be fulfilled, a Being-understanding (*Seinsverständniss*).

Some critics have suggested that Heidegger might be trying to repudiate his earlier decision to root Being in the Nothing by surpassing this negative notion of the Dasein's transcendence toward a more powerful, though occult conception of Being as a dionysiac presence. I have already indicated my disaccord with this conception. I have admitted, however, an evolution of Heidegger's thought in the sense of a profounder rooting of early tenets; the case at hand is a splendid example of this. Heidegger himself has stated in later years that he is now attempting to found more positively the conceptions that were formulated in reaction to metaphysics in the early years.[1] The

---

[1] See chapter IV in this book.

notion of the Dasein's transcendence as ground for Being is no exception. This does not mean that the notion of "the Nothing" will be abandoned; it will be subsumed into a richer analysis of the Dasein's Being-understanding that takes full account of the whole fabric of action which this existence can reveal. Because the dimension of the Nothing does remain in the most recent works, and because we must be sure to recognize its final contribution in Heidegger's most mature conceptions, we should examine carefully the two lectures of 1929, *Vom Wesen des Grundes* and *Was ist Metaphysik?* in which the "ontological difference" and the *Nichts* play such a key role.

The *Grund* in question in the title very evidently refers to the fundament of metaphysics invoked when Heidegger spoke, in reference to Kant, of a *Grundlegung der Metaphysik*. Heidegger is obviously not the first to think of metaphysics as having a "ground." The traditional conception of "ground" that Kant himself inherited goes back at least as far as Aristotle: Metaphysics is grounded in "sufficient reason."

The moment one poses a question, as the lecture in question evidently has, concerning the essence of this ratio, one discovers a very curious thing: The grounding of metaphysics in ratio being considered self-evident, the whole question of the *Grund* has always been more or less taken for granted. When repeating (for here is a good example of what Heidegger means by *Wiederholung*) the traditional notion, that is exactly the error we want to avoid; we must not take for granted the meaning either of ratio or of ground.

Heidegger assumes that the most rationalistic version of the traditional conception will therefore be the most revealing, though what is there discernible could probably be found in even the most realistic theories of ground. This is why he chooses to meditate upon the Leibnizian formulas of sufficient reason. He intends, however, to aim his criticisms at all the systems that have existed in the past. The heart of the difficulty encountered by all the traditional positions is the same: an inadequate, unfounded conception of truth, which manifests itself in the notion, apparently common since Aristotle's time, of truth as a "conformity of intellect and thing." As long as this remains the starting point of an ontology, its way back into the ground of a metaphysics is blocked, because its way back into the ground of *truth* has been closed off prematurely. The accent on conformity signals to Heidegger a common failure to ask in *virtue of what* is it possible for there to be that presence of thing to intellect that makes a conformity possible in the first place.

In *Vom Wesen des Grundes* Heidegger reaffirms in the strongest possible language a capital lesson of *Sein und Zeit*, and in so doing he marks once again his intention to situate his meditation out beyond the metaphysical, "conformity" tradition. He first recalls the fundamental distinction between the two kinds of truth, the truth of the discovery (*entdecken*) of objective things (*Vorhanden*), and the truth of intimate, phenomenological self-discovery (*erschliessen*). This essential distinction alone shows up the inadequacy of the conformity theory of truth. We are reminded that both the categorial analysis and the existentiale are rooted in the "illumination of Being" (*Enthülltheit des Seins*) which "first makes possible the openness of the things that are."[2] In the language of *Sein und Zeit*, ontic truth is rooted in onto-logical truth as the condition of its possibility; any grasp of the nature of metaphysics requires that I first understand funda-mentally the *vor-ontologisch* possibilities of there being through me, any knowing in the first place. Or, in traditional language: the "intentionality" of the knower in relation to the things-that-are depends for its possibility on the ontological structure of the knower as transcendence. Truth is then, more than a "property of expression," as was once said; it is the essence of the exsistent.[3]

It is against this background that Heidegger launches his attack on the effort to conceive truth in terms of a relation of subject and object, a kind of "bridging the gap" of an imaginary metaphysical crevice opened between me and the things I transcend. In place of an object Heidegger would affirm the direct presence of the thing, known in and for itself, not as "object of my knowledge," but as "thing" known and tran-scended. "What would be depassed (in an act of transcendence) is straightaway the *Seiende* itself, which the Dasein has or can uncover, including especially the thing that the Dasein itself is."[4]

---

[2] Heidegger, *Vom Wesen des Grundes*, pp. 12-13.
[3] *Ibid.*, p. 15.   [4] *Ibid.*, p. 18.

FOUNDING A WORLD

In transcending the thing that lies open before me, I discover myself. My very selfhood is constituted by this act of transcendence, which secures both Dasein's independence from, and presence to, the things-that-are.[5] In the language of *Sein und Zeit*, the *Befindlichkeit* of Dasein is that of a Being-in-the-world whose Being-there is fundamentally the projection of a Self among the things-that-are. By transcending his very nature, Dasein does not depass simply this thing or that thing, but the grand totality of things, everywhere and always, thereby declaring his absolute fundamentality in founding the whole world.[6]

This fundamental act of founding a world, basic to there ever being a "truth" or a "metaphysics," Heidegger terms a *Worumwillen*.[7] It is not a concrete will act, not an act of comportment; it is the fundamental act which makes all will acts and all comportment possible. It is not *a* free will act, but *the* act of freedom itself. "In this transcendent holding-of-oneself-in-opposition, which is the *Worumwillen*, the Dasein manifests itself in man, essentially engaging itself in its existence, that is, so that it can be a free self."[8] Existence and truth are freedom. And freedom is freedom to ground (*Freiheit ist Freiheit zum Grunde*).[9]

Heidegger wastes no time in reminding us again that we have to do here with a finite freedom; this is the real key to understanding Dasein as Being-in-the-world.[10] For we must remember that it is the finitude of Dasein that establishes the necessary reciprocity of *Sein-Seienden*. This accounts for the complicated reciprocity of the founding act itself—for to know things we must be with things which we discover and do not create, and we must know things before we can even become aware of ourselves. This necessary relation of the Dasein to the *Seienden* is what alone makes it possible even to pose the "transcendental question," i.e., the Being-question itself: "Why basically is there something rather than just nothing at all?"[11] The act of founding, consequently, is a complex, reciprocal relationship

[5] *Ibid.* [6] *Ibid.*, p. 19.
[7] "Das Dasein existiert umwillen seiner." *Ibid.*, p. 35.
[8] *Ibid.*, p. 40. [9] *Ibid.*, p. 41. [10] *Ibid.*, p. 43. [11] *Ibid.*, p. 44.

of Dasein, Being and the things-that-are—the ultimate sign that we have to do here with a finite being which finds, but does not basically create its object. Heidegger sums up the moments of the founding act in this way: It is because founding (*Gründen*) as ratio is also instituting (*Stiften*) the reality of the world of *Seienden* that the intentional act of establishing (*Begründen*) can take place. But the act which fulfills the founding, namely the act of establishing (in the sense of the assertion of the truth of *Seienden*) is not the fruit of an unlimited knowing process. Precisely because the freedom which is at the root of the whole act of founding is finite, the act must issue forth not only in *Begründung*, establishing, but in its accompanying opposite, *Anweisung*, the exclusion of things which Heidegger terms in a later essay,[12] the "Untruth."[13] As *Vom Wesen der Wahrheit* will explain, our finite freedom as ground of truth is a freedom to let things be as they are; but, being both finite and free, it must also be freedom to *not* let things be as they are, i.e., it must at one and the same time unveil and dissimulate those things which it discovers only partially and cannot create.

The essence of real transcendental fundament has three aspects: (1) world-projection (*Weltentwurf*, which is the name for the result of *Grunden*); (2) involvement in the things-that-are (*Eingenommenheit im Seienden*), which corresponds to the act of instituting (*Stiften*); and (3) the providing of an ontological, intelligible sense for the things-that-are (*ontologische, Begründen des Seienden*). These three aspects of fundament owe their unity as one act to their common source in the Nothing of Dasein's finite freedom. The notion of a threefold founding act grounded in Nothing invokes, of course, the central ontological discovery of *Sein und Zeit*: the reality of finite Dasein as foundation of the threefold extases of temporality. The underlying structural unity of the threefold act of providing a ground or ratio corresponds to the very structural unity of Time itself, the complexus of Dasein as *Sorge*.[14] The act of founding a world, of discovering the things-that-are, and of endowing them with a sense is made possible by the Dasein's exstatic nature, his ability to project beyond the here and now and to separate

[12] *Vom Wesen der Wahrheit.*   [13] *Vom Wesen des Grundes*, p. 46.
[14] *Ibid.*, p. 47.

himself from a purely physical involvement by anticipating the things that will be. The transcendence of Dasein is entirely the result of this ability to live afar, to anticipate, to be beyond the too-absorbing exigencies of a narrow here and now. Da-sein can, then, as in *Sein und Zeit*, be conceived as care (*Sorge*), because he is, as Heidegger beautifully describes it, *ein Wesen der Ferne*—"an essence that dwells in the distance."[15]

Heidegger sums up in this way the results of the analysis of transcendence as it develops in the lecture we have just been considering:

The [traditional] principle states, "Every existing thing has its *ratio*." From what has just been seen it is now evident *why* this is so: because Being natively (*von Hause aus*) and primordially discovers itself in understanding. Each thing as thing presents itself on the basis of its type of *ratio*, whether this can be grasped in itself and adequately determined or not. Because *Grund* is a transcendental, essential characteristic of Being in general, the principle of reason is valid consequently for all the things-that-are. The *ratio* (*Grund*) belongs to the essence of Being because Being *is* only as the transcendence which is *Grund* world-projecting, self-discovering as *there*.[16]

With this analysis, which is here only briefly summarized, Heidegger has effectively laid the ground for a completion of the task Kant set for himself but was not able to achieve—a critique of metaphysics in its fundament.

DASEIN AS TRANSCENDENT HORIZON

Traditional metaphysics sought the Being of the things-that-are and the ground of their intelligibility, their sufficient reason, in another *Seiende*, a super-thing existing in a world beyond the senses. Heidegger now shows that this "Being," this "principle of sufficient reason," is "no thing," no substance, no creativity on the part of an ideal absolute, but the Dasein-founded possibility that there be a world in which things "can be" and "can be discovered." If this possibility lies in Man it is precisely because he is cabable of being more than "thing," more than "substance," without being infinite absolute, yet without being merely "present" as a tree or a house is "present." This

---

[15] *Ibid.*, p. 50.   [16] *Ibid.*, p. 47.

freedom of Dasein which Heidegger wants us to discover is freedom to be *not* just another thing present, but to be the presence of all things present. This difference which the Dasein enjoys lies in the abyss of understanding, waiting to be filled up by the things-that-are, an ek-static abyss opened when Dasein, through projection, extends himself forward between the two poles of his exsistence, between the *Befindlichkeit* which brackets the beginning, and the death which terminates the span.

This entire reality of Dasein as transcendent horizon, is what the traditional metaphysics missed in their search for the "Being of the things-that-are." The error accounts for the tradition's transcription of Being into terms that never took cognizance of the importance of temporality. A false eternalization of Being, achieved by tearing the exstasis "now" out of its temporal frame so that Being was conceived as eternal presence (*Anwesenheit*), masked the futurity of the Dasein's existence as fundamental characteristic of the horizon of Being itself. The very nature of the traditional metaphysical questioning hides the true sense of Being's transcendence, though this was never realized before Kant's time. All metaphysical inquiry, Heidegger points out in the beginning of *Was ist Metaphysik?*, always questions the whole of the possible object, *ens qua ens*; and, consequently, the questioning always involves the questioner, since he is one among these possible beings. What metaphysicians have never understood is that the reason why metaphysical questioning *must* involve the whole of reality is that it is interested in the transcendental horizon itself, and hence in everything that is or can be within it. This always involves *me*, not as a thing but in a special way as Dasein, thanks to whom alone the "totality of the things-that-are" (*Seienden als Ganzen*) with which metaphysics has always been concerned is gathered up and brought into question. As Dasein I have the ability to open a transcendental horizon from out the Nothing.

The tradition failed to establish the relation of Dasein to all things because it failed to realize the ambiguity of the notion of the totality of the things-that-are.[11] Obviously, the metaphysician can never hope to know every possible thing. But this has never really been what he was after. The metaphysical question actually originates in the experience of a potential relation between me and all existing things. The metaphysician never discovered that the fundamental experience of the basis of this relation is that *anguish* before my death in which I am afforded a compelling grip on the reality of my contingency. In the vision of the last moment I see literally everything slipping away together, dissolving in the gloom of an all-pervading Nothing. It is thus that I come to see that the presence of anything and everything before me is a united whole, as I also see that it is due to nothing other than my own finite horizon-projection.[17] I see for the first time clearly, that the *Seienden als Ganzen* could not "be" without my Da-sein, and at the same time I realize that the apparent solidity of that "world" of things offers no lasting thing upon which I can depend as a protection from the dissolution of the world in death.

This special concern with the "all" is precisely what distinguishes metaphysics from the physical sciences. Sciences are content to function through instrumental relationships with mere segments of the *Seienden*, never asking the fundamental question "Why is there something at all, rather than just nothing?" In contrast to this narrow-minded satisfaction with instrumental success, Heidegger introduces in *Was ist Metaphysik?* the *dreadful* aspect of our essential finitude—the total helplessness of science and, by implication, of the traditional metaphysics before the reality of transcendence. For both depend on that transcendence for their reality, though neither discovers its true essence. Each pronouncement of science and each decision of the traditional philosophers is a new revelation of the "totality of things-that-are" pulled out of the Nothing. "Projecting into Nothing, the Da-sein is already beyond what-is-in-totality."[18] Hence every human revelation and every human act affirms the transcendent supremacy of the Nothing, whether it realizes it or not.

Nothing is that which makes the revelation of things as sucn possible for our human existence. Nothing does not merely provide a conceptual opposite of the things-that-are, but also is an original part of essence. It is in the Being of the things-that-are that the nihilation of Nothing (*das Nichten des Nichts*) occurs.[19]

Just as we have seen Heidegger build upon and depass Kant, we now see him borrow a phrase from Hegel and transform it,

[17] Heidegger, *Was ist Metaphysik?*, pp. 29-30.   [19] *Ibid.*   [18] *Ibid.*, p. 35.

to render it a fuller meaning in keeping with the spirit of "destruction":

"Pure Being and pure Nothing are thus one and the same." This proposition from Hegel[20] is correct. Being and Nothing belong together, but not, as the Hegelian point of view would have it, because both are one in their indefiniteness and immediacy, but because Being itself is finite in essence and is only revealed in the transcendence of Da-sein as projected into Nothing.[21]

Being is finite. The transcendence of Dasein, who, because he can grasp the Nothingness of his own death, can possess himself, provides the opening in which the things-that-are can appear, that is, can *be*. Hence the question of Nothing provides the answer to the question of Being, fulfilling thereby, as they have never been fulfilled before, the requirements established for *the* metaphysical question: (a) it envelops the totality of everything that is; (b) it involves *me*, in my very essence, as ground through finite freedom of the horizon of the question itself.

The old proposition, *ex nihilo nihil fit*, then, needs to be reformulated. It "will then acquire a different meaning, one appropriate to the problem of Being itself, so as to run: *ex nihilo omne ens qua ens fit*, every being, so far as it is a being, is made out of nothing."[22] Going beyond the totality of things-that-are into the Nothing of their transcendental ground is the task of Dasein. The answer to the question "What is metaphysics?" is simply this: "Metaphysics is the ground phenomenon of Da-sein. It is Da-sein itself."[23]

The Inaugural Lecture marks the first result of the preliminary effort announced in *Sein und Zeit*—the sweeping away of the old to make way for the sound erection of the new. The result is preliminary because what is accomplished later in a more detailed and more profound fashion is here achieved only in general and, indeed, rather sweeping terms. These sweeping results Heidegger himself sums up in the closing lines of the original lecture. The effort has been made, first, to release philosophy from any tendency to approach timidly only a part of the things-that-are, so that it might march boldly toward its true object, the *Seienden im Ganzen*. Secondly, it

---

[20] Hegel, *The Science of Logic*, I, WW III, p. 74.
[21] *Was ist Metaphysik?*, pp. 39-40.   [22] *Ibid.*, p. 40.   [23] *Ibid.*, p. 41.

invites us to "let ourselves go"—into the *Nichts*, to sweep away with one blow the insupportable incrustations of the past. Heidegger speaks flamboyantly of *das Freiwerden von den Götzen, die jeder hat und zu denen er sich wegzuschleichen pflegt* (freeing oneself from the idols we all have and to which we are wont to go cringing). This achieved, the third step may be realized: holding ourselves in suspense in the Nothing, we may be able "to swing continuously back into the ground of metaphysics," which is wrested from the Nothing itself.[24]

The nature of that ground remains in question. To posit the reality of the *Nichts* is evidently not to answer all the questions involved in a search for "the essence of fundament"; in fact it is hardly even a beginning. With the idols of his youth destroyed—the entire metaphysics of the West, the physical science to which it has given birth, and the God of Christian civilization which has been identified as the source of Being's "necessity"—there remains as valid then, after the searing blast of the Nothing unleashed in *Was ist Metaphysik?*, only the final word of the Inaugural Lecture itself. This word, which is the Being-question itself, continues to thread through the works of Heidegger today: *Warum ist überhaupt Seiendes und nicht vielmehr Nichts?* (Why, in general, are there things, and not rather Nothing at all?)

[24] *Ibid.*, p. 42.

IV   The Positive Accent of a Negative Doctrine

THE shift in accent which occurs in his works after 1930 marks Heidegger's concentration on developing the positive side of the doctrine of finite Being. The Being revealed by the Dasein's existence is historical; the sum total of the historical destiny of mankind composes the immeasurably rich treasury of concrete human possibility, which, in the form of the progressive illumination of the *Seienden*, can also be seen as the Being of the things-that-are. But the Dasein *is* finite; the negative element, so strongly emphasized in the works we have just been examining, cannot be ignored. It but joins with the positive to paint the chiaroscuro picture of a revelation of the things-that-are that must remain at the same time always a dissimulation.

In the Postscript to *Was ist Metaphysik?*, written in 1943, some thirteen years after the Inaugural Lecture itself, Heidegger seeks to equilibrate the black and the white of what was said in his original discussion of the Nothing. After having admitted that *Was ist Metaphysik?* is "thought in transition"—a thought which has not born its full positive fruit and which remains too much in reaction against the traditional ontology—Heidegger seeks to show that what was written there is nevertheless basically sound. He proposes to allay three "misgivings" that have troubled critics of the work, intending to show that the lecture may, and indeed should, be interpreted in a way that leads past the forbidding negative assertions to a positive doctrine of Being. 1. The affirmation of the Nothing is not nihilism, but recognition of that which is at the heart of the essence of Being. 2. If the work is anti-logical, it establishes that there is another thinking more fundamental than logic. 3. If a philosophy of *Angst* paralyzes the will to act, it leads Dasein to grasp the meaning of his Being. These criticisms, as Heidegger treats them, are of particular interest; not only do they show the points about which the philosopher has lately become sensitive, but also, through the answers he furnishes to each, they demonstrate vividly the advances which he has made in coming into full, positive possession of the ontology he would found in breaking with the past.

THE NOTHING AS THE UNFATHOMABLE

After reviewing the analysis in *Was ist Metaphysik?* that led to the affirmation of the Nothing, Heidegger rejects any possible nihilistic interpretations of his intent.

It would be immature . . . to adopt the facile explanation that Nothing is merely the nugatory, equating it with the nonexistent (*das Wesenlose*). We should rather equip ourselves and make ready for one thing only: to experience in Nothing the vastness of that which gives every being the warrant to be. That is Being itself. Without Being, whose unfathomable and unmanifest essence is vouchsafed us by the Nothing in essential dread, everything that "is" would remain in Beinglessness (*Sein-losigkeit*). But this is not a nugatory Nothing, assuming that it is the truth of Being that Being never essentializes itself without *Seienden*, and *Seienden* cannot be without Being (*das Sein nie west ohne das Seiende, dass niemals ein Seiendes ist ohne das Sein*).[1]

The opening of a transcendental horizon is not, indeed, a nugatory nothing, but neither is it the work of a "something"— a *Seiende* in its *Seiendheit*. When the philosopher wishes to introduce into history the proper presence of the presence that opens a horizon and requires him to distinguish his conception of being from the traditional metaphysical conception which always begins with *things as things*, then clearly the first effort at expression is bound to be negative: Being is not *Seiendheit*. Even when Heidegger affirms that it is anguish which reveals that Nothing is at the heart of the transcendence of Being, he is not nihilistic in the usual sense. Indeed, anguish *is* the grasp

[1] Heidegger, *Was ist Metaphysik?*, p. 46.

of the radical finitude of our freedom, but it is that freedom, in and through its finitude, which makes possible that presence of the things-that-are which we call "Being." The accent then is positive when Heidegger declares that it is because we can grasp our own finite end in death that we can stand-out, *Ek-sist*, in a projection which makes it possible to render a sense to things. The Nothing, he points out, is *abgründig* in the sense that it is not an infinite absolute, there being none necessary in order that Being might be; it is "unfathomable" because of the vastness of our transcendence of the things-that-are, and because of the vastness of the sum total of the things-that-are themselves, a vastness not of infinity, but of great extent (*Weiträumigkeit*). In a word, finitude does not, for Heidegger, necessarily imply a nihilism, because Being can be fully real, fully transcendent, without needing to be infinitely absolute. The Dasein's freedom and the totality of the things-that-are are nonetheless "real" for not being either eternal or unmoving. They constitute a positive something, without breaking through the negative bonds of finitude.

ORIGINATIVE THINKING AS THE ACT OF FREEDOM

Heidegger answers the objection of illogic by developing the notion that there is a more originative thinking than logic, a thinking upon which logic depends. He analyzes the derived, non-fundamental knowledge that we use in everyday life in terms of calculation. Calculation begins its operations upon a whole that is already given, and interests itself only in terms of its sums and parts, which it dissociates and reassembles, following the schemes it has erected out of the necessities of daily life.[2] That whole which calculation ignores "in its wholeness"—*because* it is incalculable—is nevertheless "always closer to man in its enigmatic unknowableness than anything that 'is,' than anything he may arrange or plan." This awareness can sometimes put the essential man in touch with a thinking whose truth no logic can grasp:[3] the more fundamental, originative thinking that "gave" this whole in the first place.

Heidegger contrasts the consuming character of calculation

[2] *Ibid.*, p. 48.   [3] *Ibid.*, pp. 48-49.

with the originality of essential thinking; this distinction is very central to the philosophy we are considering. The same distinction—rooted in the fact that all human activity must either get to the root of things or not, either unfold in view of the originative freedom of the Dasein or not—is at the heart of the authentic-inauthentic dichotomy. It provides the two poles of the necessary dialectic which must constitute the "undifferentiated structure of the Dasein" in all of its determinations. All thinking must abound in the calculative, but this is possible only because of the fundamental originative unveiling; all existence must abound in the inauthentic, but this is possible only because we can project freely in view of our true natures.

"Calculation uses everything that is, as units of computation ready in advance, and in the computation uses up its stock of units."[4] Calculation achieves an appearance of productivity because its units can be multiplied or divided indefinitely. Originative thinking (*anfängliche Denken*), however, creates anew, adding to the richness of the treasury of Being. In a very difficult passage of the Postscript, Heidegger seeks to describe this thinking which is, in the Heideggerian meditation, the ultimate ontological reality. Ultimates are hard to describe precisely because there is nothing beyond them in terms of which they can be described. The originative thinking, through which the *Seienden* come to light for the first time, through which new ways of seeing things are invented out of Nothing, is the very act of freedom itself, pushing back the darkness in an extension of the kingdom of light.

The thinking which not only does not calculate, but is absolutely determined by what is other than the *Seienden*, is called "essential thinking." Instead of calculating on *Seienden* with *Seienden*, it expends itself in Being for the Truth of Being. This thinking answers to the demands of Being, in that man surrenders his historical Essence to the simple, sole necessity (*Notwendigkeit*), whose necessitation does not so much necessitate (*nötigt*) by simply constraining, but rather creates the Need (*Not*) which is consummated in the freedom of the sacrificial offering. The Need is that the Truth of Being be verified and protected, no matter what can happen to man and the things-that-are. The sacrificial offering is freed from all constraint

[4] *Ibid.*, p. 48.

because it comes forth from the abyss of freedom, as the surging abandonment of the human essence to the verifying protection of the truth of Being on behalf of the existing thing.[5]

Heidegger has recourse to religious language here because he is trying to express what has always been the concern of religion.[6] Religion has always concerned itself with the ultimate in virtue of which and for which we live. Sacrifice has always represented a willingness to accept the charge of this destiny intended for us by the root of our existence, to shoulder our "vocation." But just as metaphysics has always looked *meta-ta-phusika* for the ground and reason of the *phusika*, so religion has also sought the *Heilige*, the source and end of the call, in a Transcendent that is beyond man. But to Heidegger the ultimate that is "beyond man" is *Da-sein*, the Being-there among the things-that-are that is founded in the ultimate transcendence of our finite existence. In the language of the paragraph just quoted, the "sacrificial offering" which we must make lies in devoting our existence to the Being achieved in the wedding of the things-that-are with the temporal, transcendental horizon. This devotion, in its purity, is the end of authentic existence. The authentic existent, finding in his nature the place where Being becomes, where shines the Light that lets *be* the things-that-are, offers himself to the ultimate reality, the *Wahrung der Wahrheit*, the verifying of truth. The thinker sacrifices himself to think, the artist offers up himself to create.[7]

As in all religious situations, the authentic religious grasp is founded in need, for our freedom is grounded in necessity. The more advanced religions always recognize the human essence to be free. But this freedom, they realize, is not absolute; it is finite. It functions in terms of the necessity of the essence. Nietzsche spoke of the necessity of freedom, but Heidegger's advance is in seeing that this *Notwendigkeit* is indeed a *Wendung* in the *Not*, a wandering in the need. And this need is the thirst-for-Being of a finite *Seinsverständniss*.

Let us try to clarify this notion. Being, interpreted as the

[5] *Ibid.*, p. 49.

[6] He calls this *das Heilige* in his analyses of the poetic act of originative thinking.

[7] In analyzing the work of Cézanne, Mérleau-Ponty speaks in this sense of "the difficulties of the first word." *Sens et Non-Sens*, p. 36.

Light which shines on the *Seienden* in the projection of a transcendental horizon, arises from the exercise of the freedom generated by our originative need. This need is that of a positive freedom seeking to fulfill its needs, born of finitude, from out its strictly limited resources. When Heidegger insists that *das Nichts* is not a purely nugatory Nothing, he is thinking of the positive generation of light originated by the call of that need. The Being disclosed in the opening cleared by nothingness, by the need grounding freedom, is that Being by which and for the sake of which we exist: hence the justification for the religious language. It is this that the religions of the metaphysical epochs sought to express in terms of their absolutes. In appropriating the religious language of the past, Heidegger would render the traditional religions their ultimate—their finite—significance.

In sacrifice there is expressed that hidden *thanking* which alone does homage to the grace wherewith Being has endowed the nature of man that he might assume in his relationship to Being the guardianship of Being. The originative thinking is the echo of the favor of Being, an echo in which it illumines the unique occurrence[8] and lets itself prepare for Being's own advent, *that the Seiende be*. This echo is man's answer to the Word of the soundless voice of Being. The speechless answer of his thanking through sacrifice is the source of the human word, which is the prime cause of language as the enunciation of the Word in words.

If the reader is still tempted to see in phrases which suggest that man is related to Being an indication that Being transcends man in the sense that an infinite transcendent absolute founds the things-that-are, then he is interpreting Heidegger's doctrine as though it were another sample of subjective metaphysics. Being and Dasein are more than man, because they involve both man and *Seienden*, as well as a tradition which goes beyond this particular individual man. The exact nature of the relationship Being-Dasein-man is very complex. Let it now suffice to understand that for Heidegger it is the originative erection of the thing, enabling it to be by providing it with a horizon, to which man must devote himself. His thanking

[8] "Unique," in that there is nothing else like it, and "unique occurrence" in the sense that it is only thus, in Dasein's act of originative thinking that anything ever happens (*geschieht*).

sacrifice is wordless because it is, in the form of devotion, the attitude that precedes, wills, and thus makes possible the Word, the Light, the Thing. The Word "comes home" in the word of common language, the final incarnation of most originative thinking. This conviction puts the problem of language at the very center of Heidegger's meditations.

In a continuation of the same paragraph Heidegger offers more insight into the nature of the act of thanking sacrifice.

If there were not in the various times [i.e., exstases] a revealing thinking in the fundament of historical man, then it would never be possible that there should be a thanking, assuming that all consideration (*Bedenken*) and memory (*Andenken*) must be grounded in thinking (*Denken*), which must originally think the Truth of Being. How else could mankind attain to original thanking unless Being's favor preserved for man, through his open relationship to this favor, the splendid poverty in which the freedom of sacrifice hides its own treasure? The sacrificial offering is the farewell from the things-that-are on the road to the preservation of the favor of Being. The sacrificial offering can be made ready by doing and working in the midst of the things-that-are, but can never be consummated there.[10]

The *Nichts* can never be far when we touch authentically on matters concerning finite thought. The originative thinking that lies at the base of temporality is rooted in the "splendid poverty" of freedom, i.e., its essential *Nichtigkeit*. Originative thinking is achieved only by realizing freedom through getting at the ground of all Being, which implies thinking out and beyond the things-that-are. A thinking that remains a calculative thinking among the things-that-are can never achieve the goal which the traditional metaphysicians were seeking. Not that calculative thinking is without value. Thinking and working among already revealed *Seienden* prepares the way for an originative thinking of that which has not yet been revealed, just as the epochs and epochs of metaphysics have prepared the way for thinking originatively the Truth of Being itself.

But calculative thinking dangerously tends to become parasitic, egotistical, and destructive, blindly ungrateful to its source of nourishment. Heidegger terms originative thinking a "sacrifice" to contrast it all the more with the calculative

[9] *Was ist Metaphysik?*, p. 49.   [10] *Ibid.*

thinking that can only feed on the light already won by previous "sacrifice."

> Calculation always miscalculates sacrifice in terms of the expedient and the inexpedient . . . the search for a purpose dulls the clarity of the awe, the spirit of sacrifice ready prepared for anguish, which takes upon itself kinship with the imperishable.[11]

What does Heidegger wish to signal by the term "the imperishable"? The imperishable is what the Dasein preserves through its act of standing-in among the things-that-are. The imperishable is the past, maintained in the present by the Dasein's recalling. It is the reality of *Seienden* maintained in time by the Dasein's exstatic act of founding Being in time.

Heidegger, then, has discovered that relationship of man to the things-that-are that is more fundamental than logical relationships and in fact makes possible the act of founding a logic. The "misgiving" of illogic can be answered squarely by saying that Heidegger does not envision his theory as illogical, but as prelogical. It attains the source of logical thinking and the rules of grammar in that basic encounter of Dasein with the things-that-are that grounds the Word in language. Heidegger says that the maintenance of the Word of Being in language grows out of care (*Sorge*) in the use of language (*es ist die Sorge für den Sprach-Gebrauch*). It is on this note of the ultimacy of the Word that the Postscript ends.

> Out of long-guarded speechlessness and out of a careful clarification of the domain which it must illuminate, comes the thinker's *Sagen* (pronouncement). Of like origin is the poet's *Nennen* (naming). Because things can be "like" only if they are also different, poetizing and thinking are poles apart but similar in this respect: They both take great care of the Word. The thinker pronounces Being; the poet names the Holy (*Der Denker sagt das Sein; der Dichter nennt das Heilige*). How—when conceived in terms of the essence of Being— poetizing and thanking and thinking exclude one another and are distinguishable remains an open question for now. Presumably thanking and poetizing spring in different ways from originative thinking, which uses them when yet unable to be for itself a thinking.[12]

The suggestion that neither poetizing nor the fundamental attitude of devotion to Being (for thus we may interpret

[11] *Ibid.*, p. 50. [12] *Ibid.*, p. 51.

tentatively the hardly obvious notion of "thanking" as Heidegger uses it in these texts) achieves the ontological fullness of a *Denken* must not be accepted too readily until we can examine some slightly earlier texts in which Heidegger treats at greater length the relationship of *Denken* and *Dichten*. In these texts we shall learn that both poetizing and thinking are rooted in a fundamental *Dictare* which is originative thinking considered essentially. We can understand neither thinking nor poetizing in the less fundamental sense until we have deepened our conception of what occurs when the "thing" is erected in an act of originating thinking.

ANGUISH AS THE ULTIMATE INTENTIONALITY

The preceding discussion has presented something of the positive richness of a doctrine of essential finitude. It is only against this backdrop that the third criticism of *Was ist Metaphysik?* can be approached. The suggestion that a philosophy of *Angst* paralyzes the will to act is one of those questions that tends to test, as nothing else can, the human soundness of an ontological explanation. We are now in a position to see why Heidegger puts anguish at the centre of things, and what this imports. We must through anguish grasp the meaning of our being—its whole structure—before we can project any act authentically, and, therefore, before we can render to the act of originative thinking in particular its full meaning and true place, consequently before we can comprehend anything about a possible answer to the "Being-question." It is anguish which must lead us to that grasp of the structural whole (or in a word to *Sorge*) because of what we are: finite freedom. Thus anguish is not a blind feeling; it is the ultimate *intentionality*. Anguish is the act of intentionality in its self-penetration and self-comprehension that is rooted in the nakedness of human finitude. The grasp of our freedom—a freedom that can peer into the abyss of its own Nothingness, a freedom that "needs"—is not, in Heidegger's view, an invitation to inactivity, but a call to render our activity its full responsibility—to itself and to "Being"; it is an invitation to an *authentic* activity.

We have now seen that none of the three misgivings, when presented in the form Heidegger gives them, is fatal if we fully understand Heidegger's doctrine. But as far as we can see now, Heidegger's answers still do not allay every doubt we can raise on the score of nihilism and quietism. These, however, are questions of final evaluation.

For now, we can summarize the effect of this effort to come to grips with the most fundamental objections that can be raised against Heidegger's philosophy by saying that our earlier impression of what Heidegger is basically trying to accomplish has been vastly reinforced. Writing of the true significance of Heidegger's philosophy, DeWaelhens comes to the heart of the matter in these words:

If up to now all values have appeared to humanity as linked to God, the dismissal of God threatens to cause a collapse of values which will throw a man into a sink-hole of anarchy. This is why the affirmation of the death of God must go hand in hand with an effort to transform values, with the pretension of endowing them with a sense which, in the older philosophy, then appeared to derive only from God.[13]

This is the sense of what Heidegger is trying to do, and it explains why he uses a religious language to do it. It is why he repeats that the totality of the things-that-are is mysterious in its richness, and that the light which we cast to make them be in our temporal horizon is also mysterious, finite, and ultimate; the mysterious and the limited are united in a world view that would incorporate all that is real, but that refuses to fly to a transcendent in order to explain it.

It is only in this positive sense that we can interpret the final lines of the Postscript. "One of the essential stages for speechlessness is anguish in the sense of the terror in which man, in the abyss of the Nothing, stands determined. The Nothing as the Other to *Seienden* is the veil of Being. Each destiny of *Seienden* has already been fulfilled originally in Being."[14] The two aspects of finitude are revealed in this passage: The Nothing as limit of totality, but revealing the very possibility of the opening of the light of Being, and the positive implication of all for all. If we recall what has been said concerning authentic temporality, namely that the nature of the authentic past is to be a recalling of the concrete possibilities of Dasein as basis for originative

[13] DeWaelhens, *The Philosophy of Martin Heidegger*, p. 354.
[14] *Was ist Metaphysik?*, p. 51.

projection of the future, then we shall understand: Every destiny is always partially fulfilled in the Being achieved by past Dasein. The Postscript concludes on this note:

The last poem of the last poet of the originative period of Greece— Sophocles' *Oedipus in Colonnus*, closed with the Word that harks back far beyond our key to the hidden historical destiny of these people and marks their entry into the unknown truth of Being:

But cease now, and nevermore lift up the lament:
For in all times and in all places it happens that the event
Protects a determination of the fulfillment (*Vollendung*).[15]

[15] *Ibid.*

V Originative Thinking as Essential Thought and Poetizing

THE philosophy of Heidegger begins as a search for the ultimate ground of the Being-question that can permit the founding of a fundamental ontology. The conviction that this quest must carry the seeker out beyond the traditional philosophy, though present from the beginning of Heidegger's efforts, grows and deepens with each succeeding work, until the problem of achieving an *Ueberwindung* of metaphysics becomes so developed that even the term "ontology" is finally deemed unsuited to the philosophy that is to appear. The new philosophy, in the later works, is spoken of in the terms which made their appearance in the preceding chapter, as an "essential thinking" (*wesentliche Denken*). Describing this fundamental thinking, the Postscript to *Was ist Metaphysik?* spoke of: (1) a "thanking" by sacrificial offering through utter devotion to Being for the sake of illuminating the things that are: (2) a poetizing that names the Holy; and (3) a thinking that pronounces Being.

This language is new to us; what we have learned from our study of *Sein und Zeit* does not very well unlock the significance of these highly poetic utterances. But this much we have been able to conclude: the originative thinking that is at stake here, being the very presence of Dasein opening himself to Being, is at the center of Heidegger's philosophic effort: It expresses the rapport between the existent and the things-that-are that achieves what Heidegger calls the *Wahrung der Wahrheit*, i.e., Being's own self-essentialization. Originative thinking builds truth and protects what is gained in the process. The coming to be of new Being takes place in the revelation of the Word of Being, whose proper expression is the human word. "Language is Being's House," as Heidegger declares in a now famous formula, *Sprache ist das Haus des Seins*. Fundamental thinking, fundamental poetizing, and the "thanking" devotion to Being are, then, somehow rooted in the same endeavor touching the very soul of the new philosophy. The whole fruit of the existentiale hangs from a tree whose roots are in this deepening conception of the nature of the Dasein's involvement with the Being of the things-that-are.

The strange new poetic language encountered in these discussions has its origin in the poetry of Frederick Hölderlin, a contemporary of Hegel, a Romantic poet and one of the most difficult in any language, any time. In the decade beginning in 1935, Heidegger, searching for truth concerning the poetic nature of man's fundamental act of opening Being's horizon, engaged in what Beda Allemann has termed a *Zweisprach Hölderlin's und Heidegger's*.[1] This veritable cooperation between philosopher and poet illustrates that affinity between essential thought and poetizing which Heidegger, from 1935 on, is so concerned to point out.

But why is Hölderlin especially chosen as the source of Heidegger's new philosophical-poetical vocabulary and as the prime example of originative poetizing? Heidegger does not claim that Hölderlin is the greatest or the most originative of all poets. The early Greek poets and thinkers who evolved the beginnings of the West's philosophical language would most probably better deserve this credit. But, as Heidegger explains in the essay "Hölderlin and the Essence of Poetry," Hölderlin has, more than any other thinker, meditated on the nature of the poetizing act.[2] It is this "poet of poetizing," as Heidegger calls him, who established the originative explanation of the fundamental act of interpretation itself. This is the historical reason why, as we turn to consider the root of *Denken* and *Dichten* in the fundamental interpretative act that brings Being

---

[1] Beda Alleman, *Hölderlin und Heidegger*. Heidegger made it clear publically while he was at Cerisy in 1955 that he considers this treatment of his relations with Hölderlin definitive.

[2] "Hölderlin and the Essence of Poetry," in *Existence and Being*, p. 294.

to language, we confront the distinctive and difficult expressions of the poet.

DENKEN AND DICHTEN

In a recent essay, "Was heisst Denken?"[3] Heidegger again makes it clear that *Denken* and *Dichten* are not to be considered one: "The poetizing pronouncement and the thinking pronouncement are never the same thing." But, he adds, "Both can, however, say the same thing in different ways."[4] How do they differ and how are they alike? Heidegger warns us of the great difficulty involved in clarifying this distinction, and in so doing excuses, as it were, the lack of clarity in his own discourses on the matter. The difficulty arises from the fundamental nature of the subject under consideration. Bluntly put, to think the essence of the poet's "Word" would be to think Being in the essence of its Truth. It would be, in short, to surpass metaphysics.

But in addition to the inherent difficulty of the subject, interpretation of Heidegger's pronouncements on the relationship of *Dichten* and *Denken* is further complicated by a certain shift of perspective that occurs between the writing of the essay "On the Origin of the Artwork" (1935), in which important remarks on the subject are made for the first time, and the more recent pronouncements, especially those contained in an essay on Anaximander written in 1946. The confusion is enhanced by the fact that the two essays, though separated by eleven years of development, were published together after the War in the collection of short writings entitled *Holzwege* (Forest trails). Indications in these two essays manifest a consistency, but also a definite evolution in Heidegger's thought. An analysis of these matters will lead us to a clearer formulation of the relationship and common root of thinking and poetizing.

In "On the Origin of the Art Work" Heidegger affirms that Truth manifests itself in many ways.

One way Truth essentializes itself is as the established fact. Another way Truth comes to light is in proximity to that which is

[3] Heidegger, *Merkur, Deutsche Zeitschrift für europäisches Denken* (1952), pp. 601-11.

[4] "Was heisst Denken?," p. 607.

not a *Seiende* but the *Seiendste des Seienden*, the most "thingly of all things."[5] Still another way Truth grounds itself is the essential sacrificial offering. Still another way that Truth becomes is the questioning of thinking which, as thinking of Being, grasps Being in its question-ableness.[6]

Why is *Dichten* not mentioned here? Do all of these ways that Being has of coming to be—as fact, as speculation about God, in creative art, in questioning about Being itself—ground themselves somehow in a fundamental, original *Dichten*? In this same essay Heidegger declares that all art is basically an originative poetizing, but whether all original thinking can be so considered is a question that this essay leaves open.[7]

However, the affirmation *is* made in the same essay that it is *Sprache* that brings every existing thing as such into the open.[8] This means then that language, taken in the large sense that can include the language of a musician as well as that of a poet, grounds all the various ways that Truth manifests itself. But since "language itself is poetry in its fundamental sense," it would follow that somehow "thinking" must be a "poetizing."

This is just what Heidegger affirms unequivocally in the essay on Anaximander:

Thinking, however, is poetizing (*Dichten*), and indeed not just a kind of poetizing (*Dichtung*) in the sense of poetry or song. The thinking of Being is the fundamental manner of poetizing. In thinking thus considered, language comes to be language primordially, i.e., in its essence. Thinking pronounces the *Dictare* of the Truth of Being. Thinking is the fundamental (*ursprüngliche*) *Dictare*. Thinking is the root-poetry (*Urdichtung*) from which all poesy follows, also all that is practical in art, insofar as art comes in its activity into the region of language. All poetizing in this very wide sense, and also in the narrow sense of poesy, is in its ground a thinking.[9]

This unequivocal statement helps us formulate the change of perspective that occurs between 1935 and 1946. The earlier work seems to suggest that thinking was one of the many ways

[5] God, or the ultimate *Seiende* as viewed by a metaphysical system.
[6] *Holzwege*, p. 50.　　　　[7] *Ibid.*, p. 60.
[8] *Ibid.* See also Parts IV and V of *Hölderlin und das Wesen der Dichtung* (1936), pp. 38 ff.
[9] *Holzwege*, p. 303.

that the truth of *Seienden* could manifest itself, and that all possibly had their common ground in poetry in the widest sense. "Ten years later in the essay on Anaximander," as Alleman says, "this relationship is to some degree changed, to some degree maintained—retained in that poetry keeps its earlier meaning 'in the wide sense'; changed insofar as thinking is not subsumed into the same step, now that it is indicated as the most fundamental kind of poetizing."[10] In other words, all hesitancy today has disappeared. The originative act of Dasein relating himself to the things-that-are by bestowing them a meaning in language—the *ursprüngliche Dictare*—is at the root of all poetry, thought, art. It is the originative thinking referred to in the Postscript, the act through which Being itself comes home in language (*Sprache*).[11]

The hesitancies of the earlier work Heidegger himself would ascribe to their still "too philosophical" nature. He feels that his thinking back into the pre-Socratics—especially the essay on Anaximander, where he is forced to go back beyond the beginnings of metaphysics—has really plunged him into the nature of the originative thinking that makes it possible for philosophy even to begin to exist. In rethinking the accomplishments of the "thinkingest thinker," as Heidegger calls Anaximander, he finds himself at the point where the root philosophical notions of the Western tradition are originally forming themselves, as Anaximander creates the language that is to bear them. Anaximander is supremely poetical, because in thinking he brings the Word to be.

In this vein Heidegger claims that "a poet becomes all the more poetical the more thinking he becomes."[12] We can see now that Heidegger does not insist that the poet convert himself into a pseudo-philosopher, but rather that he must abandon himself (or, in the language of the Postscript, "sacrifice himself") to an ever deeper communication with things on the level where one finds the roots of language in its primal role as the "House of Being." The poet and the thinker share the responsibility of "bringing Being to house" in forging language. This, indeed, is the most properly human of all human activit-

[10] Alleman, *Hölderlin und Heidegger*, p. 100.
[11] *Holzwege*, p. 61.
[12] In a letter to Emil Staiger, cited by Alleman, p. 100.

ies. "In this housing dwells man. The more thoughtful and the more poetic are the ones who make this housing flourish."[13]

How can this dramatic situation of the poetic compounding of language as the root act of Being-revelation be compared to the position concerning language which Heidegger earlier developed in *Sein und Zeit*? In the fundamental work the foundation of language was declared to be discourse (*Rede*), which with *Befindlichkeit* and *Verstehen*, was declared to be a basic form of authentic existence.[14] In the recent Postscript to *Was ist Metaphysik*? the role assigned earlier to "authentic discourse" seems to have been deepened into the conception of the primacy of the Word that "language, as the elaboration of the Word, first casts into words."[15] Dasein's essential act of authentic existence is to engage in that thinking which, as Heidegger puts it in the letter to Beaufret, "in its pronouncing merely brings the unspoken Word of Being to language."[16] We can take the description of the Word in the recent essay *Bauen Wohnen Denken* as though it were a description of the issue of authentic discourse: "The word corresponding to the essence of a thing comes to us from out of language, if it is understood that we are thereby attending to a veritable essence."[17]

These developments are in keeping with the basic motive proposed in *Sein und Zeit*, i.e., a more fundamental ontologizing of our thought. I think it would be fair to say that the course from *Sein und Zeit*'s description of speech in terms of the "expression" of "discourse," to the recent declaration that language is the house of Being marks an increasing ontologization of the human word. Just what this imports for Heidegger's whole philosophy will become more manifest when, in our coming analysis of the "destruction" we watch Heidegger gathering up the fruit of Being that has been sown in history, precisely by rethinking historical words. In fact, as Heidegger sees it, in our attempt to achieve a repetition (*Wiederholung*) of the past we have to turn to a historical heritage consisting only of words, plus what the artist's language has left to us in the form of music and art objects. Getting the Being out of these

---

[13] Heidegger, *Humanismusbrief*, p. 5.

[14] *Sein und Zeit*, para. 34, "Dasein und Rede."

[15] *Was ist Metaphysik?*, p. 45.   [16] Heidegger, *Humanismusbrief*, p. 45.

[17] Heidegger, *Bauen Wohnen Denken*, p. 73.

remnants, or better yet, keeping alive the Being which these traces represent, is the very heart of the task of "remembering." The problem is acute, for the deeper meaning of words is constantly corroded out of them by daily usage as the purely calculative thinker drains the sense from them, pulling them down to his level of conception, without ever awakening any fresh meaning in them. The only way to bring the word back to life is to develop an active interest about it, a kind of *Wortmystik* that will induce the thinker to reawaken the sense of Being that might have once coursed through the halls of a historical work.[18] "The force of the most elementary words, in which the Dasein expresses himself," must be maintained![19] This is what Heidegger has in mind when he attacks the problem of understanding the "meaning" of a word from a faraway epoch. The critics who attack Heidegger's philological arbitrariness often forget to attack the root of the problem— what the meaning (*Bedeutung*) of a word represents in Heidegger's eyes. As receptable of past Being, a historical word finds meaning in its role as "the foundation of possible Being in word and speech,"[20] an expression which underscores as dramatically as possible the position that, just as "Being" in general only has meaning in terms of my own being and my own possibilities, so the meaning of a historical word always has to be meaning for me as Dasein. When Heidegger therefore attempts the *Andenken*, for example, of a Greek philosophy, his effort to breathe new life into the "most elementary words" takes a personal form, i.e., its course is dictated by the *projection* upon which the repetition is based, a desire to view in the "elementary word" a sign of the epochal revelation-dissimulation of Being. Heidegger's approach to Anaximander's *Logos* or Parmenides' *En panta* is not arbitrary, however personal it may be. The existentialist admits the decisions that are guiding his quest for meaning; he brings them out into the open so that we may judge their validity in terms of our own engagement in reality, instead of keeping them hidden, perhaps even from himself, as anyone who claims to be objective in historical analysis must do.

In attempting to reawaken the primitive force of an elementary Greek word, Heidegger will range the length and breadth

---

[18] *Sein und Zeit*, p. 220. [19] *Ibid.* [20] *Ibid.*, p. 87.

of Greek literature, seeking any key that can help unlock the Pandora's box so firmly closed by centuries of custom and mediocre interpretation. He then examines all of the progressive stages of the word's evolution in a wide sweep of history; he endeavours to view each as an epochal stage in the gradual devaluation of the word, but he also uses this devaluation as a kind of negative revelation of the potentialities of the original conception, hidden in its earlier indefiniteness.

When dealing with German words, Heidegger likes to reinvent something of the feeling of the "ancient forests," first by splitting these words into their components, and also by returning to the old forms (*Seyn* for *Sein*, *Thing* for *Ding*); this at one blow cuts underneath the accumulations of habitual interpretation, opening the field for a fresh "*An-denken*." The end of such *Wortmystisch* efforts is not to achieve depth by merely obscuring simple words. Simple words are often really not simple, though sometimes their obscurity will appear only when we attend to their implications. No, in awakening fresh meanings, Heidegger seeks precise meanings, as Alleman assures us: "He would *fix* the aggregate of meanings that come into language (in a word), and so would achieve a return through the philosophical speech in all its originality to a precisioning of speech, so that it may fulfil the sharp needs of thinking in the domain of the Being-question."[21]

These reflections on Heidegger's approach to the word illustrate a point that we might, in our concern to stress the originative, forward-projecting nature of new revelations of Being, tend to forget: Essential thinking must also, of its very nature, through its originative projections, look to the past, reawaken it, and protect it. The origination of language, as an act of authentic existence, must maintain integral each exstasis of the temporal horizon. The originative thinker's task is not to bring Being to be in the Word from out of a vacuum, but from out the course of the revelations of the past. Though *An-denken* can only occur because of projection in interpretation, projection, to avoid discontinuity and blind arbitrariness, must be rooted in the *Nach-denken*.

We shall return to consider further the fusion of different temporal elements in the creation of the "word" and the

[21] Alleman, *Hölderlin und Heidegger*, p. 105.

erection of the "thing." It is important that we not lose sight of one exstasis while emphasizing another, as we turn to push a little deeper yet into the consideration of the originative element in *Denken* and *Dichten*.

"The thinker pronounces Being; the poet names the Holy." The relationship of *Denken* and *Dichten* can perhaps be clarified if we consider what it is that is "pronounced" and "named."

"Being" and "the Holy" are not related to one another, Heidegger assures us, as two species to a higher genus, nor is one in any way subordinated to another. Rather they are correlative aspects of the same reality. Being is the result of the historical existent's letting-be the things-that-are. The Holy is the dimension of that *Lichtung* which is the very illumination of the *Seienden*. Following Hölderlin's lead, Heidegger agrees to term the dimension of the illumination of the things-that-are "the Holy," both because Dasein's originative act of letting-things-be is what in all reality is "most high," and because it is what actually is truly *transcendent*, in this sense: the supreme fulfillment of man's nature, as well as of the things. In the meeting of the mortal Dasein and the finite thing a historical-destiny which transcends the birth and death of *this* particular man and the annihilation of *this* concrete thing is forged within given horizons; these horizons, because they are horizons, always implicitly suggest the existence of "something more" than that which has already been explicitly interpreted.

"The Holy, which is the essential stage (*Wesensraum*) of divinity (*Gottheit*), which again is only the dimension for the gods and God, comes to appear only when a prior and long preparation is achieved by Being itself illuminating itself and being experienced in its Truth."[22] Like Being itself, the dimension of the *Lichtung* is not often present to man's awareness. Only in favored times and after long preparation do we come to see that Being is rooted in the transcendence of Dasein, and only then can we hope to understand the nature of that "ever more" of the Holy, which is the transcendence of Being in finite illumination. The Greeks, we might say, enjoyed a kind of primitive, unsophisticated awareness of the transcendence that lies behind the definite; they expressed it in their awe before the gods. Later times, seeking to reconstruct the unity

[22] *Humanismusbrief*, p. 26.

of the world which the last Greek philosophers had tended to disintegrate, found this unity and transcendence in the God of the Jews. The absence of God in our times is the ultimate sign of the "forgetting of Being," that exaggeration of the role of the *Seienden* and that affirmation of the arbitrary which destroy any hope of contemporary man's feeling the mysterious holiness of the transcendence of Being.

In the same letter to Beaufret, Heidegger asks how we can expect the dimension of the Holy to reappear in our times as long as the very dimension it represents—the opening of Being —is so totally ignored.[23] The same historical "uprooting of values" which climaxes in the "uprooting of values" (*Entwertung*) of Nietzsche is responsible for "the forgetting of Being" and "the closing of the dimension of the Holy." The situation is not, however, absolutely hopeless. When later we consider the essence of Truth as a "wandering in need," we shall see that Heidegger conceives finite truth to be a revelation of Being that inevitably makes us forget Being at the same time. The Holy as *Lichtung* is subject to the same law of finitude as the thinking of Truth. In *Holzwege* Heidegger declares that *Unheil als Unheil spürt uns das Heile* ("the unhappy as such makes us feel the happy"), just as darkness serves to make us feel the reality of light in the need we felt in its absence. So, in wandering farther and farther from Being, in closing more and more the dimension of the Holy, we become so isolated from Being and the Holy and what they necessarily import that their absence starts to make itself unmistakably felt.

Pursuing further our effort to understand the significance of this conception of the *Lichtung des Seins*, we must continue to eavesdrop on the *Zweisprach* between Hölderlin and Heidegger. Heidegger's interpretations of Hölderlin are so many efforts to find traces in the great poet's works of this "illumination." For example, writing of the poem "Feiertag's Hymne," Heidegger says: "What Hölderlin here names 'nature' dominates the entire poem to its very last word." He then proceeds to interpret "nature" (and through it the entire poem) as a revelation of Being, by reading the entire poem as though it spoke of Being's way of illuminating itself in time. Some critics might complain that Heidegger's interpretations in this and

[23] *Ibid.*, p. 37.

many similar examples are imaginative but entirely too fanciful. Such criticisms do not go to the heart of the matter. Heidegger conceives of the poem as Being that has come to be in words and, in this case, in a very special way. Here is revealed something about the very dimension of Being's *Lichtung*. The effort to think these traces of Being even more originatively requires that the thinker make more explicit what is only implicit in the poem, perhaps because the poet himself only half saw the implications of his inspiration. As Heidegger himself puts it, there is no question "of misusing the poem as a mine of discoveries for a philosophy. Rather it is the central Need to think soberly, in what the poem has pronounced, that which remains unspoken. This is the road of the historical-destiny of Being." The effort to understand the nature of the *Lichtung des Seins* as it is interpreted in Hölderlin's poetry, in Allemann's words, gets "on the road of the *Geschichte des Seins* when it itself is thought as a further step in Being's self-revelation and, as such, a kind of supreme *self-Lichtung* which can only be understood in the large framework of an *An-denken* on the whole sweep of Being's revelation in the Western tradition."[26]

To sum up: Being comes to be when an exsisting Da-sein within its transcendental horizon illumines the things that are. This illumination is of two kinds (as existence itself is both authentic and inauthentic). Most often it is mere calculation, the thinking that can only arrange and rearrange things that are already given, i.e., historically interpreted, within an illuminated totality that is itself assumed and inherited. Never seeing the totality for what it is, a finitude that can disengage its contours against the black background of the Nothing, derived, calculative thinking ignores the fundamental reality that makes the totality possible. That reality is Being itself, the light in virtue of which the derived thinking can see in the first place to begin its calculations. Hence it is always limited to the language of the market place which it finds and treats purely instrumentally.

[24] See chapter 7 of this book. The notion of the *Not-wendigkeit* of Truth has already been touched upon in passing.

[25] Heidegger, *Holzwege*, p. 252.

[26] Alleman, *Hölderlin und Heidegger*, p. 119.

Essential thinking, on the other hand, pulls the *Seienden* from the darkness of night into the light of Being. Heidegger, as we have seen, emphasizes the originativeness in this, the act of interpretation. Far from being a passive process of objective impression, interpretation demands that Dasein radiate the light of new intelligence from his own resources, i.e., from out of the Nothing, to illumine the *Wesen*, capturing the new meaning that it discovers there in that house of language which Dasein has built to protect Being's revelation in time. Dasein gathers up from the past the light that other generations have brought to bear on the *Seiende* and then, extending the range of previous insights, prolongs the tradition toward the future, which it thus builds-out existentially. So it is that *das Sein kommt nach Hause.*

The *ursprüngliche Dictare* and the act of essential thinking are one and the same. All other thinking and all forms of poetizing are derived from this source, for they depend on the *ursprüngliche Dictare* to illuminate the things-that-are by capturing their Being in words. When Heidegger speaks of the poet as "thinker," he refers to the poet's act of forging new meanings in forging new words. In this same sense the thinker is poetic, too, for he needs new words for new thoughts if Being is to be revealed through his efforts. When poet and thinker turn to interpret the central existential act, the *ursprüngliche Dictare*, though remaining closely bound to one another, they emphasize its two different aspects. "The thinker pronounces Being," i.e., the philosopher discovers at the root of the essential thinking the freedom of Dasein which makes possible the origin-out-of-nothing of new interpretation. "The poet names the Holy," i.e., the poet, in bringing the Word to be, places the thing in the dimension of greatest reality, where past and present and future meet, to transcend this man or that, this time or that— the dimension of the pure act of illumination itself, which in its total reality transcends the thing, the man, the epoch to become what is lasting—for that is what is "Holy." What it is that does not change through the annals of time and the flow of years is, as Kant already saw, Time itself. That which makes Time possible makes Being possible. That is what the metaphysicians sought when they spoke of the divine as the "thingliest of things."

Denken and *Dichten* are epochal because they are finite. And because they are finite, dissimulation accompanies their revelation in "pronouncing Being" and "naming the Holy." That is why the poets of metaphysical times named the Holy with the name of God, just as the thinkers sought the ground of the things-that-are in the thingliest of things. A deeper investigation of the epochal nature of the finite revelation-dissimulation of Being and the Holy will bring us to the very essence of truth.

ESSENTIAL THINKING

We must turn now to three recent essays in which all of the aspects of the originative discovery of the *Seiende* are woven by Heidegger into a definitive statement that clears up many uncertain spots and remaining doubts left by the earlier analyses. Equipped with a fuller understanding of the revelation of the thing, we shall be able to penetrate to a very solid grasp of Heidegger's conception of "the essence of truth," which is so important for a comprehension of his entire philosophy.

In the essay "Das Ding" (1950)[27] Heidegger shifts from the point of view of the essays we have just considered, where attention was concentrated on the thinker and the poet, to an attention on the "thing" as the centrum where the light of illumination and the darkness of the brute *Seiende* come together to form *das Ding*. While all thinkers recognize the importance of the *Sachen selbst*, no one, says Heidegger, has meditated on the thingness of things.[28] The failure of the tradition to do so is one of the most striking manifestations of the "forgetting of Being."

How can we think the essence of thingness through its manifestation, for example, in this water jug? If we try to examine what the jug really is—in what the jugness of the jug really consists and how it fulfills its role as *this thing*—we shall see that it serves as a kind of epicenter for a gathering-in process, becoming the nucleus of a whole set of new relevancies.

[27] The three essays we shall now consider are published with several others to form the volume *Vorträge und Aufsätze*.

[28] *Vorträge und Aufsätze*, p. 168.

First of all, it is something definite, impermeable, enclosing a certain space, filled with air. Its hardness, coupled with its form, gives it a certain capacity to contain; it can hold water, gathering in the rain; it can hold wine, gathering in the sunshine and the earth from which the grapes drew their sugars. But it not only gathers-in; it offers, too. It offers drink to man. It has a utility for mortals—and on this level it has meaning for them; but deeper meanings hide in the thing, too, for *real mortals* who view the thing through the deeper eyes of anguish. As a "something definite" it also suggests the presence of the unknown, and should be thought of, therefore, as a kind of gift conquered from the realm of what is never completely laid out before us. "In offering the grace of a drink the godlike comes to linger here. . . ."[29] The essence of the jug lies in its gathering into one the earth, the heavens, the godlike and the mortal in a way that makes them together, and only together, come to linger as that manifestation which we call the "thing." The thingness of the thing is this binding together which renders their sense to each member of the fourfold unity (the "square" [*Gevierte*], as Heidegger calls the relationship).[30]

The "forgetting of Being" has resulted throughout the course of the Western tradition in the thing's being thought always in terms of one aspect of the "unified square." The surpassing of this tradition toward a thinking of Being requires that we understand the *Gevierte* as it is, each aspect requiring the other three to give it its meaning. In the essay now being discussed and in another, "Bauen Wohnen Denken," Heidegger employs the same formulas for each of the aspects of the fourfold unity:

1. *The Earth* is the constructing supporter, the rendering-near fructifier, preserving waters and stone, flora and fauna.[31] "If we pronounce 'earth' then already we are thinking the other three without the unity of the four."

2. *The Heaven* is the Sun's course and the path of the Moon, the shining of the stars, the times of the year, the light and evening of days, the darkness and brightness of the night, the favour and unhospitableness of the weather, the blue depth of the ether.[32] Again Heidegger announces the same formula, "If we pronounce (*sagen*) Himmel. . . ."

[29] *Ibid.*, p. 171. [30] *Ibid.* [31] *Ibid.*, pp. 149, 176. [32] *Ibid.*, pp. 150, 177.

3. *The Divinities* (*Göttlichen*) are the fleeting messengers of the Divinity (*Gottheit*). Through their hidden rule appears God in his essence, which, with each comparison with the present (*Anwesende*), slips away from us. This time the "pronouncing" of the formula is changed to "naming" . . . *Nennen wir die Göttlichen, dann* . . .[33]

4. *The Mortals* are men. Man alone dies, animals simply come to an end. They have death neither in prospect nor in retrospect. Death, as the coffer of the Nothing, protects for man the realization of Being in itself ("*Der Tod birgt als der Schrein des Nichts das Wesende des Seins in sich*").[34] The Mortals are the essentializing relation of Dasein to Being as Being. Again the formula, "If we pronounce 'mortals' then we think the other three without the unity of the four."[35]

As enigmatic as these short pronouncements are, on the basis of what little we have already seen we can draw a number of firm conclusions about what Heidegger is saying in Hölderlinian terms. The assembling unification of the four which makes it possible for each to linger in the common light is evidently the thing thought in the dimension of Being. All the aspects of Being-revelation which we have already encountered are here: the *Sagen* of the thinker and the *Nennen* of the poet. The threefold *Sagen* and the poet's *Nennen* must be brought together so that each can cast its light on the other, and the four together can constitute the "thing." Heidegger speaks of this relationship as a "coming-to-pass interplay of mirrors" (*ereignenden Spiegel-Spiel*). It is this interplay which he calls here "the World."[36]

The world owes its existence to the Being of the "mortals" whose grasp of the nothing makes possible the unification of the four. In the earlier essay on "The Origin of Art Work" the inner dialectic constituting Being was pictured simply as an interplay of earth and world. The essays now under consideration do not contradict this analysis but enrich it by searching more profoundly, in the form of a discussion of "the thing," into the details of what *Vom Wesen des Grundes* had termed, still earlier, *stiften eine Welt*—the instituting of a World. The twofold relationship *Sein-Seienden* had since *Sein und Zeit* always implied a third, *Seienden-Dasein-Sein*; the essay on fundament elaborated

[33] *Ibid.*   [34] *Ibid.*, p. 177.   [35] *Ibid.*, pp. 150, 177.   [36] *Ibid.*, p. 178.

the complications of the relationship likewise in a threefold way, speaking of the *Stiften-Grunden-Bodennehmen* relationship in a way that presented each aspect of "founding a world" as corresponding to one of the three exstases—past, present, and future, of the temporal horizon. The position in "The Origin of Art," namely that the art work is rooted in the earth from which it is only partially pulled into the light of a human world, could also suggest this threefold nature of the *Verhältniss* (relationship): the earth, the light which comes to shine, as the temple is rooted in the earth, and the Dasein who is at the root of the situation as founder of a world.

But how can we coordinate the previous doctrines, all implying a threefold exstatic temporal horizon, with an explanation of the erection of "the thing" that insists, following a suggestion of Hölderlin, on a "fourfold gathering-in"?

First, we must notice that three of the four can be identified as elements present in one form or another in all of the earlier analyses.

The earth, the "fructifier," which provides the solid base for the "rendering-near" of the thing, is the mass of *Seienden,* the stones, plants, and animals from out of which and among which man must build his kingdom. We must not think of the "earth" or brute *Seienden* in terms of the Aristotelian *hyle,* because the *Seienden* are not "pure potency," though they provide the basic stuff of a world. Rather they enjoy an "actuality" which, entering into union with the other elements in the *Gevierte* through "*Inständigkeit,*" in part really constitutes the thing. The fundamental extasis of the earth is the present of that which is present, the now of the fundamental encounter with the things-that-are.

The light, which shines forth from heaven; termed in the earlier works the *Licht des Seienden,* then (for example, in the *Anaximander Satz*), the *Licht des Seins,* now undergoes a further deepening as Heidegger, inspired by the late poems of Hölderlin, writes: "The poet calls forth all brightness from a glance at heaven and endows every sound with its way and its air in singing word, and brings thereby to light and to sounding forth the called-for one (*Gerufene*)."[37] The glance of light, then, comes through the poet—the "mortal"

[37] *Ibid.*, p. 200.

of the four—from out the heaven by way of poetizing. The twofold sight-sound imagery employed here is Heidegger's signal that we are witnessing in illumination the birth of language, which is always indifferently seen or heard. Thus Heidegger will often interchange light and sound imagery, speaking on one occasion of the light which shines forth from heaven, and on another of the "quiet voice of Being." The "light in view of which" the things that lie open before us are seen is essentially the light of what transcends the now, chiefly of a past that must be made present through the projections of the mortal. In consigning the light mainly to the exstasis of the past I ask the reader to remember that each exstasis infers the other two, and that each is a matter of accert. Plato recognized in the mortal's ability to gather up the light of the past to make it shine on the present, as Aristotle did in memory, the very foundation of knowledge. But Heidegger sees that we must explain the *how* of the making present in terms of an origination that is more than a passive retaining. Hence the central position afforded to the third exstasis, the futurity of the mortal's projection, to which *Sein und Zeit* assigned the fundamental role of establishing all temporality.

The mortal then is the poet who makes the light of the past present by opening toward the future from out the originative source of his own nothingness a gap where Being can occur.

But what of the fourth element, the *Göttlichen*? Are there not but three exstases possible in a temporal horizon? Certainly; but then there is the whole, and even the *more than* the whole, if we may for a moment speak in terms as mysterious as Hölderlin's. The structural whole is Being, but Being is more than what has been revealed and what has been held up to now. Because of the finitude of Dasein, what is present, i.e., what has been gathered up through a projection toward the future from out of the past, is never all that has been, all that can be now, all that can be projected. Hovering around the thin aura of the intelligible light of the Dasein's day lies the night, unknown, implied, suggested, always being conquered and always conquering. What is present owes very much to the light of what has been, hence the eternal association of the really-real with the light of heaven. But what is said is always less than what is unsaid and needs to be pronounced. When the poet names and the thinker pronounces, he does so always in view of something; hence he always hides as he illumines, so that every assertion is also in part a falsehood (one thinks of Gide's remark in his journal, "When I think of the stupidities uttered in an average day by the intelligent man, I am tempted to complete silence"). Every positive predication, as Hegel said, posits at once a negation. The always-more, the always-hidden transcendent is the *Gottheit* of which Heidegger speaks when he names the fourth of the *Gevierte*. Its awful and mysterious kingdom lies beyond the outlines of the all of the *Seienden als Ganzen*, for it is the nothing from out of which the something is withdrawn. Hölderlin's "Was ist Gott?" begins:

> Was ist Gott? unbekannt, dennoch
> Voll Eigenschaften ist das Angesicht
> Des Himmels von ihm. Die Blitze nämlich
> Der Zorn sind eines Gottes. Jemehr ist eins
> Unsichtbar, schicket es sich in Fremdes.

In interpreting this text Heidegger declares:

The poet calls, in looking toward heaven, whatever in shining-forth lets that which hides itself also appear . . . but appear only as the self-dissimulating. The poet calls in familiar manifestations the unfamiliar, wherein the invisible is destined to remain what it is: the unknown.[38]

What is unknown lies beyond the limits of the heavens, because the heavens mark the limit of the light we have gathered up to now. But this light, by the very fact that it is limited, suggests a *more*. This is why poetizing inevitably faces man with the realm of the unknown. As we have already poetically "measured the things-that-are" and gathered them into new light, we can also expect in the future to render familiar more of what remains just now still foreign (*fremd*). This making familiar by measuring in the light of heaven against the backdrop of the unknown is precisely the fundamental *Dictare* itself.[39]

The poet poetizes only when he grasps the proportion in which he speaks (*dict*) the Glance of Heaven, the manifestations of which he adapts, as the Unfamiliar wherein the Unknown God "offers himself." The customary name for Glance and "*Aussehen*" is

[38] *Ibid.*   [39] *Ibid.*

"Image" (*Bild*). . . . Because poetizing grasps each mysterious proportion[40] in view of heaven it can speak thereby in "images." Therefore poetical images are "imaginings" in an extraordinary sense: not simply fantasies and illusions but image-ings in the form of revelatory notes from the Unfamiliar gleaned in the glance of the familiar. The poetizing saying of images gathers together the Bright and the Toneful of the heavenly manifestations in unison with the Darkness and the Silence of the unfamiliar. Through such glances God surprises. In these surprises he reveals his unceasing Nearness.[41]

A few lines farther on Heidegger furnishes the key to understanding what he is expressing here in the difficult language of Hölderlin: the proportion and measure[42] of the poet is of the nature of heaven; but "heaven is not idle light. The flash of its height is in itself the Dark of its all protecting Vastness." The phrase, "all protecting Vastness," was identified earlier as a description of the Nothing—as the *Weiträumigkeit* of the finite totality of the *Seienden* viewed projected against the nothingness that enfolds a limited reality. It is again through anguish, in the surprising revelations of the nearness of *das Nichts* that "the glance of heaven—the light of historical Being —manifests itself as the backdrop for its *Erscheinungen* (manifestations).

Once again we must realize that the bringing together of the four elements to form the thing is not automatic but a responsibility of authentic Dasein. Heidegger introduces a new word for the Dasein's authentic maintenance of the four exstatic elements of the *Gevierte* in their proper proportion: "dwelling" (*Wohnen*). The essay, "Bauen Wohnen Denken," explains how man must bring the elements together under the guidance of respect for the *Göttlichen*, for the divine element of the transcendent *Weiträumigkeit* of the incomprehensible nothing. "To dwell" on this earth, in the way that means to have a home, is to dwell by, with, in, and from things, through the fusion of the exstatic elements in sacrifice to the holy. This is the sense Heidegger gives to Hölderlin's beautiful pronouncement:

[40] In the sense of ratio.   [41] *Vorträge und Aufsätze*, pp. 200-1.

[42] The proportion refers to the maintenance of the proper balance of exstases in the vision of the things-that-are. It is against the full temporal reality of "what is" that the Dasein should conceive.

... dichterisch, wohnet
Der Mensch auf dieser Erde

—"poetically dwells man from out this earth." It is the essential task of authentic existence to dwell, which implies building the thing ("to let be the things-that-are," is the way Heidegger puts it).[43] Transcribing each of the elements of the *Gevierte* into language expressing what we may do, "Bauen Wohnen Denken" transforms the insights of *Das Ding* into a program for that "poetical dwelling" which is the end of authentic existence:

1. Mortals dwell insofar as they save (*retten*) the earth. Heidegger renders Hölderlin's *auf dieser Erde* its deepest sense: "To let be the things-that-are" means to root ourselves in the dark resisting mass of the real *Seienden*, to call down the glance of the god's light so that they may be illumined, to protect the glory of ancient lights, that Being might be preserved.[44]

2. Mortals dwell insofar as they receive (*empfangen*) the heaven as heaven. The mortal who has tasted in anguish the great and bitter fruit of his nothingness respects the unnamed and guards the unknown. He does this by refusing to turn night falsely into day, i.e., by respecting mystery. Heidegger means that we must not "solve" the secrets of Being through the kind of callous dissimulations practised by those who erected great metaphysical systems without concern for the things that really escaped their grasp. Where the gods offer no light, the poetic dweller is patient; where they do, he guards its beam from the *gehetzten Unrast*,[45] the meaningless of the prattle of the *alltägliche Gerede*. Like the "dwelling from out this earth," the "dwelling under the stars" is also a letting be of the things-that-are.

3. Mortals dwell insofar as they wait on (*erwarten*) the Divine as Divine. Anguish should introduce care. Care is the atmosphere in which Being is revealed because Dasein is "open to" what is real. This requires that Dasein be attentive to what is present and miss what is absent. Earlier we saw that our epoch stands far from Being and that the *Heilige* stands withdrawn. The "caring" Dasein, the "mortal," must make ready

[43] In his essay on truth.   [44] *Vorträge und Aufsätze*, p. 150.   [45] *Ibid.*

the reawakening of a sense of the Holy. "The mortals wait for an indication of its [the Divine's] arrival and do not mistake the sign of its lack."[46] Authentic dwelling requires an essential thinking of the *Seinsvergessenheit*, which is the very object of the destruction of the history of ontology. Each authentic existent must make "destruction" a part of his dwelling *auf dieser Erde*, at least to the extent that he works to free himself of the effects of the forgetting of Being, which is the only way to prepare the advent of a new presence of the Holy. The cauterizing effect of a pure experience of the Nothing is brought to mind in lines reminiscent of the last words of *Was ist Metaphysik?* ("Mortals fabricate no gods and do not serve idols. In the midst of the Unholy they attend the withdrawing Holy."[47] No *Seiende* must be erected into the place of *das Sein*. The idols of daily existence and calculative thinking must be left behind.

4. The mortal saves the earth, receives the heaven, and waits on the Divine. The fourth responsibility that makes it possible for the mortal to dwell involves attention to his own mortality. The mortal must "dwell" in full view of the significance of his own death. This does not mean, Heidegger warns us, that we should establish death in the sense of an empty nothing as our goal (*nicht den Tod als das leere Nichts zum Ziel setzen*). Once again Heidegger invokes death as the nothingness of Dasein as a way of warning that authenticity lies in dwelling as we are meant to dwell, as *Aufenthalt bei den Dingen*, and nothing else. A full realization of our mortality can dissolve the bonds that tie us to metaphysical systems, freeing us for our authentic task, which is to dwell by protecting the *Gevierte* in its unity through "sojourning with things."

"Dwelling is the very mark of Being."[48] This unification of the four by "sojourning" with things *auf dieser Erde* is the very act of *Inständigkeit* which *Sein und Zeit* presented as the fundamental reality of Dasein.[49] The "saving," "receiving," and "waiting on" which constitute dwelling are rooted in the *Befindlichkeit*, *Verstehen*, and *Rede* of sojourning's authentic standing-in.

Now that the dwelling and the *auf dieser Erde* of Hölderlin's formula of existence have been explained, the mode alone remains to be commented on in the light of all that we have

[46] *Ibid.*, p. 151.   [47] *Ibid.*   [48] *Ibid.*, p. 161.   [49] *Ibid.*

seen of authentic existence—the *dichterisch*. It is in explaining
what he means by *Bauen* that Heidegger unifies the previous
rich commentary with the earlier discoveries concerning the
root of authentic existence in the originative thinking of the
ursprüngliche Dictare.

"Poetizing is not erecting structures from things already
built. Rather poetizing is the originative building as authentic
measuring of the dimension of dwelling. . . . *Das Dichten ist das
ursprüngliche Wohnenlassen*—poetizing is the fundamental letting-
dwell."[50] To dwell we must make it possible that there be
things by which we *can* dwell. The erection of the thing, understood as it has been described in the preceding pages, is the
task of originative poetizing. This is the great need of the Dasein,
to find the homeland where he can prepare for himself a dwelling. Before he can achieve this, man must first think the need
to dwell precisely as a *need*, so that it can become for him a basic
impulsion. "As soon as man considers his homelessness, this
homelessness ceases to be a misery; rather, correctly considered
and rightly held to, it becomes the authentic exhortation calling
the mortal to dwell."[51] In the following chapter the fundamental
Need that is the very finitude of the Dasein seeking its fulfillment, will become the center of the discussion of truth and
freedom.

From these remarks on poetizing are we to gather, then, that
everyone is himself supposed to be an originative poet? Hölderlin himself tells us in his poem on the theme of dwelling, "Home-
coming," that this is of course not possible. In clarification of
the way this need to build a dwelling affects the individual,
Heidegger writes:

The "Need" is the mysterious call "to" the others in the Father-
land to become hearers, in order that for the first time they should
learn to know the essence of the Homeland. "The others" must for
the first time learn to consider the mystery of the receiving proximity. . . . Out of these deliberating ones will come the slow ones
of the long deliberating spirit, which itself learns to persevere in
the face of the self-imposed, continuing failure of the God. The
deliberating ones and the slow ones are for the first time the
"care-ful." Because they *think* of that which is written in the poem,
they are directed with the singer's care toward the mystery of the

---

[50] *Ibid.*, p. 202.   [51] *Ibid.*, p. 162.

preserving proximity. Through this single turning toward the same object the care-ful hearers are related to the care of the speaker (the poet). "The Others" are the "kindred" of the poet.[52]

The strange language of Heidegger transmits to us the even stranger music of Frederick Hölderlin. Ours is a task of preparation and anticipation for an essential *hören* of what the true poet names and the originative thinker says. We are to hear and to preserve. It is not given to everyone to name the holy, but it is the duty of everyone in the absence of the God (i.e., in the epoch of de-ontologization, of *Seinsvergessenheit*), to listen as the poet names that *Nähe* (proximity) which remains ever *fern* (distant), the Being to which we ourselves are the way of access, but which we never fully discover. We can be care-ful (*Sorge* being the way to the grasp of the totality of the things-that-are), even if we cannot be truly originative; at least we can be protective of that which *is* original, keeping the way open in our civilization to a genuine dwelling with Being, not dispensing its riches and closing the way through a total abandon to purely calculative thinking. We shall be more than calculative, though we employ only calculation, for we shall see its limits and therefore be aware of the existence of a truer thinking as its foundation. Less than poets, "we others" nevertheless shall be his kindred. We shall preserve the truth of the word the poet has spoken.[53]

The poetizing of originative thinking, the dwelling by the things-that-are, and the building of the thing which makes the dwelling possible are all rooted in the essential need of Dasein, that original impulsion of the finite Da-sein to be and to reverently understand Being.

But these conceptions cannot become truly meaningful until we have explored what is at the heart of this, as well as all the problems involved in the comprehension of Dasein that we have seen up to now: the nature and meaning of the need. Heidegger reveals the essential nature of the Dasein's need in his lecture "On the Essence of Truth," to which we shall now turn.

[52] *Ibid.*, pp. 287-88.   [53] *Ibid.*, p. 289.

VI   The Essence of Truth

ALL paths of the Heideggerian phenomenology lead to the essence of truth. Every effort to get at the essence of that thing which we ourselves are has brought us to roughly the same conclusion: (1) Dasein is the "stage" of Being in its rapport with the things-that-are, that is, of truth itself, and (2) this rapport is rooted in the Dasein's finitude as need.

The most definitive presentation to date of Heidegger's effort to "think Being in the Essence of its Truth" is the short lecture "On the Essence of Truth," basically sketched out in 1930 but completed and published only in 1943.[1] This *Vom Wesen der Wahrheit* is the summit and conclusion of the existential analysis of Dasein.

The essay opens with two sections devoted to the ordinary conception of truth. Heidegger as usual presents the common, metaphysical, and, when considered, ultimate, inauthentic conception of truth, in order to take the reader beyond its limits to more essential and original thinking of that which founds and makes possible the phenomenon presented by that less fundamental position. The metaphysical conception views truth as a conformity of intellect and thing, making truth reside ultimately in the judgment.[2] Heidegger shows that one penetrating question can carry us at once beyond this limited traditional point of view: from whence the *possibility* of there being a conformity of intellect and thing?[3] It is not judgment which is ultimate, but whatever it is that makes it *possible* that there should be judg-

---

[1] So Heidegger tells us in the *Humanismusbrief*, p. 17, where he adds that *Vom Wesen der Wahrheit* "gives a certain insight into the thinking necessary for the reversal from 'Being and time' to 'time and Being.' "

[2] *Vom Wesen der Wahrheit*, secs. 1 and 2.   [3] *Ibid.*, p. 12.

ment.[4] This ground of judgment Heidegger terms the *Vorgeben*, the "preliminary gift" of "opening" itself. It is, in a word, the standing-open of our comportment (*Verhältnis*) which makes possible the "joining of representations," the conformity of intellect and thing. This standing-open itself is grounded in the freedom with which the Dasein finds himself endowed as he is thrown into the world. The Dasein freely comporting himself in opening a world founds the possibility of truth. Consequently, *das Wesen der Wahrheit ist die Freiheit*—the essence of truth is freedom.

Our analyses in the preceding chapters have prepared us amply for this conclusion: Freedom as ground of the transcendental horizon lies behind every discussion in *Kant und das Problem der Metaphysik*; in *Vom Wesen des Grundes* the "essence" in question is freedom itself; in *Was ist Metaphysik?* it was freedom which, as essence of truth, brought the Dasein before the Nothing. We have seen that in all three works the finitude of this freedom was seen as a need (*Not*) or a thirst for Being-understanding; it is this need which is the very impulsion behind originative thinking. Consequently the fundamental act of "dwelling" has been conceived as the thinking of this need as need. "On the Essence of Truth" is basic to the perspective shared by all of these works, for here, more than in any other work to date, Heidegger attempts to think the essence of the founding freedom in terms of the need which is manifested by finite existence.

Freedom, declares our author, as the *Offenbaren eines Offenen*, lets the *Seiende* be what it is. "Freedom discovers itself to be the letting-be of *Seienden* (*das Seinlassen von Seienden*)"[5] When we discover a *Seiende*, engrossed as we are in what there is to be seen here, interested in the internal reality of the thing itself (that *als-Struktur*, as Heidegger terms it), we are naturally inclined to regard the light in which the *Seiende* is revealed as emanating from the thing itself. But the *Offene* is not source of its openness; it owes the possibility of being-open to its place within the world, within a transcendental horizon. Consequently the source of light is in that which makes open the open, i.e., in the *Offenbaren eines Offenen*. This fundamental making-open, which lets things *be* in the first place, not in the sense of creating them

[4] *Ibid.*　　　　　　[5] *Ibid.*, p. 14.

but in the sense of permitting them to be discovered, this *Sein-lassen* is exposition, is existence itself. "The *Ek-sistenz* rooted as freedom in truth is the ex-position in revelation of the *Seienden* as such."[6]

Quite obviously, the fundamental freedom which here is in question in the explanation of the foundation of truth, is not the "free will" of man, which is rather dependent upon the fundamental freedom. (There could be no free choice prior to the opening of an exstatic horizon within which "truth" and therefore "engagement" becomes possible.) Rather Heidegger is trying to describe the fundamental engagement of the Da-sein, which is nothing more than the opening of a world, the root of the *Da*.

The ability to let *be* the things-that-are depends on the fundamental possibility to take a stand in regard to the *totality* of these things. Consequently, at the root of the question of truth lies the root of the question posed by metaphysics, the question of the *Seiendheit des Seienden*, the interrogation about the nature of the totality of the things-that-are. It is because "freedom possesses us," as Heidegger paradoxically puts it to explain man's servitude to Being, that we are "transcendental" in relation to the things-that-are, and it is, consequently, in the face of the experience of the Nothing that metaphysics can ask about that totality. The freedom which Dasein enjoys separates him from the mass of *Seienden*, which separation first makes it possible for Dasein to comport himself in relation to the things-that-are. This separation of *Seienden* and Dasein is effected by freedom's insertion of nothingness between Dasein and the total mass of the things-that-are—insertion which takes place when he grasps *Seienden* for the first time, not in a purely functional concrete relationship like an animal, but as *Seienden* in their "thingness" (*Seiendheit*).

When the first thinker in ancient times thought the nature of truth as *a-letheia*, *Un-verborgenheit*, (unveiledness), and asked himself then what the *Seiende als Seiende* (the *on* as *on*) was, there began the history of truth, the "historical destiny" of the Dasein.

First when the *Seiende* itself was properly swept up into its unveiledness and guarded there, first where this guarding was conceived in terms of the question about *Seienden* as such, historical destiny began. The original revelation of the *Seienden* as a totality, the question about the *Seienden* as such and the beginning of the Occidental historical destiny are one and the same and share the same Time, which itself in an unmeasurable way opened the *Offene* for every measure.[7]

Heidegger in effect is declaring that real truth was not born until man had realized his independence by grasping the freedom of Dasein. The notion of the *Seienden* as *Seienden* which followed upon the conception of truth as unveiledness could only be but a first step. To know the *Seiende* as such, fully and explicitly, means to ask about the significance of what it is to be a *Seiende*, which necessarily throws into question the totality of *Seienden*. Such a question poses a further question that carries us properly *beyond* the totality of *Seienden*: What is the Dasein's distinction from the things-that-are, and what is the nature of their relationships to one another? Today it is precisely that question which the philosophy of Heidegger is asking. That is why the history of the Dasein-*Seienden* relationship in its evolving stages (epochs) can and must become for us an ontologically significant historical destiny.[8] The history of this truth relationship is the key to all history, for all man's comportment in any epoch is mediated by the contemporary conception of his place amidst the totality of the things-that-are. The "destruction" of the *Geschichte* of ontologies holds the key, therefore, to our understanding the evolution of the conception of truth, which in turn will reveal amidst all the dissimulations something of the fundamental, authentic truth relationship.

Our approach to the history of the Dasein-*Seienden* relationship we have called a "destruction" rather than a recalling; for nowhere and in no time do we find a fully valid conception of the real essence of this truth relationship; each world view points towards a true conception of Dasein's relation to *Seienden* by its lacks as much as by its limited insights. This is inevitable because of the finitude of our freedom; any revelation, leaving untold as much as it reveals, is always a veiling as much as an unveiling. This is why we can never authentically conceive of truth without recalling its inevitable counterpart, the untruth of that which is hidden by the positive but partial affirmations

[7] *Ibid.*, p. 16.   [8] *Ibid.*, p. 17.

of finite truth. Untruth is not the accidental result of a certain negligence or indifference on the part of the knower, but rather an essential expression of truth itself as it occurs in the bounds of finitude. *Die Unwahrheit muss vielmehr aus dem Wesen der Wahrheit kommen.*[9]

Can we then never get at the heart of things? If the reader poses this question to himself, he has already forgotten the analysis of the "thing" which we examined in the last chapter. He must remember that Heidegger's is a *phenomenological* philosophy. The thing as we know it—the phenomenon—is the thing-in-itself. That means that it is always a phenomenon-in-time, made up as much by the original contributions of each fresh interpretation, as it is by the earth—the brute reality of the *Seiende* which forms the base of all experience. There is no eternal truth, existing in itself, awaiting discovery sometime, somewhere; truth is continually being created, and its possibilities are never exhausted. The problems which accompany such a position are grave.

With this in mind, we approach the texts in *Vom Wesen der Wahrheit* which treat of the essential dissimulation in the heart of the finite truth situation with some hope of understanding their deep significance.

Heidegger's texts concerning the truth-untruth relationship are, as usual, enigmatic, requiring, again as usual, considerable interpretation on our part. The grasp and interpretation of any concrete thing involves two aspects with which the man of the market place, in the midst of his daily activities, rarely concerns himself. First of all, the truth of that knowledge is rooted in my possibility for grasping and interpreting the thing, in my way of comporting myself toward things. Second, the truth of any thing is inevitably conditioned by that thing's insertion in the totality of things known. When I am concerned with the price of chickens I do not stop to contemplate the ultimate grounds of my interpretation of the relative value of this chicken. If I did, I would realize that its value is entirely in function of my taste and the taste of other men like me struggling to obtain the same chicken. I would also realize that the chicken, as the thing considered, has to be related to other chickens, to fowls, to foods in general, to other possible

[9] *Ibid.*

sensual gratifications, to spiritual sources of pleasure, etc., etc., and this without end, until I am forced to consider the chicken in relation to the whole of reality, i.e., in relation to the *Seienden als Ganzen*.

The "partial" nature of the concrete truth situation involves both of these aspects: (1) each epoch's original conception of the nature of that fundamental relation of knower to known—conception which founds not only its notion of truth but its way of approaching things in general; and (2) the tendency to describe the whole by particular affirmations (unveilings) of things, excluding and hiding other equally legitimate aspects of this whole (dissimulation). This partialness arising from the finitude of Dasein gives rise to the epochal and progressive nature of truth. It keeps us from any truly fundamental grasp of the whole.

The extraordinary nature of Heidegger's own meditation on the "essence" of truth—the quality that makes this the definitive step in the surpassing of all the epochs of the "metaphysical tradition"—lies in the fact that now truth is for the first time thought of in terms of its essential dissimulation, which means that the ultimate root of truth has begun to reveal itself. "Has begun to reveal itself," we say advisably, for a revelation dealing in ultimates must remain bathed in the mystery of Being. Our grasp of the essential dissimulation involved in all finite truth does not, for all that, abolish this finitude. The mystery remains, the *lethe* (the veil) of the *aletheia* remains in place; but now we become its respectful servants instead of acting, as the metaphysicians did, as though Being were required to drop her veil. The metaphysician who, failing to achieve the totality wished for by the Greek concept of wisdom, would construct an absolute system "explaining all" did not serve mystery but—to his own disservice—opposed it. In contrast, Heidegger's "essential thinking" achieves a kind of totality which does not violate the *Geheimnis* of Being. For the Heideggerian conception of truth disengages the totality of *Seienden* and explains how we originatively interpret *Seienden* against the background of the "Nothing" of finitude. The mystery of our "being thrown in the world," the mystery of the originativeness involved in the "naming of the *Heilige*" which always leaves more that is unnamed, and the incomprehensibility of the *weiträumige* mass of concrete things is nurtured and heightened in this "total" explanation that wishes itself incomplete, negative, epochal, and finite.

This interpretation helps us to see better that the "forgetting of Being" which characterizes inauthentic existence has two aspects, depending on whether we consider Being in terms of the essence of truth or whether we think of the interpretation of *Seienden* in terms of the totality of the things-that-are. In the analysis of unauthenticity summarized from *Sein und Zeit* we tended to concentrate on the latter. The average Dasein, engaged in daily concerns, interprets things without regard to the ultimate implications that represent his true possibilities and true role as the "opening" within which Being reveals itself. This prevents his judgments from achieving totality and therefore accounts for the wandering through history from interpretation to interpretation of the same phenomena. In our consideration of the "destruction of the history of ontology" we shall be more concerned with "the forgetting of Being" that expresses itself in the great truth conceptions of the principal metaphysicians. Both misinterpretations owe their incompleteness and dissimulating character to the same *Seinsvergessenheit*, the same failure to push the question of the nature of things far enough to discover their root in the nothingness of the finite Dasein. Both lead to "subjectivization," i.e., the tendency of man to impose himself and his arbitrary standards on things. "Man is the measure of all things" is history's ultimate expression of the form which the *Seinsvergessenheit* always takes, whether it manifests itself as idealism or as realism. "To measure thus," says Heidegger, here showing once again how far he would wish himself from an anthropomorphic subjectivism, "is to measure poorly." The result of all "subjectivization" is always the same, and it is ironic: man, wishing to subjugate Being to his arbitrary wishes, ends by subjugating himself to the tyranny of the *vorhandenen* things. Always his great constructed systems finally explain away freedom by subjugating it to some thing or kind of thing. These are of course matters for the "destruction" to consider in detail. The important thing to remember for now is that the inauthentic always leads to some loss of freedom. Happily, the loss is never total, for man by nature remains free. He remains, through all the vagaries of metaphysics, the interpreter of the things-that-are, *needing* the things-that-are to fulfill the wants of his *Seinsverständniss*, and therefore necessarily cooperating with them in his role as the place where Being comes to be. "Ek-sisting, the Dasein is in-sisting,"[10] Heidegger declares, and insisting is always a free act.

Dasein is always insisting. Dasein is always free—but in a finite way, so that his revelations of things are also dissimulations. Obviously we need a closer phenomenological look at the nature of this existential finitude. We find in *Vom Wesen der Wahrheit* (section 7) the most complete and formal treatment of the nature of this finitude—the ultimate phenomenological analysis toward which all of the other analyses, in one way or another, lead. It grounds both aspects of the "double task" proposed in the introduction to *Sein und Zeit*, i.e., both the existential of the Dasein and the concept of the historical destiny of the West that governs in the destruction. This being the case, every aspect of the section requires specially careful consideration.

This section of the essay is entitled "Untruth as Errancy"— *Die Unwahrheit als die Irre*. It begins:

In-sisting man is turned to the most readily accessible part of what-is. But he in-sists only as already ek-sisting, taking what-is for his measure. Yet, in the measures he takes he is turned away from the mystery. That in-sistent turning towards the practicable and accessible and this ek-sistent turning away from the mystery belong together. They are one and the same reality. But this back and forth movement follows the peculiar rhythm of Da-sein. Man's drifting from the mystery to the practicable and from one practic-ability to the next, always missing the mystery, is erring (*das Irren*).[11]

This "back and forth movement" from errancy to a rediscovery of the fundamental mystery of man originates in the fact that the errancy and the mystery make up antithetically the essence of original truth. Our human condition is one of constant tension between the two of them. This state Heidegger names the *Not der Nötigung*: the need of the obligation.[12] The term *Not* suggests a distressing need that constantly demands pro-visioning. This perpetual need of the Dasein—the same want that underlies the necessity of "building" a dwelling—keeps the Dasein wandering perpetually from one *Seiende* to another,

[10] *Ibid.*, p. 21.   [11] *Ibid.*   [12] *Ibid.*, p. 23.

none of which can answer his basic thirst. The only escape from the tyranny of such a vagabonding is not to cease wandering, for we cannot; rather it lies in getting a certain hold on the situation by doing what was likewise demanded in the case of dwelling—we must think the need as need.

There lies the center of the mystery of the finite Dasein, in the nature of that "need." "Freedom, understood as the insisting *ek-sistenz* of Dasein is the essence of truth (in the sense of the conformity of representations) only because freedom, itself being the originative essence of truth, stems from the rule of the mystery in the errancy." Heidegger sums up the basic situation of Dasein so considered into one short phrase: *Das Dasein ist die Wendung in die Not.*[14] The Dasein is free and wanders freely, but this errancy is an expression of the nature of that thing which he cannot *not* be. Dasein is necessarily (*Notwendig*) a wandering in need (*eine Wendung in die Not*).[15]

The "repetition of history" is the effort to understand the need as need by recalling the entire course of the Dasein's wandering. Because Dasein is, in his essence, wandering-in-need, destruction, which views historical positions as dissimulating-revealing efforts to fulfill the need for Being, becomes the essential way for man to know himself.

What does the destruction discover about the nature of this "wandering-in-need"? That "errancy (*Irre*) belongs to the inner structure of Da-sein, to which historical man is abandoned."[16] This is Heidegger's dramatic way of saying that Dasein's course through history is progressive, and that every position along the way involves some hiding of the truth. "Every relation has, corresponding to its openness and its rapport to the *Seienden* as a totality, its own particular way of erring."[17] The errancy, says Heidegger, is the very stage (*Spielraum*) of history, and the *Königtum der Geschichte*.

No previous philosophy has put such a strong accent on error. Heidegger installs error in the very essence of the finite truth situation for a very good reason. Error is the stamp of the Nothing in the heart of our finite revelation through time of the things-that-are, the necessary (in Heidegger's sense of necessary, *Not-wendig*) antipode of truth, the *lethe* in the *aletheia*.

[13] *Ibid.* [14] *Ibid.* [15] *Ibid.* [16] *Ibid.*, p. 22. [17] *Ibid.*

But for all this man is not tyrannized by error; he is not without hope simply because he is limited. Heidegger states that the *Irre* will collaborate with man "in the possibility that man has and can always extract from his *Ek-sistenz* of not allowing himself to be led astray."[18] How is this possible? By experiencing the errancy itself and by thinking it in its essence, preparing ourselves *not to forget the mystery of Dasein*.[19] In other words, it is one thing to realize that we shall never be free of all error, it is quite another to be tyrannized by it. Dasein can become instead the servant of Being in the discovery of historical destiny.

In the thought of Being, man's freedom for existence (a freedom which is the basis of all history) becomes the Word. This is not the "expression" of an opinion, but the well-maintained structure (*Gefüge*) of the truth of the *Seienden* as a whole. How many have ears for this Word does not matter. Those who do hear it determine man's place in the historical destiny.[20]

This historical destiny (*Geschichte*) reveals the twofold nature of the need, twofold because of the two-sided character of a finite truth that is both actuality and limit, presence and absence, *Wesen* and *Unwesen*. The need is both rigorous and mild (*streng* and *mild*).[21] The need requires mildness in that gentle letting be of the things-that-are, that *Gelassenheit der Milde*, which expresses itself in the fundamental need for a régime of profound silence and of which Heidegger speaks so often, that the philosopher might hear the "quiet voice of Being." But there is also rigor—for to hear this still voice the philosopher must be resolute, and this is hard and demanding. The *Entschlossenheit der Strenge* (resolution of rigor) is the rejection of the dissimulation inherent in the most innocent *Gelassenheit des Seinslassens*. This is the only way to protect the fragile revelation from the complete tyranny of an unsuspected errancy.[22]

This "innermost need of thought" in its mild patience and resolute rigor provides an excellent gauge with which to approach the traditional philosophies in the destruction of the historical destiny of ontologies. Of each we can ask two questions: Has this *Denken* let the things-that-are be what they are by "listening" to the thing as a whole? Has it brought out

[18] *Ibid.*   [19] *Ibid.*, p. 23.   [20] *Ibid.*, p. 24.   [21] *Ibid.*   [22] *Ibid.*

the dissimulation which underlies this revelation as all revelation of *Seienden*, with the protective humility that is the best weapon of an authentic thought? Having asked these questions we shall know, in regard to every epoch, where philosophy stands in relation to the necessary (*not-wendig*) task: that of thinking the need as need.

Because *Vom Wesen der Wahrheit* thinks back as far as the mystery of man as need, Heidegger can write of it as he does in the note (p. 27) appended several years after its first publication:

> The sequence of questions [here] is itself a mode of thinking which, instead of merely applying concepts and ideas, feels and tests itself as a new mode of relationship to Being. . . . It effects a change in the direction of inquiry, a change which properly belongs to the surpassing (*Ueberwindung*) of metaphysics.

This change in the direction of inquiry, this new mode of relationship to Being, was begun in *Sein und Zeit* and is advanced in the later essay by its success in thinking past metaphysical terminology and the lingering limits of metaphysical categories to the very center of the truth situation. To rethink the essence of truth, said *Sein und Zeit*, is in effect to refound the relationship of man to the things-that-are. The discovery of the transcendence of the Dasein as Being reverses the "direction of inquiry" of the metaphysical epochs, making it possible at last to get at the roots of the possibility for the *Seienden als Ganzen* to be. That possibility is founded by the freedom of Dasein in its nature as a wandering in need. A new epoch, indeed a new tradition, this one lying out beyond the metaphysics of the West, is being born. From the new vantage point of the surpassing of metaphysics we can recall the truth of the historical destiny of the West as it has never before been possible to do. This will permit us to understand the need of the finite *Seinsverständniss*, in action.

[23] The wholeness of the thing is intact only when we "build" the "thing" by maintaining all four "elements" of the *Gevierte*.

PART II

RECALLING THE HISTORICAL DESTINY OF THE WESTERN TRADITION

VII The Epochal and Eschatological Nature of Being

THE preceding exposition of the nature of the Dasein has been a long introduction to what in *Sein und Zeit* is termed the second part of the double task, "A Destruction of the Historical Destiny of Ontologies." And, at the same time, these chapters represent a part of the results of such a "destruction." For Heidegger claims that this analysis puts us en route toward surpassing metaphysics, which is, after all, what a destruction is supposed to help achieve. The analyses of *Sein und Zeit* explained that all "surpassing," insofar as it is an act of projection, must be rooted in the past which alone can deliver up the range of concrete possibilities out of which we must build toward a future. Consequently, if Heidegger's analysis of the truth of Dasein has in fact begun to surpass metaphysics, it must be that he has found in the historical destiny of ontologies, as this *Geschichte* has developed up to the moment, the ground of such a possibility. The very fact that Heidegger can talk of the need of surpassing metaphysics indicates that he is already a little beyond the metaphysical tradition. And, by the very fact that someone has started to get beyond it, it follows that this historical destiny bore within it the seed of this possibility. The actual surpassing is not determined and automatic, but the result of an originative act on the thinker's part. However, the thinker's originativeness does not occur in a vacuum, rather it is prepared by history. The discovery and the liberation of such possibility from the limitations of the past of which it is part is precisely the task of a destruction.

This gives us *a fortiori* grounds for arguing against those commentators who, observing that the last part of the projected *Sein und Zeit* has never been finished, claim that nothing has come of the talked-of destruction. In fact, from the analysis of Kant to the essays published recently as *Vorträge und Aufsätze* the work of destruction has never ceased. The published results are sufficiently complete to permit us to reconstruct almost in full Heidegger's view of history, the view that has made possible and rendered necessary the existential analysis for the surpassing of metaphysics.

To date no Heidegger commentator has attempted to organize this material into an over-all look at the course of that "wandering in need" which is the historical course of the free existent. I think it will be valuable to do so, especially since we seek to discover from the movement of what has happened (*Geschehen*) a more precise understanding of what Heidegger considers the all-important need of Dasein to be.

In his commentary on what is believed to be the first known pronouncement of Western philosophy, "Der Spruch des Anaximanders,"[1] Heidegger introduces us to the problem of recalling (*Andenken*) the pre-Socratic philosophers and, through this consideration, to the problem of interpreting history in general. Heidegger says that the basis of the problem is a difficulty of translation. Classical German philology (Heidegger is thinking, for example and above all, of Hermann Diels) has given us *wörtlicher* translations, but not *wortgetreu*: they are literal, but not true to the spirit.[2] A "trans-lation," to achieve a true *Ueber-setzung* ("setting-over" a thing from one language to another), must be a rethinking of the early thought so that the words "speak with the language of the thing itself."[3]

A major obstacle to such a "thinking-back" has been the unavoidable temptation to rethink the early philosophers in terms of Platonic and Aristotelian thought. Even Hegel (whom Heidegger esteems as "the sole Occidental thinker who has experienced the history of thought by thinking it"[4]) saw in Aristotle the summation of the meaning of the earlier thinkers. Said he, "Aristotle ist die reichhaltigste Quelle."

Aristotle interpreted the pre-Socratics as *phusiologoi. Phusis*,

---

[1] *Holzwege*, pp. 296-343. [2] *Ibid.*, pp. 296-97.
[3] "Sprechend aus der Sprache der Sache." *Ibid.*, p. 297.
[4] *Ibid.*, p. 298.

in Aristotle's time, meant a particular region of *Seienden*, distinguishable from the region of *Ethos* and *Logos*. But *Phusis* had lost by Hellenistic times the wider meaning that according to Heidegger it had enjoyed among the early thinkers. For the pre-Socratics it had signified the all of *Seienden*; while Aristotle distinguished the *Phusei onta* from the *tekna onta*, the beings produced by man. He then claimed, without justification, that the *phusiologoi* treated only of the former. This conviction preserved in the commentaries of Theophrastus (*Phusikoon Doxai*) and, much later, of Simplicius,[5] has led our entire tradition to approach the thinkers before Socrates with a bias.

This concrete and very devastating obstacle to our assuming the interpretations of early Greek philosophers, an obstacle inherited from the tradition, illustrates a more fundamental problem—the necessity of never accepting passively the histories which are passed along to us. "All *Historismus* calculates that which is demanded of it from images of the past that are determined by the present."[6] We recognize in this statement, in the domination of the present and in the term "calculates," the language describing inauthentic existence. An existence that locks itself too much in the present, docilely accepting from its contemporaries, for example, an interpretation of history without having the courage, inventiveness, and originality to project a fresh and more meaningful one, can only recreate the errors that surround it. This is why Heidegger is justified in terming such *Historismus* a "calculation"—in feeding on the fruits of the past, it is really allowing the most precious past to wither and die. It takes life on our part to make the past live. Only men with a future can hope to repossess their past, for only men who really *are* can hope to understand the real men who *were*. Since historicism was never more in command of men's thoughts than it is today, we are forced to seek a way to circumvent it to get the real *Geschichte* which lets the historical destiny manifest itself as the Being-destiny of the "Eveningland."

In explaining how this must be done in the case of understanding the pre-Socratics, Heidegger not only gives us the key to his interpretation of the early thinkers and of the place they enjoy; he also summarizes here the essence of what there

---

[5] A Neoplatonist, writing about 530 A.D.   [6] *Holzwege*, p. 301.

is to say both about the beginning and about the end of the entire Eveningland tradition.

The First of the early moment of the Destiny came then as the first unto the Last (*eskaton*), that is, unto the farewell of the until now obscure Destiny of Being. The Being of the things-that-are gathers itself up (*legesthai, logos*) in the last moment of its destiny. The essence of Being that has lasted until now perishes in its still obscure Truth. The historical-destiny gathers itself together in this departure in the form of the Gathering-together of the outer limits (*eskaton*) of the essence it had up to now. This *Versammlung* (gathering-together) is the eschatology of Being. Being itself is, as self-destined, eschatological.[7]

The implications for an analysis of history of this eschatological notion of Geschichte are decisive. We are to read the historical destiny of the Eveningland much more in its beginning and in its end than in the epochs in between. In Heidegger's own words, "If we are to think the eschatology of Being, then we must one day learn to think that which is most proper to the early times in terms of what is most proper to the world to come, in order to bring out what is most proper in itself."[8] Consequently, the propositions of the pre-Socratics are no longer only objects of historical or philological interest, something past and dead; rather they are what is *most meaningful* for us plunged in the Evening of the Eveningland preparing itself "for the Night of the World."[9]

Again we must warn ourselves not to pass judgment too quickly on what at first glance has indeed the air of a gratuitous decision on Heidegger's part. We must resolve to hear him out; as a matter of fact, the reader looking into the works of Heidegger for the first time will probably be astounded at the riches such an interpretation can find, both in analyzing the early thinkers and in viewing our era against the backdrop of the beginning of the tradition. Many are wont to say simply, "Riches, yes, but fabricated, not discovered." But such a condemnation does not come to grips with Heidegger's conception, for it takes no account of his whole notion of what it is to know for a Dasein whose existenz is exstatic. For the moment our task is to understand an exstatic conception of history. We shall leave criticisms for later.

[7] *Ibid.*, pp. 301-2.   [8] *Ibid.*, p. 302.   [9] *Ibid.*, p. 300.

The eschatological nature of Being, as Heidegger warns us, renders the problem of *Ueber-setzung* (translation) even more acute. In fact, Heidegger's translations of various pre-Socratic fragments have brought vigorous criticisms from both philosophical and philological circles. Heidegger's answer to these attacks is to be found in the essay on Anaximander which introduces the problem of translation. This essay begins with the lines to which we earlier devoted much attention, the paragraph which defines *Denken* as the *Ursprüngliche Dictare*. It continues: "The poetizing essence of thinking protects the reign of the truth of Being. Because it poetizes while thinking, translation appears necessarily violent when it lets the oldest 'saying' of thinking speak."[10] Heidegger does not try to conform his translation to what tradition says the various words mean. That he does violence to the text is rather to him a very good sign. Convinced as he is that ours is a tradition of progressive *Seinsvergessenheit*, and that his is precisely an effort to *surpass* that tradition, Heidegger must find the cries of "Violence!" almost consoling. Once again, as with the question of the eschatology, let us not pass judgment on these interpretations without considering fully the conception of phenomenology upon which they are based. Above all, we must not lose sight of Heidegger's conviction of the need for interpretation to be resolute as well as protective—*strenge*, in taking an interpretative stand based on my origination of new truth by projection, and on pitiless rejection of dissimulating past interpretations; *milde*, in basing the freedom of the projection in that letting-be of the things-that-are which guides the future by the light of the past. To evaluate Heidegger's "trans-lations" we must first understand the implications of the eschatology. To understand the eschatology, we must comprehend Heidegger's conception of the temporal nature of truth.

Why were the key terms in Anaximander's pronouncement of the words *on* and *einai* not understood by Aristotle, by Theophrastus, and indeed, by the entire tradition? Not because of any philological underdevelopment or any simple mistakes in "historical method." Rather, this misunderstanding, as Heidegger sees it, "comes from the bottomlessness (*Abgrund*) of the relationships wherein Being has come to pass in the essence

[10] *Ibid.*, p. 303.

of Occidental man."[11] Consequently, the effort to understand the Greeks as Greeks is an effort to overcome the limitations of Being's revelation throughout the course of an entire tradition. "Viewed within this destiny (*Geschick*) the Greeks become for the first time again Greeks in the historical (*geschichtlich*) sense."[12]

Heidegger is not just speaking cleverly when he says that the "Greeks must become Greek again"; by this he means that they must occupy for us their true position in time—and this position is a very special one in an eschatology of history. "Greek," to Heidegger, designates something more than a cultural or national heritage; it is the root beginning of that very special—in fact unique—destiny "in which Being itself illuminated itself in *Seienden* and seized the Essence of man in its title."[13]

The Greeks founded the sole tradition in which a true *Geschichte* has come to pass, a true *Geschichte* because the tradition has thought itself as destiny in that way which permits Being to recognize itself as Being. The seeds of this historical destiny were planted when the pre-Socratics thought Being as *aletheia*. This moment was a positive beginning because the notion of unveiling contained potentially the possibility of thinking Being as Dasein making-present the things-that-are. But these seeds were only seeds and not yet fruit, because the Greeks did not try to think the essence of the veil itself. Consequently, this first positive step, both revealing (in naming truth) and hiding (in failing to think its essence), was also the beginning of the errancy (*Irre*). Because of this beginning, the errancy itself was doomed necessarily to be misunderstood[14]—necessarily in the sense explained in *Vom Wesen der Wahrheit*, in terms of that wandering-in-need (*Not-wendigkeit*), which characterizes the finite Dasein's efforts to fulfill its thirst for Being. As the historical Dasein plunges himself more and more into the world of *Seienden*, erecting vaster and more absorbing structures, the light that makes the *Seienden* present and the building of thought structures possible, as well as the darkness out of which it illumines, is forgotten more and more in the rush of fascination. It is only when the loss of Being becomes total, and the plight of the world without it disastrous, that man can be

[11] *Ibid.*, p. 309.   [12] *Ibid.*, p. 310.   [13] *Ibid.*   [14] *Ibid.*

pulled from the farthest negative pole to a sudden awareness of the absence of what was needed from the tradition's very beginning: a realization that truth is born in need in finite Dasein, and that the *lethe* functions as an essential part of the *aletheia*.[15]

Between the pre-Socratics' dense, undeveloped conception of truth as *a-letheia*, and the nineteenth century's complete forgetting of the finitude of truth (Hegel), of the veil in the *aletheia* (Nietzsche), lie many intermediate stages of development in the history of man's relations to the things-that-are. These are the epochs with which the destruction shall be concerned.

The conception of truth in any epoch is the essential indication of the status of the revelation of Being at that moment. "The epoch of Being is thought in terms of the forgetting of Being";[16] the entire epoch takes its stamp from, and therefore must be understood in terms of, the way the conception of truth dissimulates the Dasein-rooted temporal nature of Being. "The epochal essence of Being is due to the hidden timely character of Being."[17] The essence of this hidden timeliness is precisely what the destruction seeks to grasp.

These remarks project onto the world-historical scale the discoveries presented in *Sein und Zeit* on the scale of the individual human existent. Heidegger himself tells us here explicitly that the epochal essence of Being and the exstatic essence of Dasein must be related as aspects of the same phenomenon.[18] We have seen that the key to a perfect comprehension of the Dasein's existence lies in understanding what Heidegger calls the "circle" of that existence. This invocation of circularity expresses the exstatic unity of the Dasein, which must project in order to make the past present and which must build on the possibilities presented by the past in order to project. The "circle" would be broken by an attitude that would give an absorbing priority to either exstasis at the expense of the others. The same rule holds when we shift our consideration to the historical level involving all the Dasein of a tradition. On this level the circle can be broken either by a doctrine that exaggerates the absolute liberty of the individual in respect to his tradition (which would be an

[15] *Ibid.*, p. 311.   [16] *Ibid.*, p. 310.   [17] *Ibid.*   [18] *Ibid.*

overemphasis on the future) or by a doctrine of exaggerated determinism (overemphasis on the past).[19]

Heidegger approaches history, then, by trying to recall the ruling truth relationship of each epoch. The originative element in such an interpretation lies in the original idea of reading all of history in terms of "truth." Not only is it original to look at all things-that-have-been in these terms, but the very conception engages the thinker to take a stand in regard to what he finds in each epoch. It is inconceivable that one should come to grips with the pre-Socratic, Platonic, Aristotelian, or any other conception of how we must relate ourselves to the things-that-are without acceding to and being enriched by the revelation of Being which it achieves, and without seeking to overcome the dissimulation which each perpetrates. Since the past with which we shall be concerned leads up to our own present, the stand we take in regard to each of its epochs will be governed by the choice, formed by that past, which faces contemporary Dasein as he looks toward the future. What does Heidegger conceive that choice to be?

This is a very important question. To a reader who has not followed Heidegger's line of reasoning it will look as though Heidegger is reading his private philosophical position back into the history of philosophy. This, again, is an exterior criticism. Heidegger is arguing that the tradition has unfolded in such a way that contemporary man finds himself the inheritor of a destiny that can go basically either one of two ways: the dissimulation of the relationship of Being and the things-that-are can continue its evolution; or, by reading the signs of the absence of Being and the Holy, the thinker can begin to "think beyond" the metaphysical conception of truth, thus moving toward the day when truth will be conceived as truth. The destruction is not "reading into history"; it is recalling the relationships of the various epochs to the things-that-are in order to surpass the limitations of the entire metaphysical tradition by achieving a radically fundamental truth relationship. Is this the way things "really were"—as the destruction presents them? The only way to answer such a question is to ask another: What is *real*? The metaphysical

---

[19] An inauthentic overabsorption in *Vorhandensein* in the present completes the picture of possible overemphasis in each of the exstases.

tradition really conceived things the way the destruction says it did if one chooses to read history from the viewpoint of the "surpassing of metaphysics." If one chooses nihilism, history will read as it did for Nietzsche. If one chooses to view history with the eyes of scientism, then it will look much as Marx saw it.

What matters most is not who is "right" and who is "wrong." Those terms have no fundamental sense. Whichever attitude prevails in establishing the projection of our epoch will determine the destiny of man's relationship to the things-that-are in such a way that the preceding epochs will amount to just what this notion will make of them. If Marxism sweeps over the world, history will become for us really what Marx describes it to have been.

The Greeks enjoy such an important place in Heidegger's destruction because of the nature of the projection that determines his interpretation. The decision to surpass metaphysics in order to rediscover the truth of Being through a recalling of its eschatological historical destiny of the West naturally forces the "beginning" into a place of exceptional prominence. The pre-Socratics form a beginning, because there is no conception of truth before the *aletheia* which we can still recall, and because the original Greek conception of truth has put its stamp on the conceptions of succeeding epochs, which have developed as actualizations of the potential positions present in the dense, ambiguous original conception. The choice that faces contemporary Dasein as he founds tomorrow was latent in that handful of critical Greek conceptions which Heidegger, in rethinking them in the context of all that has happened since, would seek to "recall." From the *eskaton* in which we live, we turn to that other *eskaton*, the Greek beginnings, for ultimate perspective. There the "surpassing of metaphysics" seeks the first spark of the 2,600 years it would overcome.

VIII   The Beginning of the Destruction

GIVEN the eschatological nature of Being, all is in the beginning as all is in the end. Consequently no more ruling question can be asked by a "destruction of the history of ontologies" than this: How, in the beginning of the Western tradition, did Being reveal itself?

THE GREEKS

Heidegger's attack on the problem begins with the effort to trans-late by rethinking the thing (*Sache*) expressed in the earliest pronouncement of Anaximander.

The Greek text reads:

ἐξ ὧν δὲ ἡ γένεσις ἐστι τοῖς οὖσι καὶ τὴν φθορὰν εἰς ταῦτα
γίνεσθαι κατὰ το χρεών· διδόναι γὰρ αὐτὰ δίκην καὶ τίσιν
ἀλλήλοις τῆς ἀδικίας κατὰ τὴν τοῦ χρόνου τάξιν.

According to Heidegger, no other text in the history of the West enjoys the importance of this, the first *denkenden Sagen*. Let us, then, examine carefully an important and typical Heidegger translation.

Anaximander's pronouncement deals with the notion of *ta onta*. How can we discover what *ta onta* meant for the early Greeks? Heidegger turns to Homer for help, seeking in the works of the great poet a passage in which the notion appears, not as it would in a lexicon, but as it comes forth from the mouth of a poet, fresh from the act of an originative naming.[1]

[1] *Holzwege*, p. 317.

For what is the sense of multiplying examples of usage, as a lexicon would, if none of the examples is actually *rethought*? In the right poetical text we may de able to gain a foothold on the thing itself, thus acquiring a base for an *Ueber-setzung* that will hand over the thing to our own time.[2]

In archaic speech one spoke of *eon* and of *eonta*. *Eon* means the absolutely singular thing. But the problem is to know exactly what was thought when one said *eon*. (We have seen already that "thing" can be conceived in many ways.) Heidegger even goes so far as to assert that "the destiny of the Eveningland depends on the translation of the word *eon*, that is, it depends on our getting at the conception of truth that underlies the word *eon-Seiend*"[3] as the Greeks conceived it. Heidegger searches for his answer in Homer, and he finds a precious indication in the Homeric notion of the seer—one who is in direct contact with truth and who knows all things in their essence. Heidegger cites this text from the beginning of the *Iliad*:

> . . . τοῖσι σ᾽ ἀνέστη
> Κάλχας Θεστορίδης οἰωνοπόλων ὄχ᾽ ἄριστος
> ὅς ᾔδη τά τ᾽ ἐόντα τα τ᾽ ἐσσόμενα πρό τ᾽ ἐόντα
> καὶ νήεσσ᾽ ἡγήσατ᾽ Ἀχαιῶν Ἴλιον εἴσω
> ἣν διὰ μαντοσύνην, τήν οἱ πόρε Φοῖβος Ἀπόλλων·

Kalchas "the seer" is here described as the one who "has seen," (ὅς ᾔδη), the pluperfect emphasizing the importance of the past in this act of vision.[4] "Having seen what has come to pass, he can see ahead." He can see ahead only because of the light that makes present in him things already seen. "The 'having seen' of such seeing can only be seeing that which is present in the unveiled (*das im Unverborgenen Anwesende sein*)."[5] What is it that becomes present, that is essentialized there in being unveiled before him? The poet names a threefold reality: *ta eonta*, the *Seiende*; *ta t'essomena*, the becoming-*Seiende*; *pro t'eonta*, previous *Seiende*. The first names a present presence (*gegenwärtig Anwesende*), the second and third two *ungegenwärtig* presences. The *gegen* in the *gegen-wärtig*, Heidegger warns, must not be understood in the later terms of the opposition of object (*Gegenstand*) and subject, but as the "open *Gegend* (confrontation) of the unveiledness,"[6] that "arrival next-to" of true

---

[2] *Ibid.*   [3] *Ibid.*   [4] *Ibid.*, p. 319.   [5] *Ibid.*   [6] *Ibid.*

presence. The three aspects of *eonta* all take their reference from the special way each stands in true presence, in the openness of unveiledness (*Unverborgenheit*). Consequently we can assign as the meaning of *eon* "presence in the unveiledness"—*anwesend in der Unverborgenheit.*[7]

But the nature of this presence remains ambiguous, and this again necessarily, thereby planting a seed destined to flower slowly through the course of the Western tradition. The present present and the two kinds of unpresent presents, past and future are all three named *eon*. "Both the present present, and the unveiledness that realizes itself in it, which itself is dominated by the essence of the absent as unpresent present," are indiscriminately named by the same word, *eonta*. The accent is therefore put entirely on the present, which is allowed in its ambiguity to hide the distinction that must be made between what is presently present and the truth horizon, the presence that renders it present.[8] Hence, from the earliest Greek enunciation of *eon-eonta*, Being has been forgotten.

The analysis of the notion of the seer continues in this vein, heightening the ambiguity of the notion of presence—which confuses the two concepts of present and presence. The seer is the "frenzied one" (*mainomenos*); he is the man who is "beyond himself," en route; he is the one who frees himself from excessive concern for what lies out before him, "he is on his way" from the merely present present toward the still absent, bringing the present together with the future and the past.[9] "For the seer all present and absent are gathered together in one presence and therein protected."[10] Thus the seer is also the protector, the guardian, the warden, of the God's present, the gift of truth. The illuminating-protecting (*Wahren*) gathering-together of the present and the absent as the basic reality of *Wahr-heit* thus comes to light in the early thinkers, but it remains unthought-through in its essence, the ambiguities are never resolved.

This recalling of Homer gives us a basis, then, for an *Uebersetzung* of *on* and *einai* as they were thought in this period truly ante-metaphysical, as "the present-unpresent present, made present in the unveiledness." If we are really to translate, i.e., rethink truth as it was actually thought by the pre-Socratics,

[7] *Ibid.*, p. 320.   [8] *Ibid.*, p. 320.   [9] *Ibid.*, p. 321.   [10] *Ibid.*

then the notion of the illuminating-protecting gathering-together of Being as "presence of what is present" (*Anwesen des Anwesenden*) must be thought in its integrated state, as it was before any opposition between subject and object, between truth as property of things and truth as property of mind, ever crossed the Greek spirit.[11] And we must also be careful in our conception of this "presence" to avoid driving a wedge between the present and absent present, for the pre-Socratics felt that the one essentialized itself (*west*) in the unity of a perfect continuity with the other—past, present, and future belonging together, as the very form of the Homeric quotation suggests.

From these considerations Heidegger concludes that *ta eonta* stands not for natural things, but for things for which time has some significance—for "the divine and human, the Achaean and Trojan, scorn and anger, ships and walls"—all the artist weaves onto the shield of Achilles. At the base of all acts of illuminating and gathering-together, the "blind poet" perceives the seer in the fundamental position. Homer does not elaborate a philosophical doctrine about truth; rather, pronouncing in *ein gedacht und denkend gesagtes Wort* what he himself experienced directly, he declares that all is brought together in the seer, "he who, having seen, is more present (*Anwesende*); he to whom the *whole* of the present thing belongs in an extraordinary way."[12] The poet forges the word. it will remain to the thinker to pronounce the name of truth.

In Anaximander's pronouncement the key words, *dike, tisis, adikia*, are dominated by the fundamental word *on*, which means that our grasp of this word in Homer will be the key to the translation of the passage.

Beginning with the unmutilated sentence in the passage, Heidegger takes the antecedent of *auta* to be the *eonta*, so that Anaximander is saying of the *eonta, he adikia*. Since Anaximander evidently speaks of the *eonta* here without restriction, *adikia* is said of them as a whole (*polla*); Anaximander conceives of the *eonta* as *adikia*, just as Herakleitos conceived the *En* (the Being of the things that are) as *Logos*.[13] *Adikia* then names the fundamental characteristic (*Grundzug*) of the present.[14] The translation usually given for *adikia* is "injustice"; what it suggests here is a disjuncture, that something in its "presence" is out of

[11] *Ibid.*, p. 322.   [12] *Ibid.*, p. 323.   [13] *Ibid.*   [14] *Ibid.*, p. 326.

juncture with something else.[15] What is the juncture in question here?

The juncture, says Heidegger, is that *Fuge* (fusion) of the present, achieved as the *eonta* essentializes itself by coming out of what has come before on its way toward what is to come. The present is the thing in its sojourn between the no longer present and the not yet present.[16] This "in between" is the *Fuge*, so that it can be said of the present that it is the juncture of absences in both temporal directions.[17] The persisting thing, then, to rejoin Anaximander's phrase, can never be an *Un-fuge*, a dis-juncture (of exstases), i.e., it can never be an *a-dikia*.[18]

But Anaximander does not rest with a negative explanation of the *eonta* in terms of the *adikia*; he adds *didonai diken . . . tes adikias*: it is the right that yields up the upright—the disharmony. "The actual present is actual insofar as it lets the unactual belong to it. . . . The presisting present, *ta eonta*, presents itself insofar as it lets itself belong to the juncturing right."[19] But to whom does the possibility or "right" of juncturing belong, and in what way? The remainder of the pronouncement reveals this, the ultimate key to understanding the *eonta*.

The first problem in the remainder of the text is presented by the phrase *tisis allelois*. This phrase seems to represent the source of the *Fug* to whom the present is accountable for its presence. In this "who" Heidegger recognizes the Dasein who lets Being be by achieving the fusion (*Fuge*) which makes possible the "present thing" (*Anwesende*).[20] "Only when we have thought of the *eonta* as the present, and of the present as the totality of the persistent, is the allelois conceived as what the pronouncement names: the presence of one persistent to another persistent within the opposition of the unveiledness." Heidegger would interpret the *tisis* in a way consistent with this accent on the note of "one-anotherness" that he has underscored in the *allelois*. The *tisis* stands for the regard, the backward glance, the *Rücksicht* toward that "other" which is necessarily involved in the *Fuge*.

---

[15] *Ibid.*, p. 327.
[16] "Das Anwesende ist das je Weilige. Die Weile west zwischen Hervorkommen und Hinweggehen." *Ibid.*
[17] *Ibid.*   [18] *Ibid.*   [19] *Ibid.*, p. 330.   [20] *Ibid.*

Heidegger admits that the problem of translating *tisis* is very great. He has to reject Diel's suggestion, "punishment," which is in keeping with the nineteenth-century translation of *adikia* as "injustice," for this whole approach fails to get at the root of the problem of rethinking the sense of the passage. In suggesting *Rücksicht* Heidegger is trying to revive the sense of an old German word, *Ruch* (cf. "ruth" in "ruthless") whose sense is very close to that of *Sorge* in the meaning elaborated in *Sein und Zeit*. *Tisis allelois* would stand for the basic relationship of the one persistent, Dasein, toward the other persistent, the *Seiende*, that makes the presence of the *Seiende* possible by fusing the extases to form the thing. The opposite of this care (*Ruch*), the failure to build the thing in all of its authentic dimensions, would be the *Un-fug*—the *a-dikia*, the *Un-ruch*, the care-less.[22]

There remains in Anaximander's pronouncement one key expression to be analyzed, the *to kreoon*, usually translated "necessity." *Kata to kreoon*, according to necessity: thus Anaximander expresses the relationship of Being to the things-that-are. Since Heidegger considers this, the very Being-question itself, the epicenter of the Western tradition, it stands to reason that a proper rethinking of the *to kreoon* must assume an overriding importance.

Heidegger's interpretation of *kata to kreoon* is as "eschatological" as can be. When this phrase was pronounced, he says, the Western philosophical tradition was born. Here is the heart of the dissimulation: the fundamental position of the Dasein as the "who" which achieves the *Fuge* is left unnamed. If Heidegger can now attempt to recall this pronouncement and force it to yield up the full ontological meaning which remained hidden to Anaximander himself, it is because he stands at the end (*eskaton*) of the tradition founded on this pronouncement. In the night of Being's total absence—the ultimate fruit of the whole course of the *Seinsvergessenheit* made possible by the unthought essence of the first pronouncement—Heidegger can begin to perceive what it was that was left unthought from the beginning, and he can try to bring it to light. "Only when the unthought of the Being-forgetting is experienced as that which must be thought, and the long-experienced need at its greatest length has been thought in terms of the destiny of Being, only

[21] *Ibid.*, p. 332. [22] *Ibid.*

then can the early word perhaps address itself to a late re-calling."[23]

Heidegger attempts the recalling of the key phrase in the light of what has already been laboriously called from oblivion, the notion of the presence of the present (*Anwesen des Anwesenden*). The *to kreoon* names the "how" according to which (*kata*) the persisting *Anwesende* persists—it names therefore the *eon* of the *eonta*. "*To kreoon* is the oldest name wherein thinking brings the Being of the things that are to speech."[24] The presence of the present (*Anwesen des Anwesenden*) lies in surpassing the im-possibility, the dis-junction, the *Un-fuge* of the *adikia*. This surpassing occurs when the *Fuge* is achieved, i.e., *kata to kreoon*.[25] *Kata to kreoon*, we have seen, was translated in the nineteenth century as "according to necessity." Heidegger, looking for a deeper insight into and through the words, searches its root family.

In *kreoon* lies *kraoo, kraomai*. From these we derive *he keir*, the hand; *kraoo* says: I handle something. It suggests the possibility of handling, of handing over. *To kreoon* is then the handing over achieved by the *Anwesen* (presence, *Sein*), which handing-over hands out the *Anwesende* (the present, *die Seienden*) and so keeps the present in hand, i.e., protects these things in the presence.[26]

If *to kreoon* is not the ideal word to express the relationship of Being to the things-that-are it is not really the fault of the word itself. For this relationship is unique, it is the *Einzige*, and its uniqueness belongs to Being itself. "Therefore speech, in order to name the realization of Being itself, which is unique, must find a unique word. We can see how risky it is to conceive any word as corresponding really to Being."[27] But the risk is not an impossible one, provided we realize that the problem is not to find *the* word, but rather to see that Being speaks *throughout* every language. The problem is simply to find a word that will lead to, and not destroy, even though it cannot perhaps essentially name, the essential thinking of Being.[28]

Heidegger suggests just such a word to translate *to kreoon*: *Brauch. Brauchen* means to make use of something, and *ein Brauch* ordinarily means usage or custom. But Heidegger invites us to return to a more fundamental meaning of the word, one

[23] *Ibid.*, p. 337.   [24] *Ibid.*, p. 334.   [25] *Ibid.*, p. 335.
[26] *Ibid.*, p. 337.   [27] *Ibid.*   [28] *Ibid.*, p. 338.

corresponding to the Latin *frui*, "to let something present (*Anwesende*) as present be present (*etwas Anwesendes als Anwesendes anwesen lassen*) . . . to let something deliver up its proper essence and so as present be kept in the protecting hand."[29] The *Brauch* stands for the *Fuge*, as care, letting the present be present.

Our author himself admits that it is difficult to justify this translation "etymologically."[30] But to quibble over philology is, in Heidegger's mind's eye, to miss the whole point of a recalling. Remember what we are trying to do: We are trying to think essentially something the Greeks named but did not think through. Hence philological exactness is out of the question, since we can never know what *to kreoon* meant in the sixth century, for the simple reason that the Greeks themselves did not know. If they had, the Eveningland destiny would not have been launched on the course of Being-forgetting which has been its lot these twenty-six hundred years. Consequently the chosen word, *Brauch*, is justified simply because it does not do violence either to the word being translated nor to the thing (*den Sachen*) described, and that is what is important. *To kreoon* named a flash of Being-revelation, unique, as all such events must be, the significance of which has never been "thought essentially." In trans-lating *to kreoon* by *Brauch* Heidegger tries to come to grips with this event, to re-create it, under the aegis of the destruction's rethinking of the whole course of the *Seinsvergessenheit's* destiny.

Since *to kreoon* is the earliest name for the Being of the things-that-are, it is not surprising that Heidegger should want to relate it to the other fundamental names which Being received from the early Greeks. Thus *to kreoon* is "the first and highest expression" of what the Greeks under the name *Moira* experience as "the portioning-out of the apportioned"—the fundamental destiny of Being underlying all things as the basis of their unfolding. Likewise *der Brauch* is the same illuminating-conserving gathering-together which the Greeks name *Logos*. This Heracleitan *Logos* in turn is the same reality conceived as the unifying unity, *En*, which corresponds in the thought of Parmenides to the *to kreoon* of Anaximander.[31] The unity of this unification Parmenides conceives expressly as *Moira*.

[29] *Ibid.*, pp. 338-39.   [30] *Ibid.*, p. 340.   [31] *Ibid.*

Consequently, the *En* and the *Moira* of Parmenides and the *Logos* of Heracleitos have been previously thought already in the *kreoon* of Anaximander.[32]

So Anaximander, Heracleitos, and Parmenides, strongly contrasted and opposed to one another in the histories written at the end of the last century, are reunited in the "recalling" of Heidegger. All think Being in keeping with the tenor of the first epoch, the epoch in which Being is *Anwesen* conceived as the unveiledness itself. All share the same dependence—dependence upon the *Zuspruch des Seins*, the words of Being. The greater this dependence on the fundamental words, says Heidegger, the greater the possibility that the freedom of thinking might fall into ready-made error by thinking Being according to the words that have previously been pronounced without realizing what lies hidden in these pronouncements, still essentially unthought.[33] This is what happened to the fundamental word "truth" itself. The veil (*lethe*) in the "unveiledness" (*aletheia*) remaining unthought as the nature of the presence of Being remains hidden. And this is why it becomes the destiny of the thinkers who followed closely after the great pre-Socratic age to begin the wandering in the *Seinsvergessenheit*.

Plato's conception of Being as Idea and Aristotle's as *energeia* are direct results of the essential unthought naming of Being as *Anwesen des Anwesendes* by the pre-Socratics. Heidegger would reverse the relationship of the later to the earlier thinkers as conceived in the histories of the last century. He would not see the pre-Socratics through the eyes of the first book of the *Metaphysics*, but would view the dialogues and the metaphysics through a recalling of the early thinkers. From the early thinkers, both the conceptions of Being as Idea and as *energeia* have inherited this: their starting point is the already un-veiled as unveiled, as *ein Hervor-gebrachtes*.[34] They conceived Being as the presence of the present without ever thinking essentially the "making-present"; nor when they conceived truth as *aletheia* did they ever *think* the veil in the heart of the unveiledness of truth.

If Plato and Aristotle inherited from the pre-Socratics this *Seinsvergessenheit*, the form that the "forgetting" takes in their works is very radically different. What they do advances the

[32] *Ibid.*   [33] *Ibid.*, p. 341.   [34] *Ibid.*, p. 342.

tradition so far beyond the pre-Socratic positions that Heidegger is almost tempted to think of the later philosophies as constituting a new epoch. In thinking the presence of the present as Idea and as *energeia* (and the root of *energeia* as the thought of thought) they think for the first time the Being of the things-that-are explicitly as a *Seiende* lying beyond the sum total of physical things. The early Greeks did not look *meta-ta-phusika* for the ground and explanation of the things which surge up in the *phusika*. For the pre-Socratics all was one in the primordial presence of what is present. They did not make explicit the presence as the "one" or the "good," as "thought of thought" or as *actus purus*. For the simple reason that they did not think it as explicitly as Plato and Aristotle, they did not actually compromise the distinction of *Sein* and *Seienden*. But they did pave the way, by their failure to actualize the potentiality of the conceptions they left unexplained, for the graver *Seinsvergessenheit*, which itself becomes a decisive step in the gradual effort to think the "of" of the distinction "Being *of* the things-that-are."

THE MIDDLE AGES

The full meaning of that beginning, because of the eschatological nature of Being, can only be seen in the end, in that fulfillment of the metaphysical tradition which is occurring in our own day. Consequently, though a long essay is devoted to each of the major pre-Socratics, Anaximander (in *Holzwege*), Heracleitos, and Parmenides (in *Vorträge und Aufsätze*, with two essays there being primarily concerned with Parmenides), and a whole book to Plato's conception of truth, no single essay is devoted to the Middle Ages, to Descartes or any other thinker before Kant. If Heidegger has much to say, here and there, about Descartes, it is always in the context of a description of the whole movement of the tradition. The work of no intermediary thinker is ever treated explicitly in its own right.[35]

Consequently, we can be most faithful to the spirit of the "destruction" as it has actually been elaborated if we simply

[35] A recent essay, *Der Satz Von Grund*, like the earlier essay, *Vom Wesen des Grundes*, does put an accent on late metaphysics, esp. Leibniz's formulation of certain principles.

summarize the general character of the forgetting-of-being's movement from antiquity to the beginning of modern times with Descartes.

Antiquity, we have seen, thought the truth of Being as unveiledness, without thinking the nature of the veil, i.e., how the presence makes present. Consequently, the early thinkers did not clearly conceive the difference between the things-that-are and the Being which renders them present. As Plato and Aristotle proceeded to try to conceive more clearly what the pre-Socratics had only felt, namely that the things-that-are as present are not their own explanation, they turned for the explanation they lacked and required to something that would be at one and the same time objective and metaphysical. In other terms, failing to see the importance of the Dasein as the opening within which the unveiling could take place, they sought for a "thingly" explanation for the presence of the things-that-are. They concluded that some thing of a different nature, beyond the "physical" world of the things-that-are, must sustain and hence account for their intelligibility. Translating Aristotle's *energeia* into *actualitas*, the Middle Ages remained faithful to the basic movement of this explanation. What accounts for the presence of that which is present must be pure actuality itself, the thingliest of things (*Seiendste des Seienden*), the pure intelligible light which makes things be and lets them be known. Truth, following the theological-metaphysical conception, necessarily becomes ambivalent. On the one hand, it becomes confused with the transcendental presence of the present, so that the godhead becomes truth itself made into a thing; on the other hand, since there remains the problem of explaining what it is for a human being to know, the truth of the human existent comes to be conceived as a conformity between the intellect and the things of creation. Such a conception is not "wrong" in Heidegger's estimation. It is simply not fundamental, because it stops short by accepting ready-made things as already present and thus fails to think the presence of what is present in terms of the Dasein's opening a transcendental temporal horizon. Consequently, the conformity theory of truth is sown with the seeds of destruction. Starting with two givens, a knower and the known, and with the possibility of their relationship essentially unexplained, it became tempting in post-medieval times to try to explain how it is that one is brought into conformity with the other. Because it is the subject who knows and judges, it is only natural that eventually it should be the subject who would be thought to determine. The conformity theory of truth leads to that "subjectivization of the subject and objectivization of the object" which characterizes the beginning of modern times in the *Meditations* of Descartes.

Epochally, then, this is all that the Middle Ages seems to mean to Heidegger—a bridge between Plato and Aristotle and the beginning of modern times *chez* Descartes. The truth conceptions of Bonaventure, Thomas, and Scotus modify and theologize either Plato's or Aristotle's; they achieve no revolution from the Greek positions into a new epoch. The Christ, to read the essays of the destruction, might as well never have existed as far as the history of thought is concerned; it is conceivable that the Middle Ages could have developed somehow without Him by refining Aristotle and by translating *energeia* into *actualitas* and the thought of thought into *actus purus creativus*, the notion of the *Seiendsten des Seienden*. In a sense, the absence of the Living God and of his Saints from the destruction of the historical destiny of ontologies is an index of how Kierkegaardian Heidegger's concept of a Christianity would have to be if he were to believe in Christ. It is as though our author were reflecting the Protestant thinker's thought, when he tells us that the Christian is an isolated phenomenon, outside the current of history, voluntarily cut off from the realm of *Denken*, plunged into the night of nothingness, beyond all *Seiende*, alone in the depths of mystery where the singular encounter with the Singular God may take place. If we were to search Heidegger's writings exhaustively for some sign of the Living God, we would be ill rewarded. There is an enigmatic remark in the enigmatic *Feldweg*, a short lyrical writing—a poem or a prayer more than a formal philosophical pronouncement—and an unpublished and expressly unauthorized university lesson (c. 1925) on the relationship of philosophy and theology, which Heidegger refuses to have formally considered today.[36] There

[36] Henri Birault has made this article the basis for a discussion of a possible rapport between theology and Heideggerian philosophy. See "La Foi et la pensée d'après Heidegger," in *Recherches et Débats*, No. 10, March,

remains only a single, quite formal remark in *Holzwege*. There *Christentum* and *Christlichkeit* are distinguished. The first, the Christian world, joined to the worldly power and structure of the Church, develops itself into another *Weltanschauung*, a vision of the world like the others, subject to the same propensities for *Seinsvergessenheit* as any metaphysical system, for it is part and parcel of the metaphysical tradition. In his study on Nietzsche in *Holzwege* Heidegger writes:

Christianism in this sense [in the sense of a *Weltanschauung*] and the Christianity of the New Testament faith are not the same thing. Even a non-Christian life can give its approval to Christianism and utilize it as a power factor; inversely, a Christian life does not necessarily need Christianity. Also, to clarify one's position in respect to Christianism is not necessarily to combat Christian life, no more than is a criticism of theology forcibly also a criticism of the faith theology would be the explanation of. As long as these essential distinctions are despised, we shall never cease to evolve among inferior visions of the world and of the combats that are unleashed there.[37]

Those who, like Birault, would keep open the possibility of accepting Heidegger's philosophy without relinquishing the faith will find some basis for their position in this text. It is quite evident that the "Christianism" with which we have to do in the destruction—the "Christianism" which the destruction, in preparing the surpassing of metaphysics, would leave behind— is not the life of faith, but the medieval world views born of theological speculation.

But, on the other hand, it is also clear that a Christian will never find in the Heideggerian *Denken* the intellectual footing a life of faith always requires. The Christian who would be at the same time a Heideggerian will have difficulty compartmentalizing his life. For the Heideggerian philosophy is, in my

1955, pp. 108-32. Birault's conclusion: "Hostile to every natural theology, a stranger to any revealed theology, [Heidegger's] thinking of Being surpasses, though in a very different way, both Metaphysics and Belief. Necessarily attentive to Metaphysics, necessarily indifferent to Belief, that thought leads us toward the living sources of Being and the Holy. . . . But the voice of Being is not the voice of God; it is a voice which delivers us up to the original stupor of the "There is something"—the obscure and clear dwelling place of the gods and the mortals" (p. 132).

[37] *Holzwege*, p. 203.

opinion, not just neutral to the notion of a transcendent; it sets out to explain *without* the transcendent everything that has up to now needed a transcendent for its explanation.

Consequently, we can probably better gauge Heidegger's position and what the Heideggerian *Denken* purports to achieve by a statement such as the following which occurs in the essay on Anaximander (also published in *Holzwege*): "Philosophy has not come forth from myth. It originates only in thinking as thinking. But thinking is the thinking of Being. Thinking originates nothing. It is insofar as Being essentializes. But the fall of Being into science and belief is the bad destiny of Being." [38] The full force of such a statement will not become clear until we examine, in the coming chapters, Heidegger's convictions concerning the technique as Being's final fall, the ultimate development in the long line of *Seinsvergessenheit*. That faith should be put on the same level is a warning to those who would search in Heidegger's works for some sign of faith's insertion into life, or at least a tolerance for it as a possibility.

It has been necessary in this chapter to consider the pre-Socratics, Plato, and Aristotle, as well as medieval thought, because the significance of philosophers lies in what they engender. The "recalling" in which we are engaged as part of the effort to surpass metaphysics can bring sense to the early positions only by watching the potentialities they represent worked out across the span of a certain amount of temporal perspective. Our task is evidently only begun. We will not be able to stop for breath until we arrive at the very "end," the *eskaton* in which we ourselves are living. There is no point, then, in pausing here to criticize what we have seen, neither, for philological considerations, to ask whether the reconstruction of the early thinkers is not outrageous, nor to protest against the rather brusque treatment afforded the Middle Ages. We must hear the destruction out, up to the point where it brings us to today in proposing something for the future. Heidegger has repeatedly affirmed that the recalling has meaning only in terms of existence, i.e., in terms of what we ourselves are and want to become. Taking him at his word, we shall complete the survey of the destruction and then consider the whole on precisely those grounds.

[38] *Ibid.*, p. 325.

IX Modern Times

Ours is an age of maximum transition. The years we live in represent not only the end of an epoch—a period of twilight within the same course of the same sun—but also the end of an entire tradition. It is the dimming of the sun itself that is responsible for the present *Götterdämmerung*. For the full course of Being's revelation of itself as thought, truth begun in the first dawn of Greek inquiry and continuing into the presence of the present, is coming to an end. The last of the epochs in the Greek tradition—Heidegger calls it the *Neuzeit* (modern times) —which began with the Copernican revolution, started to end with Hegel and Nietzsche and is now giving birth to a new tradition—is a tradition that is no longer simply Western, but *planetary*: the domination everywhere and in every compartment of life of the *Machenschaft* of technique. When meditating on the beginning—Anaxmiander's pronouncement—Heidegger asked about the end that was to follow from it:

> Do we stand in the very late afternoon of the most monstrous change affecting the whole earth and the very time of history's vital-space? Do we stand before the evening introducing the night that precedes another dawn? . . . Is the Eveningland to spread its domination over Occident and Orient and thus become the place of origin of the beginning historical destiny?[1]

Heidegger is not just reaffirming the principle that Being is eschatological. He is saying that we ourselves are destined to live in the moment of the *eskaton*. Understanding modern times so that we may take a stand in respect to the world now in formation becomes, then, the epicenter of the vocation of the

[1] *Holzwege*, p. 300.

Denker in dürftiger Zeit ("thinker in time of need"—the phrase of Hölderlin applied by Karl Löwith to Heidegger).

The central phenomenon of the *Neuzeit* is physical science. In the essay "The Time of the World-Image" ("Die Zeit des Weltbildes"), published in *Holzwege*, Heidegger exposes at length his views concerning the domination of modern times by the scientific spirit. Science, explains Heidegger, is grounded in projections establishing determined regions of objects, which are then investigated by methods corresponding to the various objective divisions. Scientific research then must be understood in terms of the reciprocal, interlocking relationship of projection and rigor, method and instrumentation.[2] The question to be determined, that we might pass from an analysis of science to an understanding of modern times, is this: What kind of a conception of the things-that-are and what kind of an idea of the nature of truth stand behind the scientific notion of research?

The basic condition of research is objectivity, which is achieved by reducing the *Seiende* to an object that can be controlled with certainty by the investigating procedure.[3] "This objectivization of the *Seiende* manifests itself in a *Vorstellen* [normally translated as "representation;" which unfortunately loses the sense, so strong in the German, of an activity of *placing* the ob-jectum *before* or out in front of the subject], which has as its purpose to bring the particular thing before the calculating man so that he can become better able to control it, more 'sure' of it, i.e., 'certain' in his relationship to it. So science as research becomes a reality only when the conception of truth has changed to become the certitude of representations (*Gewissheit des Vorstellens*)."[4] This change in the conception of truth, which made science possible, occurred in the philosophy of Descartes. It is he who achieved the "objectivization of representation" for the sake of certitude. Consequently, the whole metaphysics of modern times, including the philosophy of Nietzsche, becomes dominated by the objective and certain conception of truth.[5]

Modern times, precisely because it is governed by a conception of truth as research—as objectivity and certitude—becomes a tissue of struggles between subjectivism and objectivism. On the one hand, the search for certitude leads to the

[2] *Ibid.*, pp. 79-80. [3] *Ibid.*, p. 80. [4] *Ibid.* [5] *Ibid.*

individualistic problems connected with the *ego cogito*; on the other, the objective reality achieves a quality of impersonality and collectivity of values which never before existed in any truth situation.[6]

The subject is substituted for—i.e., becomes the trans-lation for—the Greek *hupokeimenon*, the "sub-stantia," as that *upon which* everything is based. For the Greeks the *hupokeimenon* was conceived as an ontological reality of the things themselves, independent of the knower. But now it is the subject that is conceived to provide the ground and truth of everything known.[7] This change indeed is so great and the implications, both for modern times and for the epochs yet to come, so fundamental that Heidegger can only characterize the evolution that leads to the view of man as Cartesian subject as "a change in the essence of man in general."[8] Recall that in connection with the possibility of surpassing metaphysics Heidegger has said that such a surpassing would require a change in the essence of man. What Heidegger means is quite clear. The essence of man as existent changes when the basis for the fundamental projections governing his relationship to the things-that-are changes. To surpass metaphysics truly, man will have to change his concept of what it means to be a man, and to leave behind the last traces of the projections which, from Descartes to Nietzsche, have underlaid all relations of the exsistent conceiving himself as subject to the *Seiende* conceived as *Vortsellung*, as *Gegen-stand*, as *ob-jectum*.

What gave birth to this phenomenon of modern times? Whence this insistence on the subject as source of certitude, which, when it appears in Descartes, already bears all the signs of a mature development? Heidegger traces this development to the breakdown of the authority of the Church in the end of the Middle Ages.[9] The primary result of the breakdown of confidence was a shift of accent away from the search for assurance of salvation in the certitude of the continuing revelation of the Church to the search for a sure ground of certitude accessible within the individual knower. This could be assured only through an effort to distinguish what is really knowable from what is not, that is, by determining what certitude should mean. "The metaphysical task of Descartes was just this: the liberation

[6] *Ibid.*, p. 81.   [7] *Ibid.*   [8] *Ibid.*   [9] *Ibid.*, p. 99.

of man for the sake of his own freedom as certain self-determination in order to create a metaphysical ground."[10]

The *ego cogito* is the seat of this certainty. *Vorstellen*, understood as the act of *ob-jectivization* making present that which is represented, means, *von sich her etwas vor sich stellen und das Gestellte als ein solches sicherstellen*, "to present something from out of oneself before oneself and to certify for the representation as such."[11] This is the active objectivization and "rendering certain" achieved by the *cogito*. The whole current of the knower-known relationship is reversed, then, from what it had been since Greek times. In Heidegger's conception Descartes is the true *Umkehrung*—reversal—in Western thought. The existing thing from his time on is no longer the present, nor is knowledge the grasp of what is present. The note now becomes one of aggressivness on the part of the subject, who has to set the object out before him and assure its presence *there* as something for the certainty of which it can make itself responsible.[12] But this new note of assuming responsibility for the presence of the *objectum* sounded in the Cartesian opus makes of the Frenchman's thought not only a reversal, but also a fulfillment of the Greek quest for a ground *meta-taphusika* that could account for the truth and presence of the totality of *Seienden*.[13] The complicated positive-negative reciprocal relationship that underlies Heidegger's conception of history as the unveiling-dissimulating *Geschichte* is perhaps nowhere more striking than here, at this midpoint in the *Geschick* of the West. Remembering that the course of that history stretches from a beginning in which the problem of Being is posed with an unexplicated density fecundating a fatal ambiguity in its womb to an end in which the child is born as today's twofold possibility, we can see that a central point, such as that represented by the philosophy of Descartes, must advance toward the working out of both poles of the original, ambiguous proposition. The Greeks thought Being as the presence of the totality of the things-that-are, but without thinking the nature of the presence. By Descartes's time the effort to think the nature of the *des* in the relationship *Sein des Seienden* has both taken us farther away from what Heidegger himself would consider the essence of truth and advanced us closer to the day when it might become possible

[10] *Ibid.*   [11] *Ibid.*, p. 100.   [12] *Ibid.*   [13] *Ibid.*, p. 91.

to think that relationship in its essence. It has taken us farther away because the sense of the presence as a rich surging-up before us of the totality of the things-that-are moving through the properly temporal horizon of Dasein has been lost in favour of a subject-dependent objectivization of a regionalized thing as certain re-presentation. The dark-light, ontologically rich fabric of a dynamic, temporal reality has ceded to a "scientific" landscape, clearly and distinctly divided into research regions soon to be viewed as owing their values to the will of a subject. But it has taken us closer, too, by hastening the day when man will look no longer to a supersensory world for a thought of thought, *Agathon* or divinely sustained *ego cogito*, as ground *meta-ta-phusika* of the things-that-are. The *cogito* has opened the way, a difficult and potentially fatal way, to be sure, as it passes through the transcendental Ego and the *Wille zum Willen*, yet a way to an eventual discovery of Dasein as *ouverture* for the revelation of Being. Consequently Descartes is the father not only of that technique which threatens to rule the planet in the grips of the ultimate *Seinsvergessenheit*, but also of the eventual move beyond metaphysics to a discovery that Dasein is at the center of the truth situation.

With the Cartesian conception, the notion of man as "the measure of all things" undergoes a considerable metamorphosis, and with it a new conception of freedom is born; man's essential nature changes.

Man is no longer *metron* in the sense of a focal point for the integration of the persisting englobement of the present which is present to each man. As subject man is the *co-agitatio* of the ego. Man now finds himself the measure for all measurements with which all measurings (calculations) can be made certain, i.e., can be made true and valid for things.[14]

Freedom then becomes the freedom of a *subjectum*, i.e., the *co-agitatio* as the assuring assembling of representations.[15]

A fundamental consequence of this view of freedom as *co-agitatio* is the notion that the world can be represented in a "world-image" (*Weltbild*). The *Neuzeit* is referred to in the title of the essay we are considering as "die Zeit des Weltbildes." This describes it unequivocally, for it is unthinkable that the world should ever have been considered representable in a *Bild*

[14] *Ibid.*, pp. 101-2.   [15] *Ibid.*

by the Greek or medieval man. To medieval man the whole of the things-that-are, *ens creatum*, could only correspond to the plan of the divine cause and would be representable only by Him, the Infinite.[16] The Greek man considered himself the interrogator of the things-that-are precisely because the *Seienden als Ganzen* retained for him an air of profound mystery, something that could never become the subject of an image.[17] But when in modern times man becomes essentially not interrogator but representor of the things-that-are in their objectivity, then the thing itself must be considered fundamentally an image (*ein Bild*). Thus it is no longer unthinkable that the totality of things should be represented by a *Weltbild*; rather, the exigencies of logic require that they should be.

The phenomenon of "system" is a direct result of the oncoming of "the time of the world-image."[18] By "system" Heidegger means more than an artful arrangement of a series of givens. He refers rather more essentially to the fusion of the *Vorgestellten* (the represented) resulting from the projection that governs the objectivization of the things-that-are.[19] Since the way of conceiving that makes possible such a phenomenon as the "world-image" did not exist either in the Middle Ages or in Greek times, it follows that a "system," as Heidegger uses it, could not have existed then. A system is based only on modern man's projection of himself, that projection as unifier of representations which determines his nature by determining his way of relating himself to the things-that-are, the very nature which the "surpassing of metaphysics" is out to change. Each of the great systems in its own way, with its own peculiarities and particularities, represents a different subject exercising its act of unification, be it as the *subjectum* of Descartes's *cogito*, the Monadology of Leibniz, the transcendental idealism of Kant, or the infinite *Ich* of Fichte. Act of a "subject," the system should yet not be termed "merely subjective," as though it represented (as a positivist would say) nothing but the fancy of a purely arbitrary constructor erecting tableaux that have nothing but a curiosity interest. On the contrary, the "systems" are the very *world* of modern metaphysical man, expressive of the essence of his relationship with the things-that-are. If they appear today *dépassé* this is only because the nature of the

[16] *Ibid.*, p. 83.   [17] *Ibid.*, p. 84.   [18] *Ibid.*, p. 93.   [19] *Ibid.*

fundamental relationship of contemporary man to *Seienden*, and thus the nature of man itself, has changed sufficiently to render the systems archaic. The system has become archaic both for the positivist and for the Heideggerian, but for opposite reasons: for the positivist, wandering in the night that succeeds the evening of the Eveningland, it is archaic because he is engaged in another kind of subjective affirmation, that of the technique; and for the Heideggerian, resolutely projecting in the light of an early dawn, it is archaic because he looks back on system as the quintessence of the metaphysical subjectivism he wants to surpass.

Another essential aspect of subjectivized objectivization in the "epoch of the world-image" is its conception of the things-that-are in terms of "values."[20] This is one of the most important results of that "loss of Being" which Heidegger says the *Seienden* underwent in their transformation into "representations." "This loss began to be felt, unclearly and uncertainly, so that one began rather quickly to endow the object and the thus-affected existing thing with a certain 'value,' which values were then held to be the end of all activity."[21] The Heideggerian destruction shows "values" to be virtually pieces of Being disintegrated by the *Seinsvergessenheit* which forgets the true source of the oneness of reality, the exstatic unity of Dasein as care. The objectivization of Being by subjectivism, with its growing emphasis on certainty secured by the will, can have no other source of unity than the individual act of will. Values are the incremented remains of Being offering themselves as desirable objects for these will acts.

The other face of this process is the transformation into "culture" of the activity of daily life. Directed toward the de-ontologized and revalued *Seienden*, creative activity seeks to accumulate "worth-while things." Time becomes money, a commodity, something to be spent in order to acquire a maximum quantity of these things. The time here referred to is only a reflection of man's new temporal horizon, of man's new basic relationship to the *Seienden*—temporality which forms the latest cast of "history's vital space." So-called "cultural values" become the highest end of the creative activity exercised in what Heidegger calls "the self-assuring function of

[20] *Ibid.*   [21] *Ibid.*, pp. 93-94.

man as *subjectum*.[22] From that point it is only a step to making the values themselves into objects. The value is the objectivization of the exigent ends [*Bedürfnis-Ziele*] of representing self-establishment in the world-as-image."[23] The full consequence of this separation introduced between the things-that-are and their values—which really amounts to an impoverishment of the thing itself[24]—only becomes apparent with the appearance of Nietzsche, and in the wastelands of positivism.

The flower of this epoch of "culture" and "value" is a form of what Heidegger termed in the Kant analysis *anthropology*, namely humanism.[25] Metaphysics and humanism in this sense coincide, for both connote a failure to push through to the essence of the truth of Being in trying to understand the nature of man in his relationship to the totality of the things-that-are. In his letter on humanism in 1946 to Jean Beaufret, Heidegger elaborates on this relationship of metaphysics and humanism:

Every humanism either is grounded in a metaphysics, or, in making of itself its own ground, becomes a metaphysics. Every determination of the essence of man which attempts to explain the things-that-are without first asking about the truth of Being is, whether it knows it or not, metaphysical. This shows why, insofar as it attempts to determine the essence of man, it is proper to every metaphysics to be "humanistic." Likewise every humanism must be metaphysical.[26]

The *Weltanschauung*, so much talked of since the beginning of the nineteenth century, is precisely the kind of cultural product in the sphere of philosophy that one can term properly "humanistic." If there is anything characteristic of the *Weltanschauung*—this most metaphysical of all metaphysical manifestations—it is its failure to get at, or even to open, the fundamental question of the Dasein's position in the truth of Being. It sets in center stage not Dasein, but a spurious *humanitas*, self-affirming, willful, constructing—the negative-opposite parody of the true Dasein. The *Weltanschauung*, grandiose schema that it is, is the *Weltbild* culture carried to its most obvious extreme. It is humanism's ultimate instrument—the world-image functioning as guide to

---

[22] *Ibid.*, p. 94.   [23] *Ibid.*
[24] "Keiner stirbt für blosse Werte," Heidegger remarks in archetypically existentialist fashion, in *Holzwege*, p. 94.
[25] *Ibid.*, p. 86.   [26] *Ibid.*, p. 12.

living among the totality of the things-that-are, in keeping with the self-determination made both possible and necessary by the view of Being as the unification of representations in the objectivization of the *subjectum*.[27]

If, as Heidegger asserts, "the fundamental event of 'modern times' is the conquest of the world as image,"[28] then it is safe to say it is for the *Weltanschauung* that we must, in the destruction of any *Neuzeit* ontology, always look behind the "thing represented." For the image, as man-made structure which represents things, does so according to the constructed pattern of a *Weltanschauung*, which serves to evaluate, distinguish, classify and organize all the things-that-are.[29] This central importance of the *Weltanschauung* and its nature as a production of the free subjectum accounts for the central characteristic of modern times: the conflict of world conceptions. The cataclysms that have torn Occident and Orient to shreds, first intellectually and now physically, are not the chance product of passing accidents. They are the logical culmination of a *Geschick*, the final expression of our metaphysical tradition. (This essential approach to the political phenomena of the last centuries permits us in passing to see why science *had* to play the central role of the *bête noire* in this drama of planetary upheaval. For science is the indispensable form of self-direction in a *Weltanschauung*-represented world.[30] It is, in effect, in its form as "research," the regionalization and concrete application of the humanistic man's self-willed relation to things through the "objectivization" and subjective assertion of a world-view.)

This conflict of world conceptions Heidegger calls "a battle of the giants." This modern giantism is, again, no accident. The gigantic is a sure mark of the *Neuzeit*, just as is its tendency to concern itself with the incredibly small. It is as though a conception of truth that loses interest in Being and ontological truth turns man's creativity, released from the humble protecting dwelling with the rich fabric of the fourfold thing, toward arbitrary spreading out in an expansion of surface power which even the globe cannot contain, and at the same time a concentrated downward search for that other quantitative ultimate which is the "un-cuttable" core of the things-that-are.

[27] *Ibid.*, p. 86.   [28] *Ibid.*, p. 87.   [29] *Ibid.*   [30] *Ibid.*

An authentic temporality conceives Dasein as protecting the transcendent quality of Being—the mystery of the Holy. When this is lost in the *Neuzeit*, when Dasein turns ever farther from a protective "letting-be" of the things-that-are, assertion of will takes the form of a desire for control of the *Seienden*. The new emphasis on quantity seems to suggest that the projections of quantitative science leave behind all the elements of the thing but those capable of calculative control in the present— those values we can try to accumulate through culture.

Let us sum up what Heidegger has said of modern times—the "time of the world-image": The conception of objectivization, as subjectivity's act of assuring the certitude of the world view, flowers as *system*. System welds the things-that-are into a world following the model of the subjective projection. The concomitant transformation of *Seienden* which must accompany this subjectivization of truth is the conception of things as values and of creative activity as culture.

While systematization and revaluing are concomitant, the philosophies that incarnate the two movements most purely follow one another chronologically. In Heidegger's view, the system of Hegel is the ultimate progenitor of the Nietzschean *Umwertung* (reversal of values). With Hegel, says Heidegger, the metaphysical tradition comes to its *Vollendung* in the *Neuzeit*; with Nietzsche the *Abend-land kommt nach Abend*. Hegel and Nietzsche introduce the *eskaton* in Heidegger's eschatology of Being. The destruction of these two great philosophies becomes, then, the indispensable portal leading to the culmination of modern times in the planetary domination of technique.

X The Consummation of Metaphysics

THE Hegelian system represents for Heidegger the ultimate development of metaphysics. Thus, in Heidegger's view, Hegel must be as far from the early Greeks as possible; yet, as the metaphysicians' metaphysician he must stand in the same line of development and therefore represent the fulfillment of a potentiality inherent in the earliest positions. He represents the fullest development in the direction of conceiving the relation of the presence to the present, never thought in its essence by the Greeks as a *Seiende*, and, since he follows in the tradition founded by Descartes, he achieves a conception which also fulfills the ultimate potentialities of the subjective position. Hegel's definition of the presence of the present as absolute *Wissen* fulfills the ultimate possibilities inherent in the assertion of the *ego cogito* as explanation *meta-ta-phusika* for the essence of that presence. And, in positing the absolutized subject as temporal explanation for the presence of all things-that-are, Hegel constructed a philosophy that forms the absolute opposite pole to an existential doctrine of temporality based on a thinking of the truth of Dasein. Hegel's affirmation of the dominance of the absolute subject becomes the ultimate preparation for Nietzsche's final devaluation of Being in the projection of the total *Wille zum Willen*. However, the philosophy of Hegel, like every revealing-dissimulating projection, while it advances us a step toward the final night of the Eveningland, the assertion of subjective will, also brings us closer to the dawn of the new phenomenology by linking for the first time a genuine conception of history with the subjective existence of man.

In "Hegel's Begriff der Erfahrung" (published in *Holzwege*) Heidegger comments on a long passage from the Introduction to the *Phänomenologie des Geistes* in order to replace Hegel within the stream of the historical destiny. The basis of Hegel's whole position, Heidegger infers, lies in his acceptance of the post-Cartesian traditional notion of what it is to represent an object.

The representation presents the object in representing it *for* the subject, in which representation the subject itself presents itself as such. The presentation, in the sense of the self-consciousness of the subject, becomes the main feature of knowledge. Presentation is an essential kind of presence (*parousia*). As such, i.e., as *Anwesen*, it is the Being of the things-that-are subjectively conceived.[1]

The *Selbstgewissheit*—the consciousness of self—which Hegel constantly speaks of is, then, the subject's unrestricted knowledge of the things-that-are born out of the interior resources of the subject itself, as source of the subject-object relationship. This is the significance of Hegel's assertion that his is not just a philosophy but a *Geisteswissenschaft*, a science of the spirit. The supreme science lies in the highest affirmation of the domination of the subjective self-knowledge which allows the *Seiende* (*to on*) to be *Seiende* (*he on*). As presence of the present it is absolute. Philosophy is science, then, because it represents the will of the absolute. It is in the willing of the subject's self-willing that it shows forth the existing thing.[2]

It is only natural that such a philosophy should follow immediately in the footsteps of Kant's *Critique*. Hegel is only fulfilling what the *Critique* left unfulfilled, determining what it left undetermined; Kant failed to think the nature of truth in its essence by leaving the true temporality of the knower-known relationship unexplored.[3] He left the nature of the *Irre*—the wandering in need along the epochs of a historical destiny—hidden in its essence.[4] He also left the nature of the certitude of the transcendental subject unthought and hence not assured. It is into this breach that the young Hegel steps. The problem of the certitude of the transcendental ego is solved by making the subject the absolute so that its affirmations become

---

[1] *Holzwege*, pp. 121-22. [2] *Ibid.* [3] *Ibid.*, p. 123. [4] *Ibid.*

the very reality of the *ens certum*. And since Kant had posed time at the center of the subject without thinking through to the essence of true temporality, Hegel conceives the relations of the subject to the object as unfolding certainly and dialectically in a line that resembles the *Irre*, only because it unfolds, but is in every other way its most essential dissimulation, as we shall see now. It is this most distant proximity which gives to the moments of the consummation of metaphysics their quality of pathos.

The phenomenology of the spirit, says Heidegger, can be considered the reverse-mirror image of the true wanderings of the historical destiny. For example, though for Hegel the concept of liberty is at the base of all subsumption of the object into the temporal structure of the absolute subject, just as it is in Dasein, Hegel's conception of the will reverses the knower-known dependency. In Heidegger's view freedom is ultimately defined as a letting-be of the things-that-are, a conception that makes it quite clear that the finite freedom of Dasein does not create the things-that-are but discovers them and is, in some way, dependent upon them in the foundation of its transcendental horizon. In the Hegelian *itinerarium* this is not the case. When the absolute wills to come to be through us, it is in this very act of will that it presents itself, i.e., the will act itself is constitutive of reality.[5] Therefore the things-that-are, which Hegel presents as *Erscheinungen* (manifestations) of the absolute spirit, are dependent as *Erscheinungen* on the absolute knowledge for their reality.

The reality of these real things, the subjectivity of the subject, is the *Erscheinen* itself. The Being of the things-that-are—the shining forth—is represented, as all Being in all metaphysics, only as the existing thing presents itself as existing thing (*on he on*). But the *on* is in this case the *ens qua ens perceptum*. It presents itself in the presentation through *cogitationes*, which exist as *conscientia*. What is represented then is the subject as subject, i.e., the shining-forth as shining-forth. The representation of shining-forth knowledge is the ontology of real consciousness as the Real (*Wirklichen*).[6]

It is only this series of *cogitationes* then which is really real. The historical series of *Erscheinungen* as *cogitationes* is the way of philosophy itself.

[5] *Ibid.*, p. 130. [6] *Ibid.*, p. 134.

This way of philosophy is the motion of the absolute.[7] This motion manifests itself in the opposition of "natural knowledge" and "real knowledge" (*natürliche und reale Wissen*).[8] Natural knowledge is the shining-forth subject, the making-present knowledge. It is itself something "real," but it is not the ultimate explanation of itself—it is not the *reality* of the real. "The real" is rather the *wahrhafte Seiende*, the truth-full existing thing.[9] The true, *ens verum*, is, since Descartes, the *ens certum*, that which is known in certitude, the known-certain present. The *ens certum* can only be known as certain when it is known as *ens*. "This occurs when the *esse* of the *ens* is authentically represented, and the existing thing is known in its Being—the real in its reality. 'Real knowledge' (*das reale Wissen*) is knowledge that above all represents the existing thing in its thing-ness (reality), the *Erscheinende* in its shining-forth."[10] Natural knowledge does not achieve this reality because it still depends on a *Seiende*, the realness of whose reality must still be sought out and affirmed. In grasping the existing thing, natural knowledge takes for granted its presence, its "shining-forth."[11] Lacking a comprehension of its own essence as light, it cannot itself be the light, but only "the representation of thingness in general and in an undetermined way."[12] The root of truth—the reality of the shining-forth itself (*das Erscheinen des erscheinenden Wissens*)— can be grasped only in the ways the representation takes place, in the way the shinings-forth follow one another, in the way the shinings-forth come to be re-presented. "In this coming-forth the *Erscheinende*, insofar as it grasps itself as the real, goes away. This unique coming and going is the motion which is consciousness itself."[13]

Heidegger presents the Hegelian dialectic in this fashion in order to underscore the ways in which it parallels the authentic grasp of the truth of Being which forms the basis of the thinking that surpasses metaphysics. The essential grasp of truth preserves, so we have seen, the sense of the Greek notion of truth as *aletheia*, but in so doing it renders it the full sense which it could not have achieved at the beginning of the tradition. The notion that Being in revealing itself dissimulates itself has been explained as the basic phenomenon of the Western historical

---

[7] *Ibid.*, p. 140.   [8] *Ibid.*, p. 135.   [9] *Ibid.*, p. 136.   [10] *Ibid.*
[11] *Ibid.*   [12] *Ibid.*   [13] *Ibid.*, p. 140.

destiny: the Dasein, in illuminating the things that are, forgets *das Sein* in its distinction from the *Seienden*. The errancy of history follows from this fact. In this essay on Hegel, Heidegger is suggesting that, much as traces of the revelations of Genesis are to be found in the pagan myths, the trace of the essential truth lies hidden in the Hegelian conception of the motion of *Bewusstsein* (consciousness). The coming and going of real and natural knowledge in the dialectical unity of *Bewusstsein* sees the disappearance of the one principle upon the assertion of the other, as the concentration on the subject always diminishes the standing of the object. Just as *Geschichte* for Heidegger is made up of the happenings in the many epochs of the forgetting of Being, so the comings and goings of the relationship of real and natural knowledge constitute the history of the spirit for Hegel. "Each movement of the coming of the shining-forth and the going of that which shines forth is the happening (*Geschehen*) itself which brings consciousness from one form to another, into the image of its essence."[15] This history is, in Hegel's words, *die Geschichte der Bildung des Bewusstseins selbst zur Wissenschaft,* "the history of the imaging of consciousness itself for science." Hegel explains in this phrase what he conceives the historicity of history itself to be. This motion of consciousness—the dialectic—is what Hegel terms *Erfahrung*, experience. In the words of the *Phenomenology of the Spirit*: "What is properly named 'experience' is the dialectical motion through which consciousness extends itself, both to its objects and to its knowledge, insofar as new true objects spring forth from this dialectic."[16]

"What is it really that Hegel names with the word *Erfahrung*?" With this question Heidegger brings us to the heart of the "recalling" achieved in the article under consideration. "He names the Being of the things-that-are . . . With the name *Erfahrung* Hegel names that-which-has-shown-forth as that-which-has-shown-forth, the ὸν ᾗ ὄν. In the word *Erfahrung* it is the ᾗ itself which is thought . . . *Erfahrung* names the subjectivity of the subject."[17] Being, as subjectivity of the subject, builds its own way, then, in the interplay between what is known (the *Bewusst*) and the possibility of its being known (the *Sein*), i.e., in the motion internal to the *Bewusst-sein*. This internal movement is the motion of conversation (*dialegesthai*) between the two principles of consciousness, natural and real knowing, the *Seienden* and *das Sein*. Conversation, Heidegger explains, is the gathering up of this tense dichotomy into the illuminated whole of consciousness as dialectrical organization of the essence of knowledge. Its two poles parallel the *ontisch-ontologisch* separation of knowledge brought to light in its full significance by *Sein und Zeit*. The dialogue between ontic and ontologic consciousness makes appear (*phanesthai*) the things-that-are. It is this self-shining-forth of the absolute spirit that Hegel calls the "phenomenology."[18] The spirit is the subject, not the object, of this phenomenology; the object is only rendered possible by "the self-organization of the conversation of the dialogue of the spirit with its *parousia*. Phenomenology is here the name of the Dasein of the spirit."[19]

These last remarks make especially clear how close Hegel is in Heidegger's opinion to the position of *Sein und Zeit*, and yet how far! An abyss separates the absolute spirit from the free Dasein grasped in the Nothingness of its finitude. That abyss is the very *Abgrund* invoked in *Vom Wesen des Grundes* and *Was ist Metaphysik?*[20]—the *Nichts* of the finite Dasein itself. One could, in fact, say that all the elements of the doctrine of *Sein und Zeit* find a place in Hegel's phenomenology but are not seen there in their essence because of the shadows of the evening of the *Abend-land*. The ontic and ontologic elements of the motion of history, though both present, are absorbed in the phenomenology by the exigencies of a fundamental conception which insists on thinking this motion as explanation *meta-ta-phusika* for the totality of *Seienden*.

The abyss separating the unconditioned will of the absolute in Hegel from the finite freedom of the Dasein in *Sein und Zeit* is not just the *Abgrund* that separates one epoch from another; it is the termination of an entire tradition. Because Hegel achieves the ultimate subjective *Weltbild*, absorbing everything that is and can be—even temporality itself—into the system, there remains only one way for subjectivism to go, and that is toward the denial of system in the affirmation of non-absolute

---

[18] *Ibid.*, p. 185.   [19] *Ibid.*

[20] Cf. DeWaelhens, *Chemins et impasses de l'Ontologie heideggerienne* (Louvain, Nauwelaerts, 1953), pp. 43-44.

subjective will. Nietzsche's nihilism will unleash the negativity needed to destroy the grounds for any future explanation *meta-ta-phusika*. With this act of de-absolutizing metaphysics the circle, based in the ambiguities of the pre-Socratic positions and begun in earnest by Plato's conception of truth as Idea, is closed forever by the absorption of the *phusika* in the *Wille zum Willen*.

<h2 style="text-align:center">NIETZSCHE</h2>

It is not by accident that Heidegger places in *Holzwege* an analysis of "Nietzsche's Wort, 'Gott ist tot,' "[21] immediately after the essay on Hegel. For Zarathustra's pronouncement announces the fall of the *Heilige* in that reversal within the heart of metaphysics which will block henceforth any sentiment of the "beyond." The last step of the destruction must then be to prepare the way for an understanding of Nietzsche's nihilism. Heidegger says "prepare the way" advisedly, for an essential thinking of the nature of that nihilism would require that we achieve definitively the surpassing of metaphysics. This is true simply because that nihilism is itself the *Endstadium*. Nietzsche is the end, the *eskaton* itself, because in the reversal (*Umkehrung*) which he effects the essence of metaphysics is fulfilled in the realization of its unessence (*Unwesen*).[22] To understand the *eskaton* would be to have mastered the eschatology of Being, which would amount to thinking the essence of the truth of Being itself.

To the casual reader it might seem that Nietzsche, as Heidegger presents him, should be considered not the fulfillment of metaphysics, but rather its destruction; for Nietzsche in a sense seems to lie beyond metaphysics, since he is its mortal enemy. But to think this is to miss the force of one of the most important and most characteristic principles of Heidegger's philosophy. The *Wesen* of anything human is its possibility. Just how important possibility is in the consideration of a free being becomes evident in a statement which Heidegger makes in discussing the nature of phenomenology in the introduction to *Sein und Zeit*. In explaining that something like phenomenology cannot be understood in its essence until the human possibilities which it represents are understood, our author

---

[21] *Holzwege*, pp. 193-247.   [22] *Ibid.*, p. 193.

makes this important affirmation, "Higher than actuality stands possibility"—*Höher als die Wirklichkeit steht die Möglichkeit*. The understanding of phenomenology lies properly in conceiving it as possibility."[23] Among the possibilities of any human activity, marking in fact its limits as possibility, is the free negation of whatever it is that characterizes its positive possibility. This "end of possibility" in the "outermost possibility," which achieves the negation and consequently the termination of the thing itself, is what Heidegger terms the *Unwesen*. The conditioning *Unwesen* of everything human is, of course, death itself, toward which the *Sein zum Tode* is directed as "most proper possibility." The outer limit of Dasein as possibility is death, which determines how far the Dasein can "go" and, in doing so, negates Dasein, letting it drop off into the nothingness which, as finite, it harbours as central to its essence. Similarly, the Dasein's conception of the totality of the things-that-are (*Seienden als Ganzen*) is possible only because Dasein can conceive the *Unwesen* of that totality, the possibility of their nonexistence, which surrounds and discerns their totality like a black background.

A tradition has an *Unwesen* too, simply because it is just another manifestation of Dasein's *ek-sistenz*. Its "end" too, is a kind of death, for it marks the negation of what the tradition stood for in the beginning in affirming the last possible position that could grow from it. This position is the tradition's *Unwesen*, in being at once in the same line of development as the original position and an insurmountable block to any further development of that line. The existence of such a thing as the "end" of a tradition is the surest sign that its history has for motive power the actuality-in-limitation, revelation-dissimulation nature of the finite truth situation. When the Greeks conceived the totality of the things-that-are as *on he on*, they revealed consciously for the first time that it was possible to think the totality of the things-that-are,[24] though they con-

---

[23] *Sein und Zeit*, p. 38; cf. DeWaelhens, *Heidegger*, p. 317.

[24] We should recall that the existence of the Being-question is a Western, i.e., Greek phenomenon. Historically it was the Greeks who first posed the question, "What is the Being of the things-that-are," in this form. Being in the historical sense of the word *on* was revealed only in this tradition.

sidered that it must be thought in its thingliness. Consequently they became aware of the *Seienden* precisely and only as *present*. Hence their projections in regard to the things-that-are represented only a certain degree and quality of awareness. Hence, also, they posed the problem in dangerous terms, leaving a suggestion that it could someday be exhausted and solved. The original position was an "actuality-in-limitations"; this dissimulating revelation, unthought through, remained a bundle of potentialities for future projections and, consequently, contained the seeds of future dissimulations. To unveil partially is to leave what is unveiled necessarily prey to dissimulation when the inevitable attempt is made to think that which remains veiled. When Plato and Aristotle tried to think the presence of what was present, they realized that the explanation must lie "beyond the totality of material things." Thus began the metaphysical search for a special thing to explain the presence of other things. This revelation, that we must search beyond the totality of things for their truth, contained at the same time a dissimulation, for the totality was thought in terms of a totality of objective, determined, graspable things. Consequently, the quest for a ground of the presence of the things-that-are took the form of a search for the thingliest of things. The last possible form of this search was Hegel's affirmation of the absolute spirit. Nietzsche posits the *Unwesen* of the entire tradition by felling all further metaphysical possibility with the affirmation "God is dead!"

This is in a sense a return to the pre-Socratic position: Nietzsche ends here the Eveningland's search for a supersensory transcendent as ground of Being; he poses again the problem of truth as it had originally been stated—as the problem of the presence of the things-that-are within this world. But Nietzsche's position is also the culmination of metaphysics, for it repeats the traditional error of grounding this presence in a thing instead of preserving the presence itself as ultimate. The thing in question is not a supersensory *Seiende* this time, but the *Wille zum Willen*; this dissipates the last equivocation that still protected the primitive astonishment and respect for the mystery of the presence of the *Seiende*. There is no more problem of Being; the quest for truth is ended and declared meaningless. The question of the *Sein-Seienden* relationship has evolved through the quest for an absolute transcendent ground for the relationship, to increasing subjectization of the real, and finally to complete negation of the problem itself in the absolute absorption of one pole of the dichotomy into the other, of the *Seiende* into the *Sein*.

Nietzsche is above all, then, the great de-mystifier, the enemy of the *Heilige*.[25] But de-mystification and *Entwertung* are essentially negative activities caught in the orbit of that which they negate. "Every purely opposing movement remains necessarily, like any 'anti-,' essentially ensconced in that which it is opposing."[26] The *Nichts* of Nietzschean metaphysics is not more fundamental than the standpoint achieved by the ontologies because it projects simply the absence (*Abwesenheit*) of a supersensory, obligatory world; Nietzsche is not the negation but the consummation of metaphysics, because he closes the question it had struggled to answer by declaring it meaningless. There is no such thing as the presence, as the Being of the things-that-are.

The resulting doctrine is the "nihilism" whose essential rethinking we have discovered to be necessarily part of a definitive surpassing of metaphysics. Though Heidegger does not pretend to be yet in a position to achieve this definitive rethinking, he does, in this last step of the preparatory destruction, come close to an essential notion of nihilism.

He first warns us that the common opinions concerning nihilism are very misleading. "Not everyone who is a Christian believer," he tells us, "or who maintains some metaphysical position, is exempt from nihilism." And, on the other hand, not everyone who speaks of *das Nichts* (Heidegger is evidently thinking of himself) is a nihilist.[27] A Christian, while believing in God, can mistakenly share the views of the "Evening" of the West, while the philosopher who speaks and writes of the "nothing" may be engaged in the struggle to surpass the metaphysical tradition. Our position in respect to nihilism is determined only by our relation to the whole movement of the Western tradition. For nihilism is nothing more than "the fundamental movement of the historical destiny of the Occident" (*die Grundbewegung der Geschichte des Abendlands*).[28] Nihilism as the *eskaton* of the entire tradition, is a summary word for

[25] *Holzwege*, p. 193.　　[26] *Ibid.*, p. 200.　　[27] *Ibid.*, p. 201.　　[28] *Ibid.*

everything that is happening and must happen at the moment of the birth of the new tradition that is upon us. All the devaluations—the birth of art for art's sake, the birth of a notion of culture, the flowering of research, the debasing of man to a unit within the complexus of the *Maschinentechnik*, the death of God— are only consequences of the *Vollendung* of the consummation in contemporary times of a long tradition, consummation which is the birth of a new era. The uprooting of the tradition touches so deeply, and the final forms of nihilism are such an all-pervasive occurrence, that this monumental change "can only be followed by world catastrophe,"[29] as the very nature of man is utterly transformed.

The essence of nihilism, is, we have seen, "that the highest values," as Nietzsche said, "devaluate themselves" (*dass die obersten Werte sich entwerten*.[30] Belief in the supersensory world ceases. All concepts are reduced to what can be explained within this world, so that nothing remains thought *meta-ta-phusika*. This destruction of the old is neither "arbitrary" nor is it purely negative in intent. It is not arbitrary, because it is the outgrowth of the historical destiny of the Occident. It is not purely negative, because it is accomplished for the sake of the new.[31] Nietzsche does not see himself as the "nihilist" in the popular sense—as the agent of the doctrine of utter nothingness. He sees himself rather as the destroyer who clears the land of the old for the sake of the construction of the new. The *Entwertung* is for the sake of, and prepares, an *Umwertung*; it can very justly be considered the completion of the true Copernican revolution.[32]

What is destroyed is not simply one set of values doomed to be replaced by another, but the very region within which the old values could spring into being—the supersensory world itself. The displacement is a displacement of *worlds* and of originative sources of values.[33] Nietzsche's whole philosophy obviously hinges completely on his conception of "value." According to Heidegger, Nietzsche means by *Wert* (value) a point of view (*Augenpunkt*), a way to see things; in Nietzsche's words, values are "*Erhaltungs-, Steigerung- Bedingungen*: conditions

---

[29] *Ibid.* Heidegger, though apparently convinced of this (as one who lives in these times can well afford to be), does not elaborate the point.

[30] *Ibid.*, p. 205.   [31] *Ibid.*, p. 206.   [32] *Ibid.*, p. 207.   [33] *Ibid.*, p. 209.

for sustaining and increasing." Or, as Heidegger puts it, "the conditions of life itself."[34] Those points of view are rooted in the will to grow—to increase and multiply, as the Bible would say—and the life that loses them loses the source of its vitality and is destined to be plowed under. Growth is a manifestation of what is for Nietzsche the central reality of all things, their becoming (*Werden*), the primordial force behind the appearance and disappearance of the things-that-are, the only true explanation of the presence of what is present. It is this force which Nietzsche later names "the will to might" (*Wille zur Macht*).[35] "Will to might, becoming, life and Being in the widest sense mean the same thing in the language of Nietzsche."[36] Thus the will to might determines the standpoints of life, i.e., the values. "The will to might is the ground for the necessity of the determination of values and the origin of the possibility of the judgment of values."[37] Heidegger quotes Nietzsche: "Values and their transformation depend on the growth power as value determination."[38]

We may then conclude from this that, to Nietzsche, what is real is that which "has value." It is the determination of values by the will to might which sets the things before us in reality. Nietzsche's position is really new, not because it is founded on a subjective determination of values—all the philosophies since the Renaissance had in fact been so; it is new, rather, because Nietzsche explicitly recognizes the subjective nature of his determination of the presence of what is present. Yet, Nietzsche's way of conceiving that subjective determination remains enslaved to the past. His reversal of values Nietzsche still understands only in terms of a reversal of the supersensory values of metaphysics. This is disastrous, as Heidegger has said, because it forces Nietzsche's philosophy to make its pirouette within a tight circle whose perimeter is the limited vision of the very epoch whose values it is busily upturning.[39]

An effort to recall more essentially the notion of the will to might can help to clarify why Nietzsche did not surpass metaphysics but only achieved the *Endstadium*. The word "might," Heidegger explains, names the essence of the way the will, as orderer of values, wills itself. "The will to might is the essence

[34] *Ibid.*, p. 211. [35] *Ibid.*, pp. 212-13. [36] *Ibid.*, p. 213.
[37] *Ibid.* [38] *Ibid.*, p. 213. [39] *Ibid.*, p. 214.

of might. It indicates the unconditioned essence of willing, which as pure will, wills itself."[40] Will for the sake of will is, then, the modern counterpart of the *ousia* (*Seiendheit*) of the subject, the *hupokeimenon* as support of that which is. It is, in Nietzsche's words, "the inner essence of Being."[41] When Nietzsche affirms that values are the "conditions" of the sustenance and growth of Being, this means that "values" represent the self-determination of will to power considered in its activity of sustaining and extending itself.[42] As "valuation" (*Schätzen*) the will to might provides the *essentia* of the things that are. On the other hand, it is the "eternal return of the similar" (*ewige Wiederkunft des Gleichens*) that provides their *existentia*.[43] This existence, which, while moving, must always move in the same way, returning to the same starting point, is circularly determined because it draws its motive force not from some transcendent scheme for life (*keinem Reichtum des Lebens*), but from out its own proper willing, *which is always the same*. Then "the two fundamental expressions of Nietzsche's metaphysics, 'the will to might' and 'the eternal recurrence of the like,' designate the *Seiende* in its *Sein*, in the same way as it has been throughout the metaphysical tradition, viewing the *ens qua ens* in the sense of *essentia* and *existentia*."[44]

This outcome of the metaphysics of modern times Heidegger views as an inevitable result of the Cartesian quest for certitude, in this way: "Insofar as Descartes sought the *subjectum* to furnish the *stabile* for the *hupokeimenon*, thereby placing the *subjectum* in the forefront of metaphysics and thinking truth as certitude, he discovered the *ego cogito* as the stable present (*ständige Anwesende*). . . . The subjectivity of the subject is conceived, then, in terms of the certitude of consciousness."[45] Starting from there, Hegel had asserted the certitude of consciousness to be the stability of history. It was left to Nietzsche, however, to achieve the ultimate development by declaring that this same self-assertion of the subject, conceived as will for the sake of will, was in fact the basis of the standing present of history, but with the supersensory, absolutistic element *meta-ta-phusika* eliminated.

It is this "ultimate" conception that leads to the famous Nietzschean assertion that art is more fundamental than

---

[40] *Ibid.*, p. 217.   [41] *Ibid.*, p. 218.   [42] *Ibid.*, p. 219.
[43] *Ibid.*, p. 219.   [44] *Ibid.*   [45] *Ibid.*, p. 220.

truth. The subordination of truth to art, or, in more Heideggerian terms, the conception of the relation of the existent to the things-that-are as an artful ordering of these things by the human will[46] becomes, then, the determining conception in the last twilight hours of the Eveningland.[47] The conception of man as the giver of values in the artful ordering of things is the deathbed bequest of the metaphysical tradition to what Heidegger calls "the long night which will follow the evening fading in the West."

Heidegger points out that Nietzsche intended the affirmation of the will to might as all-ordering art actually to surpass the nihilism of the negative devaluation of the old source of values. He intended it, in other words, to be the road to the surpassing of the metaphysical tradition itself. "The now expressed, experienced reality of what is real, the will to power, becomes the origin and measure of a new establishment of values (*Ursprung und Mass einer neuen Wertsetzung*)."[48] It is the very essence of man—his way of grounding truth—that Nietzsche would change. The manifestation of the new man, the artful wielder of the will to might, Nietzsche terms "the overman" (*Uebermensch*). "The name *Uebermensch* names the essence of mankind which, as 'modern,' begins the entry into the fulfillment of his epoch. The 'overman' is the man who *is* as a result of the realization of the will to might, and exists *for* this."[49]

Heidegger's attitude toward Nietzsche's conception of the new man is, as usual, an effort to subsume the truth that is manifested there by divesting it of the dissimulation that it necessarily involves. Just as the Hegelian dialectic had to be admitted in the *Andenken* as true, but was divested of the absolutism which saw in the dialectic the presence of a transcendent absolute as explanation *meta-ta-phusika* for the presence of that which is present, so Nietzsche's conception of the need for a new man, linked to the things-that-are by a new conception of the presence of the present, is accepted only to be essentially changed. Heidegger assumes the idea that destiny has decreed the moment to surpass the metaphysical tradition, and that this is what the New Man proposes to do, through a total transformation of his own nature. But he rejects the subjectivity

---

[46] Cf. *Ibid.*, p. 222.
[47] *Ibid.*, pp. 228-29.
[48] *Ibid.*, p. 231.
[49] *Ibid.*, p. 232.

of the *Uebermensch* conception, as source of Nietzsche's incapacity to achieve the definitive surpassing into the dawn. For Nietzsche's conception obscures how and to what extent the nature of man is determined by the nature of Being. The real relationship of the *Uebermensch* in his essence to the essence of metaphysics remains "necessarily[50] unthought."[51] The result is that ours remains the epoch of night, the epoch of world wars. The great battles are fought as part of the struggle of the will to might to gain world domination. Unthought in its essence, the will to might seeks to impose itself in now this form, now another, through a manipulative, technical domination of the things that are.[52] As long as the fundamental relationship of today's man to the things-that-are remains based on "the metaphysics of subjectivity," there will be no escape from this terrible course of events. The will to might will continue to grip the planet, armed with the instruments which the *Technik* can furnish it, determining in world clashes which party of human wills is going to dominate and thus impose the very "meaning" of things.

With these remarks on the nature of the *Uebermensch* conception Heidegger has brought us to today—or, more exactly, to *tonight*. The remaining pages of the analysis of Nietzsche need to be joined to Heidegger's later, explicit handling of the problem of surpassing metaphysics. For Neitzsche has raised the crucial question (*die entscheidende Frage*),[53] "Is man, in the essence he has had up to now, prepared to seize command of the earth?"[54] Nietzsche, surveying the modern world, saw that he was not and that he would have to go beyond himself to do so. Consequently, the effort to understand the implications of Nietzsche's pronouncement, "God is dead," which is, after all, the key to understanding what he really represents, is too intimately intertwined with the present day situation to be treated apart from the problem of the opposed possibilities facing the contemporary *Ek-sistent*, the planetary domination of technique, and the search for an existential surpassing of metaphysics.

---

[50] Necessarily, *Not-wendig*, in the sense that the time has not yet come in the *Wendang* in the *Not* to allow an essential thinking.

[51] *Holzwege*, p. 232.   [52] *Ibid.*, p. 237.

[53] Heidegger, *Vorträge und Aufsätze*, p. 106.   [54] *Ibid.*

XI   The Notion of Technique

THE declaration of the death of God does not mean that
man is to take the divinity's place. God's place, as metaphysics conceived it, is the seat of creation from which the
things-that-are are rendered present by the divine *fiat*.[1] With
the decline of the influence of the Christian version of the
suprasensory explanation for the *Anwesen des Anwesenden*, God's
place simply remains empty. Man has built a new seat for
himself, based on a very new conception of the Presence of the
Present. The *Uebermensch* functions from out the throne of
subjectivity. The divine *fiat* has given place to a new scepter
wielded by man: *die Technik*.[2]

It has become possible that man should make of technique
the very motor of the world only because, since Nietzsche, as
Heidegger puts it, *Mit dem Sein ist es Nichts*, which is perhaps
best translated by a slang expression: "There is nothing doing
for Being!" Heidegger means simply that the Nietzschean
nihilistic transcription of Being into value was the ultimate
Seinsvergessenheit. It is so *ultimate*, in Heidegger's view, that not
only is Being for the moment forgotten, but the old road to
Being has reached its dead-end, *blocked* by a conception of
Truth that can never be developed to Being's discovery since it
eliminates the search itself. This *Nicht-Denken des Seins*—this
failure to think Being—really believes that it has the secret to
the way Being actually essentializes itself, "so that all further
questions about Being become superfluous and remain superfluous."[3] To those who reach such a conclusion the value-fixing
of nihilism opens one exploring ground and one only: the search
for a better organization of values by science. The conclusion

[1] Heidegger, *Holzwege*, p. 235.   [2] *Ibid.*, p. 236.   [3] *Ibid.*, p. 239.

191

Heidegger draws from this is uncompromising: the only future for a rediscovery of Being lies in the complete surpassing of the metaphysical tradition and of its legacy, the planetary domination of technique.

The degree of oblivion of Being into which the tradition has allowed itself to issue gives some weight to Heidegger's assertion, cited above, that the Western, metaphysical historical destiny itself is fundamentally nihilistic.[4] This nihilism is not an accident of history or the peculiarity of an epoch, but the way Being has manifested itself historically. The whole tradition begins with the *Seinsvergessenheit* of the pre-Socratics, thinking Being as the Presence of the Present without thinking essentially the nature of the "of." It ends in the Being-forgetting of Nietzsche's "value-fixing" (*Wertsetzung*). It was Being's destiny to manifest itself in this way. This type of revelation was necessary (*notwendig*) because of the finite nature of Truth; "Being is contained in its Truth, and hides itself in this containment."[5] Heidegger adds, "We will probably encounter the very essence of the mystery of how it is that the truth of Being essentializes itself when we consider the self-concealing revelation of its essence."[6]

Even a quick glance at the context within which Heidegger approaches the problem of technique suffices to distinguish dramatically his attitude toward the contemporary "scientific" civilization from those considerations which seek to discover ways "to live with science," to "humanize a technocratic society," or "to combine science and gracious living." What gives the Heideggerian meditation on technique such richness and force? Essentially, the fact that it is so far from being simply an attack on some recent developments which the author finds aesthetically rather displeasing. Heidegger's analysis of the epoch of "the planetary domination of technique" is nothing less than the eschatological climax of an ontology of history, presented to us as our own existential challenge. These two aspects are inextricably linked; only when we understand the problem of technique in context, as the affair of an entire tradition that begins with the early Greek thinkers and continues in an unbroken line to our own day, will we be able to take up its challenge and project authentic-

[4] *Ibid.*, p. 244.   [5] *Ibid.*   [6] *Ibid.*

ally toward the essential thinking of Being that can alone surpass this legacy of metaphysics; Dasein can build no future that does not respect and assume the past, and the tradition, after all, is our past.

In the beginning of the tradition the Greek word for *techne* meant two things: (1) the actual doing which results in the production of objects, whether it be plowshares or the Parthenon; and (2) more fundamentally, a way of *aletheuein*, a way of discovering, of making present.[7] When Heidegger speaks of today's "technique" he chooses to think of the second, more ontological notion of *techne*. At the end of the essay "The Inquiry into Technique," Heidegger warns us that only by surpassing a purely instrumental conception of technique can we ever hope to get at its essence. In fact, even to understand technique instrumentally, as a way of manipulating and of producing, we must conceive of it as a way of comporting oneself toward the things-that-are: for the first meaning of *techne*, production, implying the bringing-together of the four causes to make something, is also a *discovery* in the form of a *Her-vor-zu-bring-ende*.[9] Any attempt to get behind the phenomenon of this discovery, to its essential explanation, is an attempt to get behind the four causes, to understand the possibility of their fusing in the production of the particular thing.[10]

[7] Cf. "Die Frage nach der Technik," in *Vorträge und Aufsätze*, pp. 20-21.
[8] Heidegger, *Vorträge und Aufsätze*, pp. 40-41.   [9] *Ibid.*, p. 21.
[10] The discussion of the four causes in an essay on technique is a classic example of Heidegger's penchant for switching abruptly from the ontological to the epistemological order. In the midst of discussing how the silversmith brings forth the form from the matter in view of the end of the thing as pitcher, Heidegger jumps suddenly onto an entirely new plane, using this as example of the four causes at work, letting the things *in das An-wesen vorkommen* (*ibid.*, p. 18); this leads immediately to an epistemological consideration, entirely distinct from a consideration of the ontological nature of the physical causality itself. For he states (p. 19): "Das Her-vor-bringen bringt aus der Verborgenheit her in die Unverborgenheit vor"—Production brings before [us] unconcealed that which was concealed. The consideration of the presence of the present as *aletheia* is certainly legitimate and is certainly fundamental. But one should not be under the impression that, because the causes bring something *to be*, and because to be produced means to be made present, a consideration of the presence as unveiling truth prvoides the ultimate explanation of all the implications of the causality itself. For the analysis of causality as transmission of concrete, physical reality is an order of consideration which examines the thing in

Modern technique in fact is also a form of "discovery" (*Entbergen*), but not in the same way as the *techne* of the *Greeks*.[11] Modern technique is not asking the things-that-are to yield up their Being; rather it demands of material things that they yield up their energy, which modern man wants to transform in a thousand ways. To dramatize how radically new and different is the approach of the *Machenschaft* to the things-that-are, Heidegger contrasts productive, energy-yielding, and energy employing machines with the simple mechanical devices and productive activities of the past. He uses as an illustration the directness of the ancient windmill, so immediately rooted in nature, at the mercy of the capricious winds, flinging its uncomplex arms open to a country sky.[12] The windmill co-operates with the paysage and is subject to the whims of the elements. Modern technique, on the other hand, destroys the field to mine its coal, and then transports the coal away to transform it into steam in a giant high-pressure power plant. The steam turns a turbine, the turbine a generator, the generator sends forth electricity a hundred miles by high-tension transmission lines; there it is converted to industrial voltages, turns a motor which turns a machine which sews a pair of shoes. Symbolized by such a contrast, the question "What kind of 'unveiling' is involved in modern technique?" becomes very evidently meaningful.[13]

The characteristic sign of this technique—which Heidegger here calls *ein herausforderndes Entbergen*,"an exigent discovery"—is that this kind of cultivation or development of things leads to a conservation, *a storing up*, of "that which presents itself under the guise of a stable accumulation."[14] A great aircraft standing at the end of the runway is, of course, an "object"; but to consider it *only* an object, as a rock is an object, would be to miss the point of its "technical significance." For it is above all a possibility for transport which must be grasped in its whole construction, which I must understand as "a complexus of its own intelligibility as already made present. That this examination might ignore the presence of the present, renders it, in Heidegger's eyes, not fundamental; but that should not be taken, as Heidegger sometimes seems to, as an implied adverse comment on the validity of all causal, "categorical" analysis.

[11] *Vorträge und Aufsätze*, p. 22.   [12] *Ibid.*   [13] *Ibid.*, p. 24.
[14] *Ibid.*

exploitable stock-parts, representing an accumulation of manipulable possibilities."[15] Everything that enters into the relationships established and discovered by the technique can be treated as technically significant and, indeed, within the limited context of this way of discovery, tends to be reduced to nothing more than that. Even man can be reduced to "manpower" or to "patients" in a modern hospital. The wood cutter who walked the forest trails his grandfather had walked can be absorbed into an enormous paper industry and become an instrument of its ravenous machines in their search for "raw material" to satisfy the hunger for woodpulp that the modern newspaper, busily indoctrinating the masses, has created.[16]

For this kind of technique, nature is reduced to a storehouse of energy, so much power waiting to be used.[17] *"Ein berechenbarer Kräftezusammenhang"*—a calculable group of forces, this is all nature represents to the physical scientist. Modern physics did not happen on the scene simply because nature required it; rather it was a *conception* of nature as complexus of forces that made physics into an experimental endeavor to uncover them as they stand.[18] Heidegger expresses this truth in a way intended to challenge the common notion that "modern science" made possible our "modern technique." The truth is that the development of modern science, of mathematical physics and of machine technique, all depended on the prior development of a new kind of truth, a new attitude concerning the relationship of man to the things-that-are. Modern science and machine technique are nothing but servants in the domination of the things-that-are conceived as forces and stocks of energy possibility.[19] If modern physics, then, finds itself incapable of intuiting the intrinsic intelligibility of a representation, this is due to the nature of the decision underlying its "scheme for positioning" (*Gestell*, a word of common usage, seized upon by Heidegger and given a new sense);[20] the scientist having originally conceived the individual thing as "stock," his experimentation will tend toward functional manipulation of possibilities rather than insight into an essence.[21]

This Heideggerian analysis of the nature of technique

[15] *Ibid.*   [16] *Ibid.*, pp. 25-26.   [17] *Ibid.*, p. 29.   [18] *Ibid.*

[19] *Ibid.*   [20] *Ibid.*, p. 28.   [21] *Ibid.*, p. 30.

characteristically brings out the epochal, *geschichtlich* nature of this kind of truth by revealing the free projection in which, as every *geschehen* in history, it is rooted. For the schematic positioning (*Gestell*) that is modern technique is nothing less than a *Geschick*, a fundamental way of bringing forth the things-that-are, of letting things happen (*geschehen*), just as the *poiesis* of the older technique is another. It is based, as every way of *letting be* must be, upon a free act of what *Sein und Zeit* called fundamental comportment.

In analyzing the technique as the fundamental truth of an epoch, Heidegger thus placed the modern discussion of science in its truly ontological context; for him, the *mystery of being* is at work there in all its complexity, as necessary interplay of revelation and dissimulation in the historical unfolding of Being.[22] This is what gives Heidegger the conviction that what is revealed there is necessary and a dissimulation, and that it is yet not a catastrophe without exit. Like everything else human, like every dissimulating revelation, the technique presents a double alternative, corresponding to the *Wesen-Unwesen* relationship that is at the heart of everything finite. A blind, absolute affirmation of the position for which modern technique stands would be, of course, the road to 1984. But a similarly blind, frightened, shrill rejection of science and everything technocratic would be nothing more than a reaction to it, turning, round, as Nietzsche did in his rejection of the supra-sensory world, within the tight orbit of that which it rejects. Rather we must look for hope precisely in the fact that the technique is a maximum, eschatological, and hence ultimate dissimulation. For the ultimate dissimulation itself is an invitation to contemporary man "above all, and more completely and more originally, to engage himself in the essence of the unveiled and its unveiledness and to experience the accustomed propriety of discovery as his own essence."[23]

The destiny of discovery brings man before these alternatives, then, as history has always brought him before alternatives of authenticity and inauthenticity. But, being the end of a tradition, ours is a *dürftige Zeit*, a period of special need when the danger is at its greatest.[24] "When destiny rules in the form of the schema of "position," then the danger is at its highest

---

[22] *Ibid.*, pp. 32-33.　　　　[23] *Ibid.*, p. 34.　　　　[24] *Ibid.*

point."[25] The sign of this danger is man's enslaving everything to the scheme, including man himself, who also becomes only a *Bestand*, a "stock."[26] All other forms of *Entbergen*, of "discovery," including the *poiesis*, are suppressed, which means that it is truth itself which is forgotten. Here lies the true danger in the technique. Heidegger makes it very clear that it is not what the technique does, not its making possible secret police control and the thirty megaton bomb, that renders it deadly. The "outermost danger" rather lies only in its blinding us to the most original truth of our own essential nature.[27]

Yet, as Hölderlin said:

Wo aber Gefahr ist, wächst
Das Rettende auch.

Where danger lies, however, there
also springs the deliverer.

The deliverer is Dasein grasping, in the night of the disappearance, the essence of the absence.

Indeed, we are not *yet* delivered. "We get a look at the danger and we see the deliverance pushing up. Therefore we are not yet delivered."[28] But because we cherish the deliverance, and as long as we continue to seek to surpass the metaphysical tradition and the technique that would reduce man to something to be manipulated, we are on the right road.[29]

Heidegger does not leave us here without any hint of how this surpassing must in fact be carried off. But the remarks he makes at the end of the essay on technique barely outline, rather than treat formally, where the possibility must be sought.

Heidegger first recalls to our attention the double sense that technique may enjoy, touching as it does the central ambiguity of the *Sein-Seienden* relationship.[30] There is only one way to escape from the modern tyranny of technique reigning in the universal acceptance of the narrower of the two senses of the word; it lies precisely in the affirmation of the fundamentality of *techne* in the more ontological of its meanings, namely as *poiesis*.[31] Again invoking Hölderlin's "dicterisch wohnet der Mensch auf dieser Erde," Heidegger reminds us of the lesson

[25] *Ibid.*   [26] *Ibid.*, p. 35.   [27] *Ibid.*, p. 36.   [28] *Ibid.*, p. 41.
[29] *Ibid.*   [30] *Ibid.*   [31] *Ibid.*, p. 42.

that has been central in the consideration of the authentic existent. All discovery is rooted ultimately in that originative thinking which Heidegger has termed "the fundamental *Dictare*," i.e., all discovery is poetic. The essence of technique is not technical—a mistake that vitiates most contemporary analyses of science.[32] We can understand, assume, and depass technique only by getting at the nature of the fundamental *poiesis* that is at the root of all discovery. This we can do best by contrasting the technique with an altogether different kind of discovery, another kind of *poiesis*, art.

Just as technique cannot be known "technically" in its essence, so neither can art be known in its essence "aesthetically." This is the heresy of "art for art's sake." Moreover, both are subject to betraying their profounder, authentic forms in a manipulative, non poetical, non originative production. But these two modes of discovery are very different. That is exactly why meditation on the one can perhaps reveal something to us of what is most hidden in the other.

How can this suggestion, however, point the way to a definitive surpassing of "modern times"? To make this clear, let us revert to Heidegger's analysis of the *Neuzeit* in the beginning of the essay, "Die Zeit des Weltbildes."[33] He lists there the essential signs that distinguish the era of the *Vollendung* of metaphysics from all the preceding epochs.

The ultimate characteristic of modern times, the culmination of all of its other aspects, is the *Entgötterung*, the elimination of God and the gods. This actualizes itself in two main series of manifestations:

1. With the emphasis on "culture," i.e. a concern for the "highest values" able to serve man's ends, comes the transformation of art into an "expression of the life experience of man," and "art for art's sake" becomes conceivable for the first time.

2. Along with the essential role of science conceived as "certifying research" comes the characteristic modern form of *praxis*—what Heidegger terms *Maschinentechnik*—the instrument by which the "objectivization" governed by a *Weltanschauung* can pass, through science, to the world of organizing activity.

The surpassing of metaphysics will depend on the destruction

[32] *Ibid.*, p. 45.　　　　[33] *Holzwege*, pp. 69-70.

of these manifestations as the ruling forms of modern life. The rediscovery of the *poiesis* dissimulated behind modern technique and modern aesthetics can make it possible to refound modern activity in the dimension of the *Heilige*. The sign that modern man has rediscovered the right toad will be a growing mysteriousness of art and technique as we penetrate into their essence, a process that should render modern man both more meaningful and more mysterious to himself. [34]

These cryptic remarks on the possibility of surpassing the domination of technique toward an essential grasp of the essence of truth in Dasein invite us to rejoin, in the midst of the darkest night of the end of the tradition, the starting point of the odyssey of destruction. The key to surpassing metaphysics is the same key that unlocks the nature of Dasein. It lies in understanding how it is that "man dwells poetically from out this earth."

It might be useful here to turn back for a moment to another *Holzwege* lecture, delivered in 1937, "Vom Ursprung des Kunstwerkes." In this article Heidegger seeks to show how it is possible existentially that there should be such a thing as a work of art. That Heidegger should insist that art exists because man has absolute need of it is not surprising in view of what has been said about originative thinking. The work of art is the field of combat between a Dasein, trying to open a world by casting forward the light of intelligibility, and the "matter" in which the Dasein must root his efforts and from whose resisting mass he must try to pull into light the thing known. The work of art is the meeting of a *World* which endows it with all of its desires and ideas and lights (but in turn finds stability and expression in the work itself), and the *Earth*, the material from which the work is moulded, be it the stone of a temple, the sonorous mass of words and musical sounds, or the colors of painting. The world absorbs these materials into its light, so that they yield up a meaning and become *Sein*. But the earth does not give itself over completely. It forces the world to sink its tentacles into its resistant soil and become a *Da*. Thus the temple takes its meaning from its site and is rooted in it. The sanctuary of Poseidon *is* Sounion and would be essentially other in any site other than this cape. But conversely the temple brings the light of its world[35] to Sounion. Its Doric stability adds motion to the waves; its silhouette, vastness to the sky; its stone foundations, life to the grey rocks jutting into the Bay of Pyraeus. In the originative work of art the Dasein forces the earth to render up meaning it would essentially tend to keep to itself.[36]

But the struggle is a struggle among pairs, and the victory is the accomplishment of both. Rather than a combat, in fact—rather than Dasein's effort to assert itself, to "express" itself in "art for art's sake"—this is a *streng-mild* dialogue in which Dasein is the earth's midwife. And the "meaning" brought forth is not "cultural value," not "meaning for Dasein," but meaning for its own sake, meaning for the sake of truth and Being, meaning higher than those who brought it to be in awe and selflessness, solidified meaning where the *Heilige* can find a home and dwell, partially unveiled, among men.

It is out of such solidified discoveries, that "practical" *techne* must build a world for Dasein to survive in, while he is not originally and actively engaged in the unveiling of new truth. This is what man must learn if he is again to understand what are the *techne* and the art he can authentically live by. Discovery is based on *poiesis; poiesis* is creative, not consumptive: it is the preserving concretion of originative thinking. Forceful though it must be, it requires immense patience and respect. Dasein-originated though it is, it implies cooperation with, not self-centered abuse of, the earth. Finite though its works are, they must find both their source and their end in the *Heilige*.

Until man learns again to build himself, from out of the earth, through *poiesis*, a home of solidified flashes of true Being, a world in which and by which he can subsist from day to day while waiting for new flashes of truth, he will not have "a place to dwell" and will roam in the cold and dark *Neuzeit*, an easy prey for "technique."

[35] "World" in this analysis is used differently than in *Sein und Zeit*; there it meant the opening of a horizon among the things-that-are so that they might be touched by the temporal illumination of Dasein. Here it refers to the rooting, in a work of art, of the ideas and aspirations already developed in and making up part of, the horizontal world of a Dasein.

[36] "Kann die Erde als das sich verschliessende in ein Offenes drängen." *Holzwege*, p. 36.

XII The Surpassing of Metaphysics

THE analysis of technique in the preceding chapter brings the destruction of the historical destiny of ontologies up to the present moment in history; there remains, then, only the work of the future. Heidegger has dramatized our position as we face that future in the terms "danger" and "deliverance." He has made it very clear where the danger lies: in the planetary domination of the technique. He has made equally clear the challenge of the future: to understand the nature of the danger itself profoundly enough to transform it into deliverance. The crucial question remains: *Can* it be transformed and *how*?

This question, we have seen, is really the basis of Heidegger's long and continuing quest, for it is identical with what we have termed the preparation for a surpassing of metaphysics. In the recent collection of essays, *Vorträge und Aufsätze*, we find included, under the very title "Überwindung der Metaphysik," what may be considered Heidegger's own gauge of that effort. The essay is in the form of a series of notes, always dense and often enigmatic, written at various times from 1936 to 1946, with one section of several pages derived from a lecture delivered as recently as 1951. That Heidegger has placed this series of notes in what baseball fans would call "the clean-up position," following the essays on Nietzsche and on technique and just before his most recent "recalling" of the pre-Socratics, is very obviously significant.

After underscoring our exact historical situation (*Metaphysik ist vollendet*), Heidegger reestablishes the gravity of the epoch. First, he dismisses the notion that this is just an ephemeral stage in history, simply another epoch now in the throes of growing pains which are bound to pass when the technocratic civilization comes of age. This notion would be similar to the concept that the world needs to pass through the fires of revolution and the dictatorship of the proletariat to arrive at the blessings of the classless society. Heidegger speaks rather of "death throes," and dramatically underscores the radicalness of what is upon us by stating, "The death throes will last longer than the historical destiny of metaphysics up to now."[1] In other words, we are not just entering another epoch in the same tradition; rather we are standing on the threshold of an entirely new era, born out of the death of the metaphysical tradition. With its own destiny to unfold along as extensive a course as the old tradition, the "death throes" could take as long as the previous tradition. Secondly, he reinvokes the crucial question which we encountered in considering the Introduction to *Was ist Metaphysik?*: "To what extent does metaphysics belong to the nature of man?"[2] The force of this question is now very evident; for what is at stake in surpassing metaphysics is the necessity to change as radically and fundamentally as possible the way man relates himself to the things-that-are, for that is what Heidegger means, as we know, by "his *nature*."

It suffices to glance about us at the seemingly systematic devaluation of everything to realize both how necessary and how incredibly difficult it will be to reinstitute Being in a world in which both poles of the *Dasein-Seienden* relationship have suffered from the *Entwertung*. At the root of this universal devaluation, the very distinction of Being and the things-that-are stands forgotten. The clearest sign of the gravity of this *Vergessenheit des Unterschieds* is the breakdown of all human distinctiveness, of all traditional distinctions. This is what has opened the door to a *planetary* domination of technique. The abandonment of Being has eliminated the importance of what is unique and what is free, even on the level of its larger projection—the nation and the historical tradition.[3] Indeed, there is nothing more *inhuman* than the modern humanism which ignores Being and, in the place of *Dasein*, asserts the *Wille zum Willen*. It would throw some light on what is involved in sur-

[1] Heidegger, *Vorträge und Aufsätze*, p. 71.   [2] *Ibid.*, p. 73.   [3] *Ibid.*, p. 90.

passing metaphysics to investigate why all distinctions are being broken down in the devaluation accompanying the planetary domination of technique. The technique opposes *Wille zum Willen* to genuine freedom. Freedom is what separates Dasein from the things-that-are. It is that projection from the *Nichts* that opens an exstatic horizon within which *Seienden* can be grasped as *Seienden (on he on)*. The highest degree of free comportment in respect to the things-that-are opens Dasein into the presence of the *Seienden* in a way that appreciates the totality and integrity of all things, as such, guarding their mystery and treating them as "holy." Realizing his finitude, realizing that he is transcendence that does not create but cooperates with the things-that-are, authentic *Dasein* contemplates and enhances, rather than dominates and destroys. The will to might, on the contrary, being based on a comportment which objectivizes things and absorbs them into the neutral, general framework of a subjective schema, must approach the things-that-are, not in their mystery and rich individuality, but only as capable of becoming objects serving the ends of the scheme. Consequently, each thing and even each person is grasped not in the unique, distinctive integrity of its whole, everescaping reality, but by one facet to which it must immediately be reduced by the technical consideration in order to be admissible into the established framework. The distinction between Dasein and the thing it absorbs is dissolved into the subjective scheme, and all freedom abolished, as the *ek-sistenz-*opening gap is ignored.

Metaphysics can be surpassed if man will cease being Will for the sake of Will; to do this he will have to rediscover in all its authenticity his true liberty. Consequently man will have to cease making the basis of his relationship to the things-that-are the technique that seeks, within the dimension of subjective certitude, assurance for the presence of a representation. The distinction of Being and the things-that-are will have to be reinstituted. The "forgetting of Being" will have to be replaced by a reawakening of the Being-question. This entails nothing less than a transformation of man's comportment with the things-that-are—a transformation of his truth—a transformation of his nature. The "destruction," recalling the metaphysical tradition in search of an "originative light," has a central role in this transformation of human nature. "Such recalling experiences the proper result of the exploration of the *Seienden*, wherein the Need (*Not*) of the truth of Being and consequently the origins of truth illumine themselves and the human essence is fundamentally brought to light."[4] By going to the heart of the historical *Seinsvergessenheit* to see what is really at stake there, Dasein can hope to come to see what is lacking in the tradition, *what is needed*. To be "delivered," man must first rethink the tradition sufficiently really to *feel painfully* the Need. What will that pain reveal? "The pain that must first be experienced and embraced is the insight and knowledge that *Needlessness* (*Notlosigkeit*) is the highest and most hidden Need that is needed from out the farthest far" (*die aus der fernsten Ferne erst nötigt*).[5] This greatest of all pains, then is a grasp of the nature of the needlessness of the era of Technique, of its feeling of smug self-sufficiency: it reflects the total abandonment of Being. This Needlessness arises because men can clutch the real and the reality (*Wirklichkeit*) which is the true (*was das Wahre sei*) without realizing wherein the truth essentializes itself. This is what we learn from recalling the traditional philosophers, for they too missed the fundamental reality, the Need of the Dasein as source of Truth.

The recalling of the Need is, then, the direct opposite of the historical abandonment of Being. The recaller must become the shepherd of Being trying to regather his flock. "The shepherds dwell out of sight and beyond the solitude of the wasted earth. . . . " In the dark of night the shepherd is alone, standing in the hills, isolated from the wastelands down below, lonely but faithful through the hours when he is forgotten of the world. "Dasein is the shepherd of Being," *Holzwege* had declared. Heidegger now brings the full meaning of the guardian's mission to the fore. From what is said in these pages on "The Surpassing of Metaphysics" we can conclude that Heidegger foresees no general reinstallation of Being, no widespread revaluation of the things-that-are through a general rebirth of understanding of our relations with the thing as a rich fusion of earth and heavens, of the divine and the mortal. Rather, we are left with the suggestion that it will be the task of the lonely individual to guard the riches of Being, to

[4] *Ibid.*, p. 79.　　　　　　　　　[5] *Ibid.*, p. 90.

keep the past from dissipating completely in a tragic forgetting that there ever was a Greece or a medieval Paris. It is the mission of the individual to push beyond the wastelands of historicism to *Geschichte*, past instrumental theories of language to *Sprache* as the *Haus des Seins*, past psychologies and anthropologies, past exploitation of manpower to *Dasein* in its full possibility as the temporal horizon within which all is illumined and made present in the fourfold building of the thing. It is the lonely shepherd who will not forget how to dwell "dichterisch . . . auf dieser Erde." Heidegger's sad and poetic conclusion reminds one of the epistles of St. Paul recalling to the Christian that he must testify in the most unhearing society to the grace of God. The shepherd of Being is the saint of a finite world, sacrificing not to a transcendent God, but to a transcendental Being, understood as Heidegger has conceived it. "It is one thing only to use the earth, it is another to receive its blessing and to become at home in the law of this reception, to dwell in the mystery of Being and watch over the inviolability of the possible."[6]

The authentic, poetic dwelling "auf dieser Erde" achieves the opposite of the inauthentic, technical consumption of things, which uses up the earth. The poetical dwelling "watches over the inviolability of the possible," in its service of the Holy. The reign of the *Machenschaft* of the *Wille zum Willen* violates it. When we dwell poetically by things we maintain the perfect balance in the fourfold fusion, rooted in the recognition that Dasein's finite freedom is devotion to the transcendent mystery of the things which it must let be as they are. The *Machenschaft*, on the other hand, seeking the absolute domination of everything by will, violates the limits of the possible, ignores the mystery of the *Heilige*, and in subjecting all loses all in the dissipation of values. The Dasein that would "watch over the inviolability of the possible," by dwelling poetically in acts of true originativeness, is able to attain the truly new and refreshing precisely because of his authenticity. Projecting always in view of the finite structural whole of the Being-destined-for-death, he achieves an authentic temporality that depends on the past and present *Seienden* in revealing the future. The holy quest for truth respects the equilibrium of the complex act of "dwel-

[6] *Ibid.*, p. 98.

ling by things." The shepherd of Being gathers his flock by reuniting in equilibrium the exstases of authentic temporality violated by the reign of the technique.

The course for the future that is poetically and somewhat dimly suggested in these passages is no simple course of action, no scheme that can transform the real. No action can be effective unless preceded by an inner transformation of man that can undo the effects of metaphysical devolution.[7] In the letter to Jean Beaufret (*Brief über dem Humanismus*, 1946), Heidegger offers some richer indications how this transformation must take place:

> [We must] turn back into the near of that which is next. The descent, once man has installed himself in subjectivity, is harder and more dangerous than the ascent. The descent leads into the poverty of the *Ek-sistenz* of the *homo humanus*. In the *Ek-sistenz* the circle of the *homo animalis* of metaphysics is left behind.[8]

What does Heidegger mean here when he suggests that the metaphysical nature of man, conceived as *homo animalis*, must be replaced by the conception of man as *homo humanus*? The key to the passage very obviously lies in the notion of a descent (*Absteig*) into the poverty (*Armut*) of humanity. In what this descent consists, and what is meant here by poverty, can only be answered by widening the focus of the discussion sufficiently to make it possible to situate the position that our author is suggesting here in relation to the traditional problem of "the ultimate"—the problem of God.

The question of God arises in this context in this way: Nietzsche having declared the end of metaphysical flight to a supersensory world with the pronouncement *God is dead!*, Heidegger is preparing the surpassing of metaphysics in a way that takes us beyond the Neitzschean *Umwertung*. But a problem arises: in reversing the reversal will Heidegger not in effect be preparing for the rebirth of the Deity? Should man, in order to achieve a definitive surpassing of metaphysics, perhaps go out in search of God?

Because this is a question affecting the future, it becomes a question of *should*. The relation of the problem of the grasp of Being to what is traditionally called "ethics" is a question that was raised—and left in abeyance—by our analysis of *Sein und*

[7] *Ibid.*, p. 95.　　　　　[8] *Holzwege*, p. 37.

Zeit. This, and the problem of the transcendent in Heidegger's thought, a problem raised and left in abeyance in Chapter 9, now find their most significant context, as inseparable from the main guiding question, *how* the metaphysical tradition must be surpassed. These questions become fully "ek-sistential" in the suite of our review of the destruction of the historical destiny of ontologies, because it is at this point that, brought up to date, we turn toward the future in an effort to determine in view of what we must project to exist authentically.

Viewed within the full perspective of the Heideggerian "destruction" the religious problem becomes the task of once again making present in the world what is, in Heidegger's *Denken*, the closest approximation to an "ultimate"—the dimension of the Holy (*das Heilige*). Evidently, if we are to understand what Heidegger proposes "religiously," we will have to see exactly what the problem of restoring the dimension of the *Heilige* has to do with the problem of a personal God, of the Christian God, i.e., where the personal transcendent stands in this the most mature moment of Heidegger's thought.

As we stated in Chapter 9, Heidegger's thought is neither directly anti-God nor in the least theistic. "This philosophy," Heidegger writes Jean Beaufret, "distinguishes itself neither for nor against the Dasein of God. It remains ensconced in indifference. Thus the religious question is to it 'all the same.' Nihilism does not achieve such an indifferentism."[9] Some Christian interpreters tend to read this passage to mean that Heidegger's philosophy protects the transcendent so perfectly that there is no question of proving or disproving anything at all about God through *Denken*. Rather, these interpreters would suggest, the openness which Heidegger would achieve to "the quiet voice of Being" (*die stille Stimme des Seins*) suggests God without compromising Him, and above all leaves open the possibility of a personal encounter with God in faith completely outside the sphere of *Denken*.[10]

---

[9] *Humanismus brief,* p. 36.

[10] Birault sees Heidegger's thought as basically religiously neutral. He clearly realizes that Heidegger's philosophy gives no positive support and provides no explicit base for a theism. But he leaves us with the suggestion that one could be philosophically a Heideggerian and still *believe* in God without any serious rational conflict.

To this position we can only reaffirm what was said in the earlier chapter, and then produce additional justification for the claim. First, anyone interpreting Heidegger in this way will have to assume the burden of explaining away Heidegger's remark in the essay on Anaximander, when he speaks of belief as "the unfortunate destiny of Being."[11] And then he will have to justify the notion that there can and should be a faith utterly unaided and unsupported by *Denken*—a faith at best irrelevant to thought. But most seriously of all, and this is the point to which we must now turn our attention, such an interpretation ignores the nature of the basic "religious" tonality of Heidegger's philosophy.

In the letter to Beaufret, Heidegger explains carefully that the "indifference" which he has tried to achieve is not an end in itself, an "indifferentism," but rather serves as a step on the road to a more positive goal.[12] In the passage in which our author speaks of this indifference he explains the two things that he is trying to establish: (1) the necessity of getting beyond the religious position of the atheism of the nineteenth century—not by opening the door to a new theism, but by getting completely beyond the God-murdering time of Nietzsche into a time when God is as irrelevant as the gods, in the way Camus's Meursault is beyond Ivan Karamazov; (2) the necessity of working to preserve the dimension of the mystery of Being, which Heidegger calls the Holy. The question of God, he states here explicitly, cannot even be raised until the "dimension of the Holy, which as dimension remains closed to us, is reopened and the illumination of Being is rediscovered."[13]

The notion of the *Heilige* is bound to remain perfectly incomprehensible to Heidegger's readers, and is destined therefore to continue to receive very personal interpretations, as long as it is not understood in the context of Heidegger's active *Denken*. It is only when we admit that Heidegger is seeking to restore the full richness of all human existence in every department of its historical manifestation, from religion to art and politics, *without God*, locating the center of the mystery of the inexhaustible richness of existence not in a transcendent God but in Being conceived as the finite relation of Dasein to the things that are, that we can hope to understand what the

[11] *Holzwege*, p. 325.   [12] *Humanismusbrief*, p. 36.   [13] *Ibid.*, p. 37.

Heilige represents. One should never forget that Heidegger wanders the "forest trails" already marked out by Zarathustra. In avoiding a realism of ready-made things endowed with meaning by a creator standing off in a supersensory world, and a subjectivism of things endowed with "value" by will, Heidegger tries to found a phenomenology of finite truth that can guard a sense of mystery.

In the "Letter on Humanism" Heidegger affirms as much quite explicitly. The fact that his *Denken* can "no more be theistic than atheistic" is due not to indifference but "to the very ground upon which this *Denken* as *Denken* rests," namely the notion of "the truth of Being."[14] The crux of the whole question of the transcendent must be sought out in the *Ek-* of the *Ek-sistenz* of that thing through whom Being reveals itself, namely *Da-sein*.[15] One cannot be much more explicit. How else, without falling into the anti-theism of the end of the metaphysical tradition, can he say that we do not need God to preserve everything in Being that can be meaningfully real, true, and beautiful. It would seem that the critics' insistence upon raising the God-problem when reading Heidegger is a sign that they are still thinking metaphysically and therefore cannot accept a genuine absence for what it is without making it into either a "preparation" or "a campaign against" a transcendent Absolute.

The mystery then resides in the *Ek-* of the *Ek-sistenz*, in the true *Mögliche*, the possibility to stand-in among the things-that-are, the possibility to ex-tend toward what is not yet. At the root of *Ek-sistenz*, at the root of Being, stands the true mystery, the nothing which makes possible the presence of everything, represented in man by the need, that thirst for Being which sends man wandering down the long destiny of the errancy. "*Der Abstieg führt in die Armut der Ek-sistenz des homo humanus*"— the descent leads into the poverty of the *Ek-sistenz* of the *homo humanus*.[16] Heidegger's philosophy is a humanism of poverty, based on finite things and the needy nothingness of a finite freedom. "To think the truth of Being means the same as to think the *humanitas* of the *homo humanus*." This *humanitas* is finitude itself.

How does such a conception affect and guide our pro-

---

[14] *Ibid.*   [15] *Ibid.*, p. 35.   [16] *Ibid.*, p. 37.

jections? Given that the *homo humanus* is based on a conception of the "poverty" of the being that projects toward death from out the Nothing, what then *should we do* now that we know that no transcendent God's will can tell us anything about our true nature and duty as men? It is authentically Heideggerian to pose this question; in fact, the very nature of this *Denken* makes it imperative we *should* pose this question. It is this apparent identity of ontological inquiry with ethical consequence that has prompted critics to accuse the Heideggerian philosophy of inextricably mixing the two endeavors. In the letter on humanism Heidegger takes up this charge.[17] The answer, he says, hinges on discerning first what ethics and ontology really mean.[18]

"Ethics" was first distinguished from "logic" and "physics" by the Platonic school. In pre-Socratic times thinkers did not distinguish the various *episteme*. That there was for the pre-Socratics no "ethics" does not mean, of course, that their thought did not touch on the "moral." As a matter of fact, the word *ethos* appears in a text of Heracleitos (frag. 119), ἦθος ἀνθρώπῳ δαίμων. In attempting a trans-lation (*Ueber-setzung*) Heidegger reads this text: "The habitation is for man the openness for the presence of the Gods."[19] Thinking truth as the presence of what is present, Heracleitos absorbs the world of doing and acting into the fundamental dimension of his thought, where it is indistinguishable from existing; to him, knowing and doing are still united as acts of the same existence. It is from this position of existential fundamentality that Heidegger endows *ethos* with the basic meaning it should have, "Any *Denken* that thinks the truth of Being as the originative element of man as an *Ek-sistent*, is itself the fundamental ethic."[20] The fundamental ethic's true place, then, is identity with the "fundamental ontology." We have seen previously Heidegger's reaction to what happened to the notion fundamental ontology in the years following the publication of *Sein und Zeit*. Critics, ensconced in the metaphysical tradition, misread consistently Heidegger's intent, substituting "ontology" each time they saw the word "fundamental ontology." Finally, Heidegger accused himself of having been a victim to metaphysical terminology while trying to think beyond metaphysics. Consequently, in the introduction to *Was ist Metaphysik?* the title

[17] *Ibid.*, p. 38.   [18] *Ibid.*, p. 39.   [19] *Ibid.*, p. 41.   [20] *Ibid.*, p. 41.

"Fundamental Ontology" was officially abandoned. The present passage in the letter on humanism does the same thing for the notion of the "fundamental ethic": "The *Denken* that inquires into the truth of Being, and thereby determines the mode of essential habitation of man from and in view of Being, is neither ethic nor ontology. Therefore the question concerning their relation to one another at this point has no more ground."[21] Heidegger's thought is at one and the same time the "fundamental ontology" and the "fundamental ethic" because it thinks beyond the traditional distinction of ontology and ethics —beyond both historically, to the time before the distinction was made, and existentially, to the *Ek-sistenz* that is inextricably *Denken* and *Tun*: "Das Denken ist ein Tun. Aber zugleich ein Tun, das zugleich alle Praxis übertrifft."[22] One must surpass phenomenologically the level where thought is "abstract" and "disinterested," and where action is merely "practical," to reach the level of the fundamental acts of *Ek-sistenz*, which are a knowing-doing, and an engaging-knowing.

It is evident that the root of this fusion of ontological with ethical and epistemological with practical lies in Heidegger's phenomenological conception of *Ek-sistenz*. The same conception, manifesting itself in slightly different contexts, determines both the form of Heidegger's explanation of the end of man and his description of what it is to know. The best way, I believe, to make the philosophical options that are at work in this conception stand out is to contrast Heidegger's notion of the "end" (*Ende*) of man with, for example, the traditional Christian conception of man's *telos*, and then examine the very different notions of what it is to know upon which each of them is based.

The Christian conception of man is rooted in a teleology which conceives the fulfillment of the human nature to lie outside man in the only object adequate to the satisfaction of the intellect and will: the Divine truth and goodness. Hence the Christian conception of man's *telos* frankly embraces an absolute transcendence, directing man beyond himself in his search for fulfillment and *raison d'etre*. The Heideggerian phenomenology, seeking to achieve an explanation of man complete without recourse to an infinite, transcendent Absolute, must

[21] *Ibid.*, p. 42.   [22] *Ibid.*, p. 45.

radically transform the conception of "end." Heidegger, in declaring *Dasein ist Transzendenz schlechthin*, declares in effect (1) that man's "end" lies not beyond but in himself; and (2) that the nature of this end is such as to render Dasein himself the fundamental source of the light of significance which endows the *Seienden* with Being. Evidently, then, the teleology of the *Sein-zum-Tode*—the teleology of the philosophy that would surpass metaphysics (if indeed the sense of "teleology" can still apply), envisions a certain internal relationship of a structure to itself, rather than the conformity of a nature to a divine idea which, in engendering that nature has willed that it should freely choose to conform itself to it as its intended *exemplar*. Rather than conform freely to the divine idea, the Heideggerian Dasein must grasp the full significance of his own finite possibilities, in order to create himself in keeping with the full range of possibilities growing out of a particular situation. The two conceptions are rooted in two very different conceptions of the existent's relationship to time. Though the Christian teleology unfolds within a temporal horizon, it directs its gaze always to an end which transcends time. Hence, upon a base of horizontal extension in time, the Christian would build vertically toward a love which, while *in* time, is not essentially *of* time. In contrast, the Dasein's finite self-extension toward a future certain to end in death requires, for authentic *Ek-sistenz*, a grasp, now, of the structural whole of what he is, based on an adequate conception of his own essential finitude. Fulfillment for Dasein lies not in transcending time, but in possessing its full reality.

Of course, at the root of these radical differences in the conception of end and the conception of time lies the more fundamental difference, disagreement concerning the nature of truth. This means that the Heideggerian and the Christian, in Heidegger's terms, engage themselves in radically different ways in the things-that-are.

The Christian conception of knowledge (Heidegger would consider it "metaphysical" in this regard) views God as the Creator both of the human *ratio* and of the *rationes* that are in things. Truth would consist, then, in the intellect's discovering the *rationes*, which is possible because of the proportion established in creation between man's reason and the reasons in things. (This notion of "proportion" is, of course, quite different from a conception of "pre-established harmony," which was invented to solve idealistic problems which do not occur in this analysis.) Ontic truth consists in the "conformity" of the created intellect with the things-that-are. It owes its "ontological" ground to the First Cause, properly Truth with a capital "T," since God is the source of all *ratio*. Consequently, the discovery of finite things does not "fulfill" the finite intellect; rather finite things send him in search of the ontologic ground itself.

Sein und Zeit attacks the categorical analysis of being and the conformity theory of truth which goes along with it as not "fundamental." The categorical analysis, according to Heidegger, does not think "the truth of Being" in our author's sense of the word, for Dasein does not appear in its role as lieu of the "opening" within which being appears, as fundament. This lack of "fundamentality" is what left open the possibility of subjectivization, finally realized in Descartes's *Meditations*. But we might ask Heidegger whether to lack "fundamentality" is to lack *all* truth. Heidegger seems to suggest perhaps not, when he declares that every revelation of *Seienden* is an unveiling as well as a dissimulation. There is no ground in Heidegger's analysis for declaring the medieval position wrong in what it declared, but only in what it did not discover; Heidegger always returns to the same charge: in lacking fundamentality, the conformity theory of truth sowed the seeds of the positions that followed.

It will be worth making some point of this, for when we come to analyze Heidegger's conception of what it is to know we shall find it not without serious problems of its own; we shall find, what is more, that its most serious difficulties arise precisely at the point where it is in greatest reaction to the traditional position.

The problem of the *telos* of the *Ek-sistent* is really one with the problem of what it means to know. What does it imply to assert that the *eigenste Möglichkeit* of Dasein is Being-toward-Death if not to say, first of all, that the Dasein must find the root of its own sense within itself, in its own freedom, which, as "letting be of the things-that-are," is originative source of meaning, the seat of the *ursprüngliche Dictare*. A finite structure, projecting out of a past toward a future which it constructs out of its own "originative" grasp of the resources of the things-that-are and especially of its own tradition, can have as "end" only that *termination* which finishes the structure, ending its course and closing the story, but which is also the basic foundation of its nature. The *Endstadium* fixes the meaning of the whole, which is just what it is, intelligible in itself. This is why, as we saw before, *Angst* is the key to the possibility of authentic projection; it permits the Dasein to base every decision on an awareness of, and direct it toward, what is indeed its outermost possibility.

It is clear now that this notion of *telos* and Heidegger's conception of what it is to know are inextricably bound up in the same philosophical options. As long as Truth is conceived to be based in the originative freedom of the *Freisein zum Tode*, the free existent cannot possibly have any other kind of *telos* than his own projection toward death. If the Dasein is truly originative, bringing something absolutely new to the knowledge act and to the grasp of its own structural whole as "end" of *Ek-sistenz*, then it must find this something deep within its proper resources. But what lies in the deepest depths of that "poverty-stricken" humanity which Heidegger sings? A freedom that is a wandering in the *Not*. Humanity is poor because its sacred treasure, the essence of its essence, is nothing but the need of Being. Humanity is indeed the poorest of the poor because it is only Being-toward-death, and death fulfills no need—it only ends it. "Higher than activity is possibility," Heidegger writes in a key phrase of his explanation of the existential phenomenology. If so, then what is ultimate in the world is a freedom casting the light of Being from out of nothing. For this is the only sense "possibility" can have in a radically finite world. The very fusion of the thing in the *Gevierte* is owed to the Naught; for (1) the brute things that are, (2) the light we can bring to them from out the past, and (3) the presence of that always-more found in every unveiling are brought together by (4) the mortal in view of a free projection which makes present that which is not yet. There can be no "existential ethic" because there is, for Heidegger, no existential end, in the sense of an end fixed beyond time, belonging to the nature that we ourselves are. Behind us there is the richness of a historical destiny. Ahead of us, there is simply Nothing.

XIII *Heidegger's Existential Phenomenology*

NO PHILOSOPHY WITHOUT PRESUPPOSITION

HEIDEGGER's philosophy occupies the opposite pole from philosophies which pretend to be "without presupposition." According to Heidegger, all interpretation, of its very nature, involves some "presupposition," at the very least, that of a point of view.[1] What makes the particular interpretation true or false is not whether it is built-out from suppositions, but whether the particular suppositions may be justified in the light of the whole fabric of the resulting explanation. This very stand distinguishes Heidegger from his master Husserl, who still felt that suspending questions of existence, the phenomenologist could know the essences of things as they are in themselves, or at least could examine the real nature of the transcendental horizon itself. Husserl did not share with Heidegger the note "existential," by which we designate our author's insistence that an act of personal engagement—a "self-extension"—roots the possibility of every act of interpretation.

Heidegger's entire philosophy is founded, then, on certain *stands*, on certain ways that Heidegger has chosen to engage

[1] "Jedes ontische Verstehen hat seine wenn auch nur *vor*-ontologischen, das heisst nicht theoretisch-thematisch begriffenen 'Einschlüsse.' Jede ontologisch ausdrückliche Frage nach dem Sein des Daseins ist durch Seinsart des Daseins schon vorbereitet. . . . Aber muss sie (die existentiale Interpretation) sich nicht selbst rechtfertigen hinsichtlich *der* existentiellen Möglichkeiten, mit denen sie der ontologischen Interpretation den ontischen Boden gibt?" *Sein und Zeit*, p. 312.

himself in the things-that-are, and, therefore, on a certain way of reading the meaning of the past and of prolonging what this interpretation finds there, toward the future which it would choose to project. As we have repeatedly indicated in this study, criticisms that merely point out presuppositions at work (presuppositions governing certain translations, presuppositions concerning the significance of certain philosophers and certain epochs, etc.) miss their mark entirely by failing to come to grips with the Heideggerian *Denken* on its own terms. Any sincere effort to comprehend this extraordinarily coherent vision of Being must try to seize it *interiorly* and test the validity of its presuppositions by their ability to offer a consistent and adequate explanation of the human phenomenon. Only then shall we be able to discern Heidegger's limitations and trace their source to certain *stands* which may not be too well justified.

Probably the most important "stand" governing the Heideggerian *Denken* was the decision determining Heidegger's location of his own thought as post-Kantian, post-Hegelian, and post-Nietzschean. This is not as obviously inevitable a decision as it may seem, for it is not simply a question of acknowledging that the aforementioned thinkers existed, but of accepting certain of their conclusions as granted. To Kant Heidegger concedes, without really raising the possibility that more factors might require investigation, that the "objective," "categorical," "causal" analysis of things-in-themselves cannot lead to the discovery of principles of reality enjoying a fundamental validity; in other words, no analysis can transcend individual projections, viewpoints, horizons, epochs, or lead to a structure of reality discovered, not projected, and which the intelligence must submit to, not re-form. From Hegel Heidegger accepts the notion that the sense of history and its unity derive uniquely from the self-extension of the source of unity unfolding exstatically as freedom. From then on he never even raises the possibility that history might reveal other significance, less relative to points of view, perhaps even offering itself as a series of points of reference upon which projections should orient themselves to avoid distorting the past to suit arbitrary designs. From Neitzsche Heidegger accepted the declaration that God is dead, a conclusion which provided him with the needed protection against Hegel's idealistic absolutism, enabling him to situate the source of the Hegelian exstatic history within the finite, temporal transcendental horizon of the Dasein. Having decided that his should be a post-Kantian-Hegelian-Nietzschean philosophy in this sense, Heidegger feels licensed to ignore any possibility that "metaphysical" analysis might retain some validity. At the same time, the field is left open for an appropriation of everything positive that could be salvaged from the metaphysical eras, ready to be transposed within a radically finite frame of explanation, devoid by definition of any recourse *meta-taphusika* for the sense of existence and the meaning of things.

It will be very revealing, I believe, to trace the development of many of the most important and most difficult positions in Heidegger's thought from their source in his acceptance of a position "beyond metaphysics." Starting from the most far-reaching, because culminating, result of Heidegger's choice of position, namely the need to explain existence and being finitely, we can proceed then to the historical problem and, finally, to the Kant-rooted problem of the nature of philosophical method, thus passing in review all of the basic positions of this *Denken* in a way that should permit us to determine something of its adequacy as an explanation of existence and Being. Should we discover signs of inadequacy in the way a post-Nietzschean philosophy must conceive of our way of comporting ourselves to the things-that-are, then we might have grounds for questioning Heidegger's accession to his predecessors.

In erecting a post-metaphysical explanation of existence, Heidegger needed to observe three conditions: (1) the explanation needed to be finite; (2) nihilism was to be avoided (i.e., this philosophy must be prepared to appropriate within the limits of a finite explanation everything positive there is about existence, so that Being can be endowed with meaning and direction); (3) the explanation needed to be based on the discovery of the fundamentally exstatic nature of existence as transcendental horizon. Nietzsche had failed to avoid nihilism without, by positing the doctrine of the eternal return, compromising the originativeness of human freedom. Yet his very effort held out hope that a calmer try, based on a more penetrating grasp of the significance of the Kantian and Hegelian discoveries, might yet succeed.

The existential-phenomenological conception of existence, intended to comply with these conditions, has formed a distinctive explanation of (a) the origin of Dasein (both individually and as a tradition); (b) the end of Dasein (both in the sense of the meaning of the individual Dasein's end, and of that of a tradition); and (c) Dasein's way of inserting himself into the world, i.e., Dasein's free opening of the exstatic horizon of interpretation. This part of the explanation deals with both the individual's self-extension through the course of his existence and, consequently, the motion of history. This threefold division of our consideration of Heidegger's positions and their problems obviously remains true to the spirit of the exstatic philosophy under consideration.

The unity of a Dasein, as of a tradition, is rooted in the unbroken intentional continuity stretching back to first origins. For the Heideggerian phenomenology, first origins can have only the meaning of a kind of given which just happens. The individual existent awakes to consciousness "thrown" (*geworfene*) in the world; the Western tradition simply begins with the pronouncement of Anaximander—we might say of it that it, too, is just "thrown into the world," understanding "world" in this case as the exstatic unity formed by the continuous tradition. That the existent has parents, and that Anaximander had progenitors, the phenomenologist does not deny. But in neither the one nor the other case does this count for something within the intentional horizon. The individual existent's projections can be guided by the past only to the extent that he can recall it, i.e., only to the extent that the past can be subsumed within his exstatic horizon, which is always temporally *this side* of the "having been thrown." Similarly, the Western tradition has remained influenced by the pre-Socratic philosophers, not as they were in themselves, but as they have been taken up in the tradition, and only as they are recalled at the time of present projections.

Since the very nature of a post-Nietzschean phenomenology can allow it to handle the question of origins only in the way described, Heidegger does not provide for the possibility that the question of the origin of our life or of the origin of human history in its proto-beginnings could be approached vitally in another way. Yet questions of origin persistently raise themselves in forms to which the phenomenologist's *Geworfenheit* does not respond at all. Heidegger leaves the impression that such questions of causal origin are at best "not fundamental"; in fact, he is so mute on the subject that we are left with the impression that such analyses have been relegated to the scrapyard of "surpassed metaphysics." Has Heidegger acceded to Kant to the point of assuming such causal analysis fruitless without further consideration?

Yet problems do arise which are neither answerable by phenomenological analysis, nor dismissable on grounds prepared by Kant's reduction of causal arguments for the existence of God to the refutable ontological argument. The significance of such questions stands out when viewed in terms of the complementary exstasis—the future.

In the Heideggerian phenomenology the future is extended by the Dasein's projection of his end. Based as it is on the decision that only what is "in the world" of the exstatic horizon (understood precisely as constitutive of the sense-giving opening), should be treated as "Being," this analysis dictates that "end" be construed only exstatically, i.e., as the termination of the process. Thus in *Sein und Zeit*, Being-for-Death is described not only as the Dasein's "outermost possibility," but as its "most proper possibility" (*eigenste Möglichkeit*) as well. When Dasein turns to project the future, he of course envisions pure possibility stretching before him; but if he is existing authentically, i.e., in view of his death, he will say that whatever his possibilities may be, they are all conditioned by one inexorable reality that throws the cold light of radical historicalness on everything: the finality of death. Consequently, when Heidegger insists that the realization of the authentic structure of existence as Care begins in my grasp of my *Sein zum Tode*, he is showing that it becomes possible to seize my existence as a whole only in encompassing its term, which, being death, not only completes the process, but must affect the perspective in which everything destined-for-death must be viewed.

So, too, one can grasp the sense of a tradition only when it has been fulfilled by an end which marks the final unfolding of the potential influence that was contained in the beginning.

A phenomenological explanation of existence turns into an eschatology when applied to history, precisely because of this need to search for meaning within exstatic bounds. One looks for a beginning when a certain position, rife with possibilities, is posited, and for an end, a kind of death of the tradition brought about by its using up the early potential in arriving at a position that permits of no further pursuing of the question as it was originally posed. Thus Heidegger sees a sense and a completeness in the Western tradition, holding its beginnings in Anaximander, and coming to an end when Nietzsche renders all further metaphysics impossible.

The future is, then, as Heidegger's phenomenology conceives it, the same *Geworfene* that we encountered in considering the past, but caught in the very act of producing itself. Though the future grows out of the past, continuing the line of tradition of a person or a people, its forward extension to the extent that it brings about something new is just as "thrown" as its first origins. In fact, the future is the same reality, only viewed looking forward toward the "not yet."

Consequently, the Heideggerian phenomenology, taking up its vantage point uniquely from within the exstatic horizon of the self-extending finite freedom, must encounter absolute limit every way it turns. Confining itself to the analysis of the self-extending intentionality as self-extending, it encounters the ineluctable boundaries of this finite existence: in the past, as it simply begins to happen (this is the sense of the term *Geschichte*, "that which just happened"); and in the future, as it happens to end, either exhausted as a tradition or death-dissolved as a person. When applied to the fundamental act of comportment—the Dasein's engagement in things—the phenomenology conceives "interpretation" in this same way, encountering the element of originativeness as an absolute beginning.

And so in the Heideggerian phenomenology everything must be viewed as surging up from. . . . From where? From whence the *Geworfene*? From whence the originative element in an *ursprüngliche Dictare*? From whence the element of the genuinely new in the temporal extension of an existent toward the future? Speaking from within the perspectives inherited from Kantian and Nietzschean times, a phenomenology cannot answer any

more than "from Nothing." Thrown into the world from out
of the Nothing, impelled forward by a thirst for Being, i.e., by
a *Not*, a Need to fill itself up, the Dasein extends itself by acts
of rigorously finite freedom toward the Nothingness of the
future, in this way opening a horizon of interpretation in which
meaning is created from the Nothingness of the fundamental
Need.

Yet Heidegger does everything possible, while remaining
within this perspective, to justify his insistence that this explanation of existence, interpretation, and Being is not only
beyond metaphysics, but beyond nihilism and subjectivism.
The *Nichts* does not stand for a *nihil negativum*, Heidegger
assures us without further explanation. In every sort of context
Heidegger seems to be trying to leave the impression that the
Nichts marks the limit of the horizon within which the light of
interpretation has shown, and beyond which, in the *Weiträumigkeit des Nichts*, lies the vast darkness of the unrevealed. The
"mystery of Being" invokes the notion of the always-more, that
which has been revealed and then forgotten and that which
has yet to be revealed. In the analysis of the erection of the
"thing" this element of the always-elusive, ever-more is strongly
accented. The "mortal" opens the horizon within which the
brute *Seiende* is illumined when he brings the light of the past
to bear on it through the action of an originative interpretative
projection, restoring a new brilliance to the past light and
letting the glance of the elusive ever-more shine for an instant
as we perceive the newness of the new. This ever-more of the
mass of unrevealed Seienden, to which the light accumulated
in the past can ever be brought, in order to illumine new facets
and aspects, by an unlimited future of fresh interpretative acts,
Heidegger terms the *Heilige*. In those texts where the *Heilige* is
invoked, we are left with the sentiment of mystery, i.e., that
there lies beyond our direct grasp the ever-more, of which
we shall continue to have glances every time a truly originative
act of interpretation pulls some new light from the Nothing, and
with the sentiment that somehow these new revelations are
a kind of gift (that *Gunst des Seins*, mentioned in the *Nachwort* of
Was ist Metaphysik?) granted by the mysterious "beyond" to the
properly disposed mortal.

Heidegger has been able to invoke within the rigid limits of a purely exstatic phenomenological analysis, then, sentiments that give a great feeling of security against nihilism, subjectivism, and arbitrariness. The Holy, mystery, the grace of Being add a note of warmth and protection without seeming to compromise the fundamental perspective of the freedom of Dasein's originativeness, the radical novelty and fundamentality of those human acts which make *Geschichte* happen, without, in a word, forcing Dasein into a position of dependence in relation to some other from which his impulsions would be derived and to which they would have to be referred for their meaning and justification.

Yet this sense of well-being is only apparent. It is fostered, in my opinion, only because (1) the Heideggerian phenomenology is not always allowed to come to grips clearly and totally with the problems it raises within its own chosen perspective; and (2) the Heideggerian phenomenology, as we hinted in the beginning of this chapter, is a *chosen* perspective whose limits have not permitted some basic phenomena of human existence to take their proper place in Heidegger's monumental *Denken*. This is what I meant when I suggested that important questions present themselves which this phenomenology has not answered, and that the apparent self-sufficiency of the Heideggerian finite explanation of Being is indeed only apparent.

In support of the first allegation, it should be pointed out that the invocations of the *Heilige*, of mystery, of the grace of Being, do not in fact dispel the nihilism and subjectivism—abhorred by Heidegger but nonetheless implied by his phenomenology of interpretation—from the erection of the thing and self-extension of history through Dasein.

Heidegger would temper the fundamental nihilism of his phenomenology of interpretation by placing great emphasis on the fact that the originative thinker does not create new meaning for things out of a vacuum. Born into a tradition and impelled toward the future by a past rich in accumulated light, the thinker has the responsibility of prolonging that light toward the future. But in contrasting the *berechenden* (calculative) *Denken* with the originative *Denken* Heidegger made it quite clear where the essence of the originative *Dictare* lay: in its ability to lay hold of the really new, by pulling the obscure from the darkness of the not-yet revealed into the light of

Being, to be preserved in the Word. If we are not very careful, we can be lulled into believing that Heidegger means simply that the authentically "originative" thinker must gather up the light of the past to apply it in a fresh way, his own freedom supplying the flexibility of application necessary to supply wonderful new meaning out of these fresh combinations. But that is really what Heidegger means by *calculative* thinking, of which he warns that it must eventually use up the possibilities inherent in the past light, much as the West has "consumed" the possibilities inherent in the way the pre-Socratics posed originatively the Being-question. For creation to posit in history real future possibility, the radically *new* is required. Because the light it generates must be brought to *Seienden* to forge the thing, it is basic to this phenomenology to hold that this newness is not abstracted from things. After all, the meaning accumulated by *Seienden* in the past is itself the result of the acts of past Dasein. The truly originative, the *anfängliche*, element must always be drawn from the substance of the Dasein's freedom. It comes ultimately, then, from Nothing.

In fact, there is no opening in the Heideggerian explanation of interpretation within which a *Gunst des Seins* can really insert itself meaningfully. It can only mean that Dasein simply *happens* to supply an originative element. The *anfänglich* element comes to dwell in the word because it is "thrown" like Dasein itself. If "mystery" there is here, it is not the mystery of the truly other that could reveal further of itself. It is rather the mystery of the absolutely incomprehensible, the final limit. Yet Heidegger's "final limit" is perhaps established at a point prior to where true mystery begins.

That the nothing should so often wear the visage of the all in philosophy is only natural. The encounter of the "too great" wears the same air of transcendence as the encounter with the "no more"—at least on the surface. The difference between the "mystery" envisioned by revealed religion and the Heideggerian *Geheimnis* is, however, decisive. Christian mystery is encountered when we experience more than we can comprehend. Mystery in Heidegger's philosophy is encountered where there literally *is* no more, because we have not bestowed meaning. The possibility for *more*, envisioned by the two conceptions, originates in opposite poles. For Heidegger it lies in the paradoxical finite-originative impulsion of Dasein, the seat of the inexplicable *Gunst des Seins*. For the Christian it lies in the transcendent who can graciously give more of himself indefinitely, infinitely.

A careful reconsideration of the phenomenology of the erection of the thing can effectively dissipate the impression that some mysterious intervention saves the day from nihilism. Heidegger asserts that the *Heilige* enters into the composition of the thing erected in the fourfold fusion of Dasein's authentic dwelling. The *Glanz* of the Holy is seen in the originative act that builds the thing, because the truly new always suggests the possibility of additional revelation of that which still escapes our grasp. A feeling of reverence before the hidden reality that surreound and yet escapes us is very legitimately underscored by the phenomenology. But that sentiment of the Holy in no way justifies a leap to the conclusion that something is offered to us by the Great Beyond. The only "giving" that makes sense in the phenomenology is Dasein's offering of himself to Being, in the sense that he employs his freedom to create new meaning for *Seiende*, and Being's offering itself to him, in the sense that his self-opening to the things-that-are can really take root in *Seienden* and flower into the thing. The only dynamic element in the building of the thing is the mortal's act of opening the exstatic horizon. The only pure gift arises from the Dasein's finite will. Again the *new* comes from Nothing. A rather external indication that Heidegger's explanation of man's originative freedom has not reached the firm ground of ultimate principles lies in the difficulty that confronts one who would try to conceive what all of this could mean concretely for someone desirous of leading a fruitful life in contemporary times. The notion of withdrawing to the hills to shepherd Being strikes one as curiously inactive, especially in view of the furious activity of the technique's exponents. That Heidegger rejects quietism on the one hand and inauthentic busying on the other, we well know. But still the concrete motivation needed even to shepherd Being is too lacking to give adequate meaning to our actions. Heidegger's political critics are perhaps troubled on more philosophical grounds than just an accusation of failure to intervene at a critical moment.

Heidegger's effort to leave the impression that the accumulations of history give a direction and a responsibility to the future extension of the *Geschehen*, and thus eliminate the subjectivity and arbitrariness of will, do not withstand examination either, and for much the same reason. First of all, the Heideggerian phenomenology of interpretation establishes that the past does not have any sense until *interpreted*, which means that it must be recalled in the light of an original projection. So, at best the past only limits the range of possibility for projection; it does not definitively guide it. But when we turn our gaze forward toward the future we begin to see just how little true impulsion comes from the past, and to what an extent we are left gazing down a dark corridor of Nothing. For, so regarded, the future is really forged by the originative acts of self-extension. Whether I apply to history, twisting it this way or that to feed my purposes, does not change the fundamental fact that I face a future that is *noch nicht*, not yet, the originativeness of whose being I shall entirely forge. The only certainty that transcends the present is my death, and that can hardly be called a positive guide. In what way then are my future-forging decisions anything but arbitrary and "subjective"?

If we accept Heidegger's interpretation of the past as our tradition presents it to us today, that is, if we accept the fundamental choice of the future to which our past has limited us, is our decision to work for the one rather than the other alternative anything but purely *subjective*, in the sense that it just *happens* one way or the other? The "destruction of the historical destiny of ontology" presents a very clear picture of the choice facing us in what Jaspers calls the *geistige Situation unserer Zeit:* we can accede to and work for the planetary domination of technique, or we can withdraw to the hills to shepherd Being. There is no question as to which Heidegger prefers. The destruction places the former under the aegis of the inauthentic, while the latter is the activity of the sacrificing hero. Yet what is the real basis for choosing the one rather than the other? If Nietzsche were to say, "It's a question of taste, mediocre in the one case and excellent in the other," Heidegger would certainly reply, "A last gasp of the metaphysical tradition manifesting itself in the arbitrariness of the *Wille zum Wille.*" But what *is* the basis for the choice? In what sense is one an *uneigentlich* and the other an *eigentlich* possibility?

Sein und Zeit made quite clear the different bases of in-authentic and authentic projection. The inauthentic existent fails to base his projections on the full range of Dasein's possibility. In other terms, he substitutes for the full exstatic reality of Dasein a truncated temporality dominated by the present. The authentic Dasein, in the case at hand, would approach the choice of the future realizing (1) that the full responsibility for the Being that is to come rests in his decision—which makes him *care-ful*; and (2) that, consequently, he must so project as to preserve the full reality of Dasein which he can only encounter by recalling the past, whose Being he alone can guard. The authentic Dasein will choose not the planetary domination of the technique, which carries with it a truncated temporality based on the present and excluding whole realms of human possibility, but will seek to become the guardian of Being.

In a word, then, the authentic is the *richer* way. But why choose the richer way? Why be "authentic"?

Heidegger has never raised this question. He would probably dismiss it as foolish if someone were to ask it. After all, inquiry has an ultimate stopping point. Or, to put it another way, every point of view, as Heidegger affirms, must have a starting point, a first principle, which makes of every interpretation a circle, justifiable only to the extent that the circle of interpretation is able to enfold all phenomena needing explanation. The "ultimate stopping point" in any line of explanation represents the stand taken so that a point of view may exist. It is a legitimate "first principle" if nothing can be found in terms of which it itself becomes explicable.

But has one reached a true "first principle," an ultimate stopping point, when one simply presents the richer range of "authenticity" in contrast to the truncated nature of "inauthenticity" as ultimate intelligible grounds for choice? Can such a position justify itself by enfolding in its "circle of interpretation" all of the phenomena that need explanation?

A sign that the explanation of the fundamental choice of existence as authenticity versus inauthenticity may not be an ultimate limit of inquiry lies in the very way Heidegger presents the matter in *Sein und Zeit*. Though everything about the inauthentic strikes us as disagreeable—be it the *Flucht vor dem Tod* of everyday prattle or the superficial stimulation of "curiosity"—and everything about the authentic has a sound, healthy air about it, Heidegger is repeatedly at pains to point out that he is passing no moral judgment, and that he does not wish to suggest that the one is in anyway preferable to the other. The phenomenology purports simply to describe factually the two ways Dasein can exist. Yet the reader instinctively feels a note of insincerity in these declarations of amorality. He cannot help but feel that Heidegger in fact is making a choice from the beginning and is presenting the "good" and the "evil," but cannot, without exiting from the strict limits chosen for the phenomenology, justify this choice. A philosopher who chooses to accept as definitive the revelations of the Kant-Hegel-Nietzsche tradition as interpreted by the destruction must, after all, be "beyond good and evil."

The explanation of human existence in terms of authenticity and inauthenticity is, then, no more an ultimate stopping point for analysis than an explanation of everything new in interpretation, the erection of the thing and the self-extension of historical existence (the three being basically the same), as seduced from the *Nichts* by finite freedom. Rather, the Heideggerian *Denken* forces us to the encounter of new questions in a way that fairly cries out for new and different analysis. That the Heideggerian phenomenology does not seem able to answer this need for further analysis is not due to a limitation in the phenomenological technique as much as to a limitation built into the kind of analysis Heidegger unconsciously chose in acceding to situate himself beyond Kant, Hegel, and Nietzsche, conceived in their own terms.

THE ABSENCE OF THE OTHER AS OTHER

The result of having chosen a phenomenology that stays within the perspectives circumscribed by Kant and Nietszche is not only an arbitrary arrestation of inquiry even within the terms established by the phenomenology, but also an incapacity to examine a whole range of phenomena which can yield other perspectives than those treated by the Heideggerian phenomenology. While the former result illustrates most dramatically (because most internally) the existence in this phenomenology of unnecessary limits to analysis, the latter effect is probably graver.

Within the chosen perspectives of the Heideggerian phenomenology, the other as pure other does not and cannot appear. This grave default cannot be brought to light, as we suggested, by internal criticism, except to the extent that it can be shown that the very choice, on the part of a self-styled "phenomenological" point of view, of a position that excludes fundamental phenomena is arbitrary and "subjective" in the worst way—a most devastating accusation in Heidegger's view. That Heidegger has so well explained the inacceptability of arbitrariness and subjectivity in a philosophy that would surpass the limitations of the metaphysical tradition is sufficient justification for our bringing to bear an "external criticism," in order to prove the need to enlarge the basic cadres of this phenomenology.

The exclusion of the otherness of the other deforms the Heideggerian notion of the *Seiende* and of the other person. In *Vom Wesen der Wahrheit* Heidegger insists that freedom consists in "letting the *Seiende* be what it is." In *Vom Wesem des Grundes* we are told that the founding of a ground takes place as an admission of the *Seiende* into the transcendental horizon, which, in turn, is only possible authentically when the possibility of horizon is grounded in the *Seienden*. In "The Origin of the Artwork" Heidegger discourses on artistic creativity as the mutual interaction of "world" and "earth," which means not only that the thing is given meaning by its absorption into the transcendental horizon, but that the meaning given by the transcendental horizon must be drawn from the thing. In "Das Ding" the earth is one of the four ineluctable elements of the authentically erected "thing." And in commenting on Hölderlin, Heidegger makes a great thing of the fact that man dwells poetically "from out the earth."

Kant, too, had placed great emphasis on the absolutely inescapable fundamentality of the empirical data in all knowledge. Heidegger has splendidly brought out this too neglected element of Kant's thought through the analysis of *Kant und das Problem der Metaphysik*. In fact, a criticism of Kant can be implied in the last chapters of that book, when Heidegger suggests that the great philosopher did not yet come to grips sufficiently with the reality of the phenomenon.

Despite this constant awareness of the reality and fundamental position of the *Seiende* as thing-in-itself, despite his
apparent realization that the otherness of the *Seiende* is somehow
a controlling factor in our encounter with things, Heidegger at
no time squarely confronts the problem of the otherness of the
thing as otherness. The lack seems even more acute when we
have penetrated the fourfold erection of the thing to the source
of all meaning, even in *Seienden* revealed in the past: it is only
the projection of Dasein which can be the source of the
"other's" meaning—i.e., a source that is not *other* at all!
Heidegger renders great service to contemporary thought by
warning us against a naive realism that would ignore the
inevitable coloration of the thing by the interpretative intentional horizon within which we encounter it, and against a
transcendental idealism which, denying access to the thing-in-
itself, would destroy the possibility of our proceeding beyond
positivism without succumbing to arbitrary subjectivism. He
nevertheless leaves us without the principles of a solution to this
twofold problem.

For Heidegger seems reluctant to bring phenomenological
analysis to bear patiently and accurately on the critical point:
the precise nature of the fusion of exstatic, intentional transcendental horizon with the thing as it is in its brute reality.
Though he seems to suggest that it is important that we not fall
into a Kantian phenomenalism, and though he grants an
important place in his work to consideration of the erection of
the thing, nowhere do we find any effort to delineate the
contribution of the brute thing and the contribution of the
exstatic horizon, nowhere a description of what it means to
"let the thing be as it is," for nowhere is an effort made to
search out indications of what things might be "in themselves."
Where careful phenomenological analysis might prove a great
contribution, we encounter only obscure poetizing echoed from
Hölderlin, passages that are indeed thought provoking, but
precisely because they seem to avoid taking a stand.

Had Heidegger directed his attention to circumscribing by
careful analysis the *Seienden* precisely in their otherness, there
is a strong possibility that he might have been led in the
direction of conclusions that would have jarred seriously with
the "beyond metaphysics" stand of his interpretation. But

he never asks: What precisely characterizes my knowledge of this tree? How does it compare to what might be called my "objective" knowledge of this person? Can I distinguish within my knowledge of Jack poles of more or less "objective" and more or less "interpretative" knowledge? We can explain the total absence of this kind of analysis only by concluding that Heidegger has set out to answer the Being-question with a method that by no means intends to come to grips with every basic aspect of our experience. Had Heidegger endeavored to underscore the elements of the other as received into knowledge, as forming part of the content of the intentional horizon rather than being formed by it, he might have been led to modify considerably (1) his notion of analysis; (2) his notion of liberty, particularly as concerns the character of its originativeness; and (3) his conception of the origin of the "new" element in human creativity.

The absence of the other kind of "otherness" from any consideration in Heidegger's *Denken*, namely the extraordinary "otherness" of another person, is even more startling. The reader can almost exhaust Heidegger's sustained analyses of the experience and reality of persons other than myself by reading the paragraph on *Mitsein* in *Sein und Zeit*. The vast and significant phenomena of human contact, love, hate, responsibility toward others, of justice and civism and war as revelations of the fundamental situation of existents, simply cannot be reduced to the suggestion that human affairs incorporate themselves in language, in which form they pass into history. That this is in part true is unimportant, and the *Mitsein* treatment and the discussions of *Sprache* in the other works never touch the essential point. It is in the rich, intrinsic reality of our contacts with the other that we need to look for indications of what we are and what he is. What is more fundamental to the question of the Being of the things-that-are than insight into what I am, sought in understanding how the other person is both like me and inexorably other?

The decisions which influence the Heideggerian phenomenology to a blindness about "otherness" result in a subtle weighting of many of our author's phenomenological analyses in a way that turns up evidence of Dasein's responsibility to himself and which, conversely, plays down phenomena which manifest our dependence on and responsibility to what is other. Thus we may contrast the sense of lonely isolation of the *Angst* with a notion of true humility inevitably suggesting a place in the scheme of things; or *Schuld*, described as a sentiment of having fallen in respect to my authentic possibilities, may be contrasted with a notion of guilt expressive of a responsibility to some other. Thus, too, fidelity, participation, vocation— notions so richly analyzed by Gabriel Marcel—find no place at all in Heidegger's phenomenology.

This absence of the other is the cause of much of the uneasiness that we experience in trying to appreciate the positive terms in Heidegger's *Denken*. Each time we have penetrated to the depth of notions such as mystery, the *Heilige*, the grace of Being, *aletheia* itself, we have been unable to retain our initial excitement, for we came to suspect that they were high-flown words hiding the real emptiness of an existence for which there is no "other." "Mystery" turns out to hide no incomprehensibly rich other, but only our own limits; the *Heilige* turns out to hold no real gift, but is rather an expression of our finite "not yet"; the "grace of Being" turns out to be no real gift, for it is drawn inexplicably from our own resources. *Aletheia* itself finally fails to be an end and motive force, to become an historical sign of our incompleteness. Penetrating far enough beyond the exciting terms to discover that there is no other, we are left wondering if perhaps Sartre was not more direct in simply declaring such an existent, who is all alone, *de trop*.

The convenience of this absence of both kinds of otherness— that of the *Seiende* and that of the other person—is that it protects the Heideggerian phenomenology from the great danger: that of encountering in the otherness of the other a kind of inexorable *obligation* that could prove compromising to the ultimacy of Dasein as framed by a post-Nietzschean phenomenology. Were one to admit into the phenomenology a phenomen which of its very nature required acknowledgment, one would by that very admission accede to the existence of a dimension of the "should." It is very evidently one of the first characteristics of a philosophy that would exist beyond Zarathustra to refuse this dimension.

The rejection of otherness as a possible source of obligation, exterior to Dasein and possibly leading therefore to the discovery of a source of originativeness other than Dasein, is directly responsible for some of the other difficulties we have encountered in Heidegger's positions, touching as it does to some degree every part of his thought. For example, we feel a lack of respect for the "other" in its own reality throughout Heidegger's discussion and practice of "trans-lation." Likewise, the idea of "going to history to choose one's heroes" suggests that no serious basis of criticism underlies the destruction, which both in spirit and in detail is more subjective and arbitrary than Heidegger would care to admit. Even granting the important truth of Heidegger's attack on the naiveté of the notion that it is possible to approach history "objectively," and though it is quite clear that Heidegger abhors a subjective and arbitrary reading of history, the problem remains that his basic phenomenology has refused the destruction the respect for otherness needed to avoid it.

An excellent example of the extent to which such arbitrariness can deform is Heidegger's refusal to accord the Jewish prophets and Christ a place in the destruction of the Western tradition. I am speaking, of course, of those aspects of the phenomena of Judaism, Christ, and Christianity which are plainly historical and which are not subject to Heidegger's objection concerning matters of "faith." In the case of Christianity I am speaking of the phenomena that do not reduce to the Aristotelianism of St. Thomas and the Neoplatonism of St. Augustine, the headings under which Heidegger appears content to dismiss Christian thought. The example is an excellent one because it involves both aspects of the problem of "otherness"—the *Seiende*-like otherness of the historical event, and the peculiarly personal nature of our confrontations with Christ.

I can see no justification, in terms of the Heideggerian phenomenology itself, for Heidegger's dividing the Christian phenomenon into a theology, whose conception of truth is fundamentally a prolongation of the Greek philosophies, and a hard core of faith, which supposedly has nothing to do with philosophy. The manifestations of that faith have taken historical form in saints, martyrs, writers, mystics, and artists in a way that makes them part of the historical tradition whether one believes or not. That one cannot without believing "re-call" the Being of these phenomena in anything approaching the full "possibility" they represent is, of course, obvious. But that they hold no meaning for the non-believer—that St. Paul, St. Francis, St. Theresa, Bach as a Christian, and Memling as a believer hold no meaning at all for someone who would recall the historical destiny of the West—is simply not true. There is certainly present in these phenomena a conception of truth in Heidegger's sense of the term—a conception of how the existent relates himself to the things-that-are—that must be coped with by the destruction, just as it has had to cope with the "truth" as conceived in other epochs. Moreover, to dismiss these conceptions of "truth" by including them all under the Thomistic notion of the conformity of intellect and the thing would be just as arbitrary.

That Christ himself does not appear historically in the Heideggerian destruction is even less surprising; for He would have had to be confronted personally. There is no other possible way to "recall" the "possibility" that Christ represents than through a personal encounter with that extraordinary "otherness" of the man who revindicated for himself the ultimate "otherness," that of being *the* Truth. Even to reject the claims of Christ is to venture onto grounds foreign to the chosen horizons of the Heideggerian phenomenology. For there can be only two grounds for such a rejection: (1) an arbitrary refusal, the legitimacy of which as grounds for a basic philosophical position neither Heidegger nor anyone else would admit; or (2) a rejection on the kind of objective grounds which implies an analysis of *other* things and other people in their otherness which this phenomenology does not recognize. Consequently, because the Heideggerian phenomenology avoids recalling the historic possibility represented by the pretended God-Man who said "I am the Truth," echoing the ancient call of Jahweh "I am that am," the effectiveness of the destruction as a phenomenology of the Western tradition is severely compromised.

The two limitations of the Heideggerian phenomenology which we have just examined—the internal (its failure to come to grips patiently and thoroughly with the problems it poses from within its chosen perspective): and the external (the failure of its chosen perspective to afford any place to the other as other)— these two limitations work to produce a conception of the human existent that is in its incompleteness to some extent colorless and unconvincing. The phenomenology, when working safely within the area of phenomena with which it is willing to come to grips squarely, is very effective in deepening and enrichening our view of man. The contrast between these marvelous parts and the insufficient whole of Heidegger's philosophy is very striking, even though the uncritical reader may never be sufficiently at home in the parts to begin questioning the whole and may thus never perceive this contrast.

The Dasein comes from we know not where, destined to an end that makes little sense, impelled by a need that cannot be fulfilled, and energized by an originativeness of freedom which draws its newness from the Nothing. The Dasein is "thrown" into the world, the origins of his having the peculiar impulses which he possesses unknown. Whatever their origin (and therefore their sense) may be, these impulses are destined to obliteration in death, except for a lingering trace of historical influence that can survive the personal annihilation. The Dasein-destined-to-die lives authentically in the fullness of the moment, projecting for the sake of that Being which escapes his death and whose roots he finds in the rich accumulations of the past made present in the existential moment. He sacrifices himself to Being, because he is impelled by a thirst for Being that can be slaked no other way—if it can be slaked at all. In fact, it cannot; the essential finitude of Dasein is the ineluctable fact, and so the *Seinsbedürfniss* is seen as the very Need (*Not*) in that *Notwendig* wandering-in-need of the errancy.

Who is this Dasein that wanders in the service of a partial and always dissimulating revelation of Being toward a death that ends, not fulfills, his quest for whatever it is he seeks? That is the worst part about the Heideggerian existent: he has no personal reality. The servant of Being, making present the past in the light of a projection toward the future, has no proper reality of his own, nothing that does not slip through the fingers like the sands of time, nothing that can *confront* the other as other because it itself is a definite someone. When freedom has no sense beyond the necessary wandering-in-need of the errancy, when the ineluctable and a-temporal aspects of the personality that make love and fidelity meaningful are dissolved in the

Nothing of imposed phenomenological limits, it is the whole reality of the existent which fades away. Can the Dasein even enter the arena of life and fight for something?

METAPHYSICS NOT SURPASSED

Heidegger again recently reaffirmed his conviction that his *Denken* remains "preliminary" to the surpassing of metaphysics. In view of the analysis just completed, I believe we are justified in going even farther, in affirming that not only has this phenomenology not surpassed metaphysics, but, because it has not secured a position beyond the subjectivism and absolutism which mark the *Vollendung* of the metaphysical tradition, it belongs itself to the last stage of "metaphysics" as Heidegger has defined it. Despite its express intentions to the contrary, Heidegger's philosophy never penetrates beyond positions which, to say the least, tend to depend on the subjectivism and absolutism which our author, as forcefully as anyone, has shown to be fatal to the truth.

The rejection of the *other* in any significant form as limit, and the failure to ground meaning in anything but free projection of Dasein, leaves the Heideggerian conception of truth open to the charge of being as subjective as the Nietzschean *Wille zum Wille*, though far more subtly elaborated. That this results in Heidegger's absolutizing the Dasein can be seen by realizing that the "freedom of Dasein" in the final analysis has no limits, either imposed from without, or built from within. Though Heidegger defines Dasein's freedom as "the letting be of the things-that-are," the deeper analysis of just how one "lets be" the "thing" reveals the utterly originative role of Dasein. Extending nothing from nothing toward nothing, all of which makes something!—that is the miraculous nature of a Dasein whose ultimacy is absolute and knows only one necessity: the need to proceed exstatically. But even this need to work within the limits of a temporal unfolding, where Dasein builds on what Dqsein has done, must ultimately be ascribed to a whim of the Dasein-absolute. For the Heideggerian phenomenology, in its chosen Kantianism, has decided that there is no meaning beyond this, "what appears just happened that way"; so truth is what Dasein does, has done, and will do. If

Dasein in fact unfolds himself temporally, is it because Dasein has simply determined to unfold temporally? The very sense of finitude is destroyed, then, in post-Nietzschean philosophy, for the Nothing dissolves even the limits of what should be limited. The most curious loss in such a situation is not the dissolving of the self into the empty *Weitraumigkeit* of the Nothing-grounded Dasein; it is the loss of meaning by death— the very sign given us in *Sein und Zeit* as the ultimate warning against inauthenticity. The dissolving of the self, the absolutization of the temporal process, the eternalization of the moment of the poetic act, all contribute to gloss over death in the total course of Heidegger's philosophy. One is left wondering, "Death, where is thy sting?" after viewing Heidegger's vision of the absolutely creative Dasein pulling meaning, that should be eternally preserved, directly from the bosom of the night.

What some commentators have considered a radical change of orientation in Heidegger's works is, rather, a consistent development of the profoundest decisions founding the original Heideggerian phenomenology. It is perhaps justifiable to speak of *a shift of accent*: As the ultimate logical demands of the basic positions began to make themselves felt more and more, it was necessary to cede even some of the valid insights with which they could not be reconciled. This is the fate of that awareness of death which dominates *Sein und Zeit* and hardly seems pertinent in the later essays, even though Dasein should be termed "the mortal" when speaking of building the "thing." In other cases, Heidegger will continue to insist on the importance of principles such as anti-absolutism and anti-subjectivism which cannot be reconciled with the inexorable demands of the hidden logic of his phenomenology.

The full monumentality of Heidegger's philosophy does not reveal itself until this unity of development is understood. For then and only then do the true conflicts within its movement begin to come to the fore. And these, we have shown, course at the deepest level of philosophical thought. It is for this reason that the Heideggerian *Denken* is truly great. Any elaborate philosophy, above all an elaborate phenomenology, is bound to present a number of insights in its analyses. Heidegger's works, we have seen, are extraordinarily rich in revelations concerning time, historicity, and the inauthentic forms of existence, in fresh and very revealing historical criticism, in profound conception of language, etc. Heidegger's philosophy already enjoys a wide reputation for these things. But its claim to greatness will ultimately rest, I believe, on the fact that it wrestles with the problem of existence and being on the level where one encounters the great philosophical positions. To accuse Heidegger of following in the line of Kant-Hegel-Nietzsche is obviously a recognition of greatness, as well as an indication of how this *Denken* should be approached. For Heidegger extends that *Vollendung* of metaphysics (as he terms it) on its deepest level. In fact, his may be the ultimate pronouncement of that tradition.

The truest gauge of the greatness of Heidegger's philosophy lies, I believe, in this fact: Contemporary thinkers who treat of fundamental problems without taking into account and genuinely confronting the positions so powerfully maintained by Heidegger, invariably leave the reader who knows something of this philosophy with the impression that what he has just read has fallen short of grappling with the real issue. It is in the Anglo-Saxon lands that thinkers still write of the philosophy of history without any apparent awareness of the fundamental questions of the time-horizon analysis posed by *Sein und Zeit*; that language is the subject of philosophical inquiry without its ontological reality coming into question; that the pre-Socratics are studied without any consideration for the rich and provocative possibilities suggested by the Heideggerian *Ueberset-zung*—which, for all its fantasies, enjoys a consistency and bestows a weight to these texts that should give pause to any historian; that "realism" will continue to speak of the principles of being of the thing-in-itself while ignoring all the importance of life as it is lived within the transcendental horizon of intentionality. The examples could be multiplied many times.

The inaccessibility of Heidegger's works could excuse the delay in coming to grips with the problems posed by this *Vollendung* tradition. But there are today, at last, those who are beginning to recognize that philosophers seeking fundamental truth cannot ignore "a different tradition" that in fact challenges the fundamentality of their perspectives. Granted English and American thought today is dominated by descendents of British empiricism and mathematical positivism; the perpetuation of a tradition in the face of charges of narrowness and superficiality is still today's choice, and one that should not be made lightly. The profound perspectives revealed by the Heideggerian phenomenology (perspectives held in many respects by some of the other thinkers who term themselves phenomenologists, sometimes without all of the difficulties generated by Heidegger's more personal decisions), once understood, should both broaden and deepen the horizons of any philosophy that will deign to confront them. To the logicians and language analysts who will probably continue to ignore the deeper and more devastating problems in the name of "scientific research," Heidegger could well declare: It is sometimes better for the spirit to lose a great battle than to win a tiny foray.

Bibliography

WORKS BY HEIDEGGER

1914. Die Lehre vom Urteil im Psychologismus: Ein kritisch-positiver Beitrag zur Logik. Leipzig, Johann Ambrosius Barth.

1916. Die Kategorien- und Bedeutungslehre des Duns Scotus. Tübingen, J. C. B. Mohr Verlag.

1927. Sein und Zeit, Erste Hälfte. Halle, Max Niemeyer Verlag. First published in *Jahrbuch für Philosophie und phänomenologische Forschung*, Vol. VIII, 1927.

1929. Kant und das Problem der Metaphysik. Bonn, Verlag Fred. Cohen.

1929. Vom Wesen des Grundes. Halle, Max Niemeyer.
Foreword added to 3rd ed. (Frankfurt, Vittorio Klostermann, 1949).

1930. Was ist Metaphysik? Bonn, Verlag Fred. Cohen.
Postscript added to 4th ed.
Introduction added to 5th ed. (Frankfurt, Vittorio Klostermann, 1949).

1933. Die Selbsthauptung des deutschen Universität. Breslau, Verlag Korn.

1937. Hölderlin und das Wesen der Dichtung. Munich, Albert Langen.

1943. Vom Wesen der Wahrheit.
Slight additions in 2nd ed. (Frankfurt, Vittorio Klostermann, 1949).

1944. Erläuterungen zu Hölderlins Dichtung. Frankfurt, Vittorio Klostermann.

1947. Platons Lehre von der Wahrheit. Mit einem Brief über den "Humanismus". Berne, A. Francke.
Platons Lehre first published in E. Grassi, *Geistige Uberlieferung*, Vol. II, 1942. The letter dates from 1946, when Heidegger answered questions posed by Jean Beaufret.

1950. Holzwege. Frankfurt, Vittorio Klostermann.

1951. Erläuterungen zu Hölderlins Dichtung, 2nd ed. Frankfurt, Vittorio Klostermann.

    Adds *Hölderlins Hymne: "Wie wenn am Fiertage . . ."* (first published 1941) and *Hölderlins Gedicht: "Andenken"* (first published 1943).

1953. Der Feldweg. Frankfurt, Vittorio Klostermann.
1953. Einführung in die Metaphysik. Tübingen, Niemeyer Verlag.
1954. Was heisst Denken? Tübingen, Niemeyer Verlag.
1954. Aus der Erfahrung des Denkens. Pfüllingen, Neske Verlag.
1954. Vorträge und Aufsätze. Pfüllingen, Neske Verlag.
1956. Hebel—der Hausfreund. Pfüllingen, Neske Verlag.
1956. Was ist das—die Philosophie? Pfüllingen, Neske Verlag.
1956. Zur Seinsfrage. Frankfurt, Vittorio Klostermann.
1957. Der Satz vom Grund. Pfüllingen, Neske Verlag.
1957. Identität und Differenz. Pfüllingen, Neske Verlag.

OTHER WORKS

Allemann, Beda. Hölderlin und Heidegger. Zurich, Atlantis, 1954.

Anteile: Martin Heidegger zum 60. Geburtstag. Frankfurt, Vittorio Klostermann, 1950.

Astrada, C., *et al.* Martin Heideggers Einfluss auf die Wissenschaften. Berne, A. Francke, 1949.

Biemel, W. Le concept de monde chez Heidegger. Louvain, E. Nauwelaerts, 1951.

Brock, Werner. Introduction to *Existence and Being*. Chicago, Regnery, 1949.

    Contains translations by Douglas Scott, R. F. C. Hull, and Alan Crick of 4th ed. of *Was ist Metaphysik?*, 2nd ed. of *Vom Wesen der Wahrheit*, and *Erläuterungen zu Hölderlins*, together with an "account" of *Sein und Zeit* by Professor Brock.

Collins, James Daniel. The Existentialists: A Critical Study. Chicago, Regnery, 1952.

Grene, Marjorie. Martin Heidegger. New York, Hillary House, 1957.

Löwith, Karl. Heidegger: Denker in dürftiger Zeit. Frankfurt am Main, S. Fischer, 1953.

Marcic, R. Martin Heidegger und die Existenzphilosophie. Bad Ischl, Philosophische Gesellschaft, 1949.

Müller, M. Existenzphilosophie im geistigen Leben der Gegenwart. Heidelberg, Kerle Verlag, 1949.

Vietta, Egon. Die Seinsfrage bei Martin Heidegger. Stuttgart, C. E. Schwab, 1950.

Waelhens, A. de. La Philosophie de Martin Heidegger. Louvain, E. Nauwelaerts, 1942.

Index